SO-ATF-390

To the
COLUMBIA
GATEWAY

The Oregon Railway and the
Northern Pacific, 1879-1884

California Railroad Museum
Old Sacramento
June, 1999

To the COLUMBIA GATEWAY

The Oregon Railway and the Northern Pacific, 1879-1884

PETER J. LEWTY

Washington State University Press
Pullman, Washington
1987

Copyright © 1987 by the
Board of Regents of Washington State University

All rights reserved. No part of this book may be reproduced or
transmitted in any form or by any means, electronic or mechanical,
including recording, photocopying, or by any information storage and
retrieval system, without permission in writing from the publisher.

Printed and bound in the United States of America
Washington State University Press
Pullman, Washington

Library of Congress Cataloging-in-Publication Data
Lewty, Peter J., 1934-
   To the Columbia Gateway.

   Bibliography: p. 190
   Includes index.
   1. Northern Pacific Railroad Company—History—19th century.
2. Oregon Pacific & Eastern Railway—History—19th century.
3. Railroads—United States—History—19th century. I. Title.
HE2791.N855L48   1987   385'.09795   87-21041
ISBN 0-87422-030-0 (alk. paper)
ISBN 0-87422-029-7 (pbk. : alk. paper)

This book is printed on pH neutral, acid-free paper.

*To the brave men who built
the railroads of the
Columbia Interior*

CONTENTS

MAPS AND FIGURES

The Columbia River and Tributaries

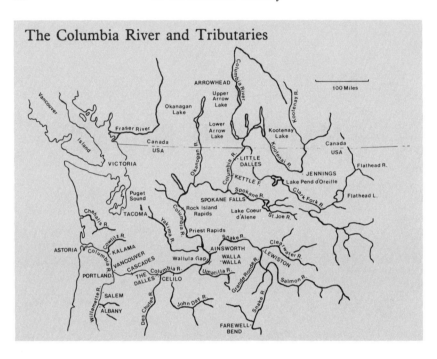

Railways in the Walla Walla Area
December 31, 1880

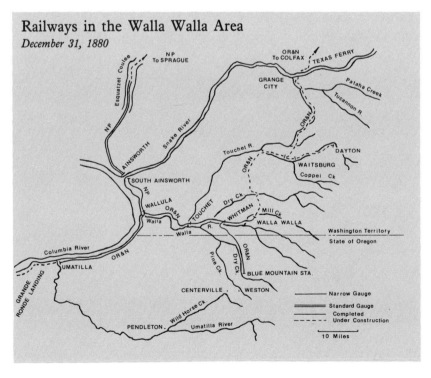

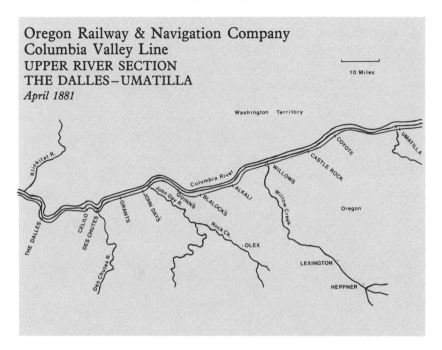

Oregon Railway & Navigation Company
Columbia Valley Line
UPPER RIVER SECTION
THE DALLES–UMATILLA
April 1881

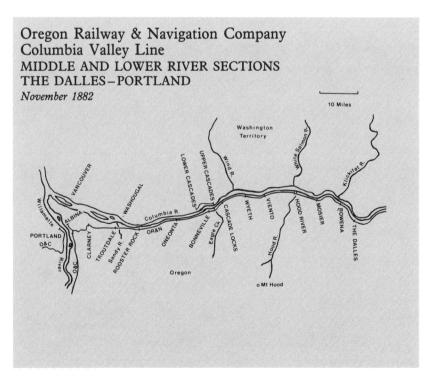

Oregon Railway & Navigation Company
Columbia Valley Line
MIDDLE AND LOWER RIVER SECTIONS
THE DALLES–PORTLAND
November 1882

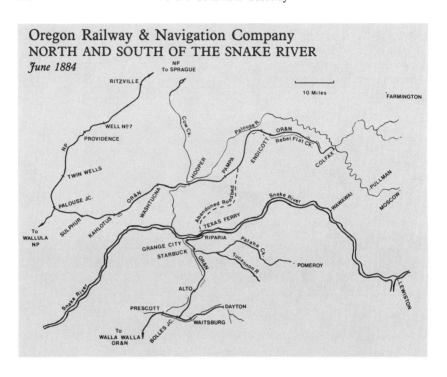

Oregon Railway & Navigation Company
NORTH AND SOUTH OF THE SNAKE RIVER
June 1884

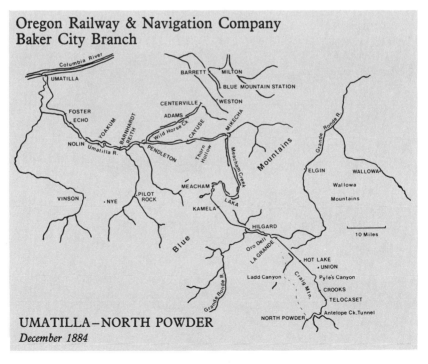

Oregon Railway & Navigation Company
Baker City Branch

UMATILLA—NORTH POWDER
December 1884

Oregon Railway & Navigation Company
Baker City Branch and Huntington Extension
NORTH POWDER – HUNTINGTON
December 1884

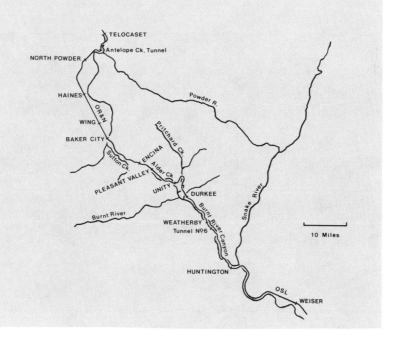

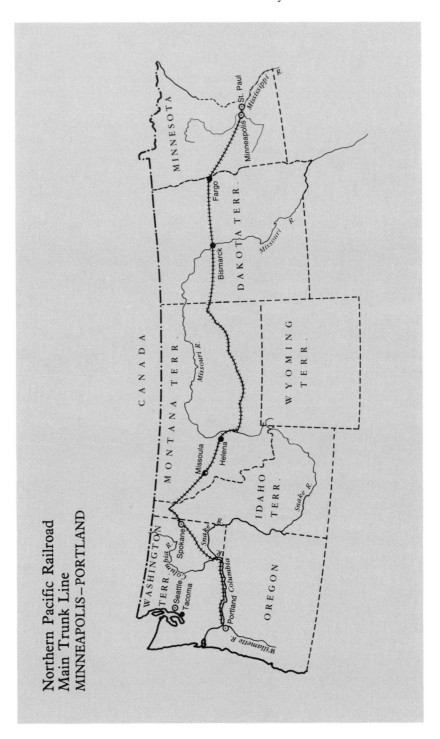

Northern Pacific Railroad
Main Trunk Line
MINNEAPOLIS–PORTLAND

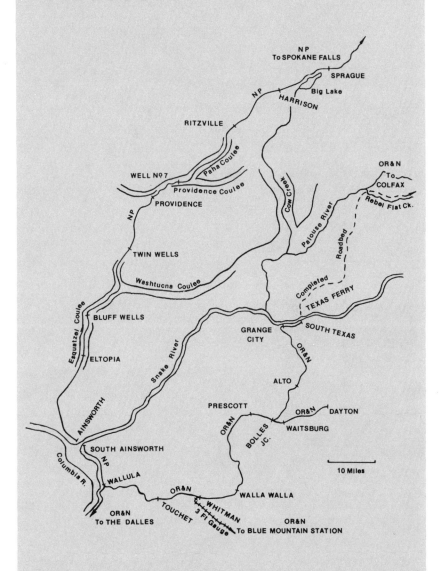

Northern Pacific Railroad
Lake Pend d'Oreille Division
AINSWORTH–SPRAGUE
December 1880

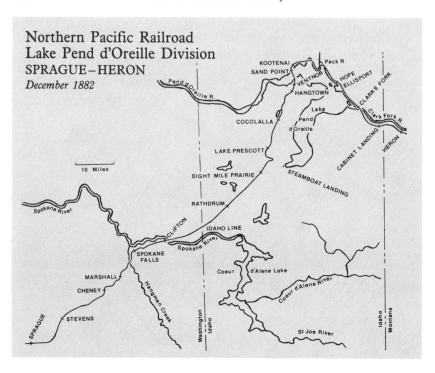

Northern Pacific Railroad
Lake Pend d'Oreille Division
SPRAGUE–HERON
December 1882

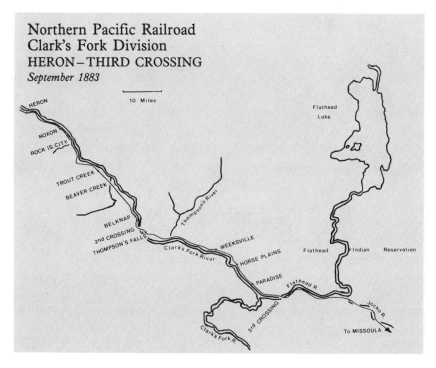

Northern Pacific Railroad
Clark's Fork Division
HERON–THIRD CROSSING
September 1883

Oregon Railway & Navigation Simplified Gradient Profile, from Pendleton to Riparia.

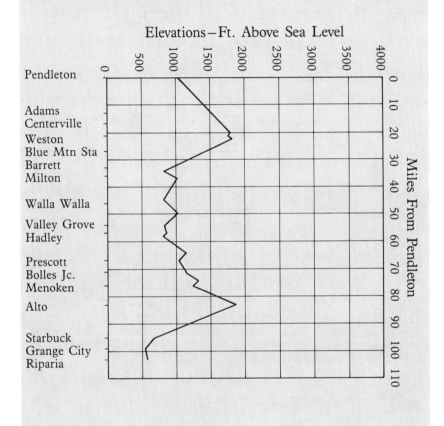

Oregon Railway & Navigation Simplified Gradient Profile, from Umatilla to Huntington.

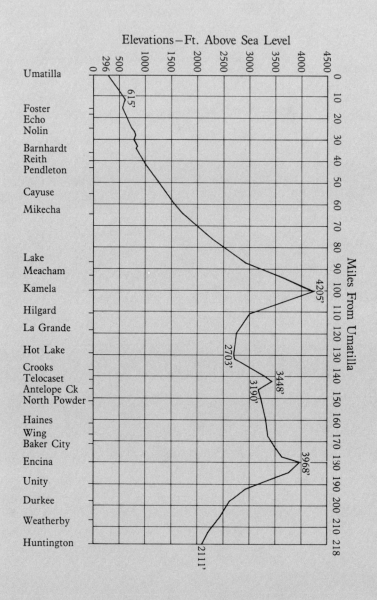

Oregon Railway & Navigation Simplified Gradient Profile, from Ainsworth to Sandpoint.

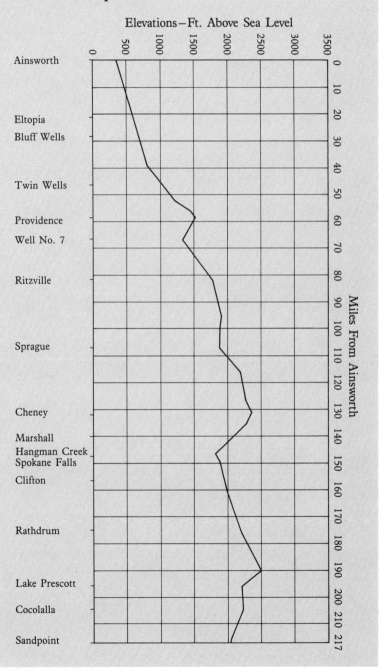

PREFACE

When I first came to live in the mountains of the West Kootenay I was surprised to find that if I followed the Columbia River southward into the state of Washington it soon brought me to a wide open prairie country, a land of broad wheat fields on rolling hills, with small towns nestling in the dry valleys between. This was certainly not what I had expected in the heart of the Cordillera, but there it was; and it extended as far as I could see, from the foothills of the Bitterroot Range in the east all the way to the Cascade Mountains hull down on the far horizon to the west. Southward it presented a great vista of land and sky.

The first surprise of discovering this country was to be followed by many more, for it is a land of surprises, which it reveals one by one. Looking immediately at maps of the Inland Northwest I was struck by the close mesh of the railway network, and at once began to wonder why such a sparsely populated agricultural area should have been blessed with so many competing lines. Before my questions could be answered there was a lot to learn, and not only about railways. Donald W. Meinig's admirable book *The Great Columbia Plain* provided me with a wealth of information. Moreover, the threads of regional railroad history, so skillfully woven into it, suggested that an attempt should be made to assemble a more detailed account of the way in which the railway system had developed. Without fully realizing what was involved, I foolhardily decided, in 1978, to write a complete story of railroad construction in the Columbia Interior between 1879 and 1914. Unfortunately, as my research progressed, it became clear that I was exploring an ever-expanding field. If I was to cope successfully with the wealth of information available from newspapers and periodicals published prior to the financial collapse of 1893, the saga would have to be cut off at that point.

Since any study of later events would have required access to railroad company archives, which I did not have, the decision was easily made. I gladly opted for further exploration of the more forthright world of the 1880s. Even then I found that there was far too much material for one book, and had to divide the work into two at the construction hiatus of 1885.

This volume, then, covers the origins of the Northern Pacific Railroad and Oregon Railway & Navigation companies, the rise and fall of Henry Villard's first empire, and the completion of overland railways converging on the Columbia Gateway. Geographically, the story unfolds along the Oregon Railway & Navigation Co. main and branch lines between Portland and both Huntington, Oregon, and Colfax, Washington, and the Northern Pacific main line between Wallula, Washington, and Paradise, Montana. Given that the events occurring in the Columbia Interior cannot be considered alone, the narrative also makes occasional excursions to points beyond the Cascade and Bitterroot mountains. In the realm of omission, only passing reference is made to the Northern Pacific line between Pasco and North Yakima, opened early in 1885. The building of that section of railway, however, seems to be a topic blending more readily with the completion of the Cascade Branch between 1886 and 1888, an account of which I hope to be able to present in a sequel to this work.

Although every attempt has been made to ensure that the historical data presented in this book are accurate, there may inevitably be some mistakes. For these I take complete responsibility and offer sincere prior apology.

Before leaving the reader with the text, I would like to acknowledge the help given to me by many kind persons during the preparation of this book. Among these I am particularly indebted to the staff of Selkirk College Library at Castlegar, British Columbia, and especially to Mrs. Arlene Ommundsen, who went to great pains to keep me supplied with reference material from elsewhere. Others deserving special mention are: Mr. Charles Mutschler of the Archives & Special Collections section of Eastern Washington University Library at Cheney, who searched out material otherwise difficult to find; Mr. Lawrence Shawver of Spokane, Washington, who generously provided information from his extensive collection of railroadiana; Mr.

James Reiser of the Union Pacific Railroad Company Division Engineers office, Portland, Oregon, who cheerfully complied with my repeated requests for civil engineering data; Mr. Craig Holstine of Cheney, Washington, who augmented the footnotes; my old friend Mr. Ernest Turner of Ottawa, Ontario, who sought out material held in the National Science Library of Canada; and last, but by no means least, my wife Beverley, and son Steven who typed the manuscript and all its ramifications several times over. To all of these wonderful people I express my sincere thanks.

Peter J. Lewty
August 1987
North Bay, Ontario

INTRODUCTION

The forging of transportation links was vital to the development of pioneer settlements in the Pacific Northwest. The steamboats that plied the waters of the Columbia Interior were later replaced by steam locomotives. These machines and the men who owned them greatly influenced the lives of all those in the region, as well as the very look of the land itself. The route of a railroad, and its depots along that route, often determined settlement patterns, townsites, and the development of other enterprises.

The U.S. portion of the basin of the Columbia River drainage system became a gateway that provided a focal point for economic activity in the late nineteenth-century Pacific Northwest. When the railroads reached the Columbia Gateway the era of exploration ended and a new era of economic opportunity began. The completion of the northern overland railways was a final link in the chain of events which began with Christopher Columbus and continued through the Lewis and Clark expedition. It was the culmination of efforts to get to the East, the Orient, by going west. The transcontinental railroads were the dream of the Northwest Passage turned into reality through determination and hard work.

1

NORTHERN PACIFIC

A first serious attempt to promote the building of a transcontinental railroad to the Pacific Northwest was made in 1845. At that time Asa Whitney, who had been based in China as a commission agent for New York merchants, proposed that a railway be built from the western shore of Lake Michigan to the Oregon coast for the purpose of stimulating trade with the Orient.[1] Whitney at first suggested that the line be built and operated by the United States Government at cost. Later he offered to undertake construction and run the railway himself, provided he was given title to all the land within thirty miles of the right-of-way. These ideas were premature and failed to gain support, but within a few years conditions changed and other schemes were put forward.

The resolution of the Oregon boundary dispute with Great Britain opened vast new areas of the Northwest to settlement, but gold discoveries deflected the mainstream of migration southward to California. By 1853 the Pacific railroad question had to be reconsidered. Rapid growth in population made California the obvious objective, but the choice of a route remained mired in the widening political gulf between the Northern and Southern states. Plans were drawn up to examine and compare five different routes between the 32nd and 49th parallels of latitude. The surveys,[2] however, were carried out largely by military engineers responsible to Pierce's secretary of war, Jefferson Davis, who was an ardent protagonist of Southern interests. The result was predictable. Davis subsequently recommended the most southerly route, and in the prevailing atmosphere of sectional jealousy no agreement was reached.

In April 1862 the conflict of sectional interests came to a head. The Southern states seceded and the Civil War began. Northern legislators found themselves able to pass measures long blocked by Southern opposition. To complement the Homestead Act and simultaneously encourage California to remain loyal to the Union, a transcontinental railroad was at last sanctioned. On July 1, 1862, the United States Congress chartered the Union Pacific Railroad Co.,[3] with a capital stock of $100 million, and gave it authority to build westward from Omaha, Nebraska, to the eastern boundary of Nevada Territory, where it was to meet the California-promoted Central Pacific Railroad.

To encourage construction of the overland railway, Union Pacific received a large grant of land and was loaned money raised by United States first mortgage bond sales amounting to $16,000 for every mile of easily constructed road and up to three times that sum for work in difficult mountainous terrain. These inducements, however, proved insufficient to attract private share capital. In 1864, therefore, Congress magnanimously decreed that the government bonds need only be secured by a second lien on the property, and permitted the company to double the available loan capital by selling its own first mortgage bonds to the public.[4] These and other concessions having been granted, construction finally got under way in 1865. As Union Pacific built westward from the Missouri River, Central Pacific, financed under similar arrangements, advanced eastward from Sacramento. The two lines met at Promontory, north of the Great Salt Lake in Utah Territory. The last spike was driven there at 12:47 p.m. on May 10, 1869.[5]

The decision to build a railroad on the central route did not for long silence demands for a line from the Upper Great Lakes to Puget Sound. The initial impetus for such a scheme came from Josiah Perham, a visionary promoter from Maine. Eventually Perham's ideas were translated into a proposal presented to Congress by Thaddeus Stevens, and this led to the chartering of the Northern Pacific Railroad on July 2, 1864.[6]

Northern Pacific was authorized to build a railway westward from the head of Lake Superior to Puget Sound, with a branch line down the Columbia Valley to the growing community of Portland, Oregon. Although Northern Pacific was awarded an enormous grant of land, it was denied financial assistance. Indeed, at Perham's own suggestion, it was even forbidden to issue mortgage bonds. Perham's naive belief that funds could be raised by selling stock to a large body of enthusiastic small investors turned out to be unfounded. When the money failed to materialize, the project foundered.

Early in 1866 the Northern Pacific charter was sold to a group of New England capitalists headed by John Gregory Smith, president of the Vermont Central railroad.[7] Initially Smith and his associates thought the Grand Trunk Railway of Canada might be used to connect Northern Pacific with the Vermont Central and other northeastern lines, thus producing a truly transcontinental road with an eastern terminus at Boston. In this way New England might have regained trade originally diverted to New York by the opening of the Erie Canal.

The members of the Smith syndicate immediately launched a campaign to secure financial aid from Congress, but, being almost exclusively New Englanders, they were unable to gain the wider political support required to offset growing public antipathy to large, costly, subsidized railway ventures. They therefore decided to broaden the company's sphere of influence. Overtures were made to several prominent eastern and midwestern railroad personalities, resulting in the so-called Original Interests Agreement of 1867.[8] Under the terms of this agreement, ownership of the Northern Pacific enterprise was divided into twelve equal parts, each costing $8,500 and carrying the right to appoint one director. The persons subscribing to this proprietary arrangement pledged their support for the struggle to obtain financial help from the government. In this way William B. Ogden, president of the Chicago & North Western Railroad; Robert Berdell, president of the Erie Railroad; William G. Fargo, vice-president of the New York Central Railway; George W. Cass, president of the Pittsburgh, Fort Wayne, & Chicago Railroad; and J. Edgar Thompson, president of the Pennsylvania Railroad, were recruited to provide the board of directors with a broader political base. John Gregory Smith, Thomas H. Canfield, Benjamin P. Cheney, and Richard D. Rice, meanwhile, maintained the New England interest.

Lobbying in Washington was vigorously resumed and carried on for two years, but the available support eventually proved inadequate. The legislators would neither grant financial aid nor provide guarantees for bond issues. The Northern Pacific promoters therefore had to settle for a charter amendment, dated March 1, 1869, permitting public sales of bonds secured by a first mortgage upon the railway and telegraph line property.[9] By a strange oversight, permission to mortgage the land grant was not included in the 1869 Amendment and had to be secured, in the face of bitter opposition, a year later.

The struggle in Congress not only delayed construction of the road but also drew widespread attention to the great handicap from which the scheme was to suffer. The initial excursion into uninhabited territory would have to be paid for by sales of bonds lacking government guarantees. Raising funds in this way was not going to be easy. Nothing but the most energetically prosecuted loan subscription campaign, conducted by first class financial agents, would ever get the project under way. The directors therefore turned to Jay Cooke & Co., private bankers, who were well known for the major part they had played in financing the Union war effort.

Before Jay Cooke & Co. would undertake the sale of Northern Pacific bonds they insisted that a survey be undertaken by their own nominees to confirm the engineering feasibility of the several alternative routes and determine the settlement potential of the adjacent lands. In the summer of 1869 two expeditions therefore took to the field.[10]

A large party consisting of Governor Marshall of Minnesota, Northern Pacific president Smith, vice president Rice, chief engineer Edwin F. Johnson, and a multitude of capitalists, journalists, and clergymen, many of them accompanied by their wives, set out from St. Paul along the Red River Trail. The majority turned back at the Red River, but Governor Marshall, chief engineer Johnson, Phillip Holmes of Jay Cooke's New York house, and C. Carleton Coffin of the Boston *Journal*, proceeded westward with a military escort to the Missouri River, where the reported approach of a large body of Indians caused them, prudently, to retreat.

The other group, which was led by the distinguished engineer W. Milnor Roberts and included Northern Pacific general agent Thomas H. Canfield, the company secretary Samuel Wilkeson, a clergyman called Claxton, and the sons of both Edwin F. Johnson and Jay Cooke's partner William G. Moorehead, inspected Puget Sound, ascended the Columbia River from Portland to Walla Walla, traversed the Interior Plain to Lake Pend d'Oreille, and proceeded by way of the Clark Fork River to Missoula. They examined the passes through the Rockies and descended the Missouri to Fort Benton. Having retraced their steps as far as Helena, they crossed the Bozeman Pass into the valley of the Yellowstone. Further progress, however, was discouraged by the hostile attitude of the local Indians. The party was therefore obliged to return to Bozeman and take the stage road south to Corinne in Utah Territory, where they were able to reach the line of the Union Pacific.

The reports prepared by persons accompanying these expeditions were enthusiastic, as Jay Cooke, with an eye to publicity, had hoped they would be. The journalists wrote long accounts of their travels and had them published far and wide. Some of the writers were especially exuberant in their descriptions, and Samuel Wilkeson, now Northern Pacific Railroad Co. secretary, was completely carried away with what he had seen. The engineers fortunately provided a more sober assessment, but even W. Milnor Roberts, cautious as he was, conceded that the land grant possessed " . . . great intrinsic value . . . " and the railway " . . . if judiciously located, honestly constructed, and properly administered . . . " would " . . . pay within a few years a fair dividend upon its cost."[11] He estimated the cost of construction and equipment, including interest on bonds during the construction period, to be $85,277,000.

The work carried out by the western expedition of 1869 clarified the choice of routes from the Rocky Mountains to the Columbia River and confirmed that Puget Sound would be the railroad's ultimate objective. Acquaintance with the Pacific Northwest, however, made the directors realize that it was going to be very difficult, if not impossible, to create a new terminal city on Puget Sound without alienating the powerful interests already well established at Portland.

Portland had grown up at a point where river and sea borne trade converged, and by 1869 was already the single most important center of commerce in the entire Pacific Northwest. The substantial citizens of that growing metropolis would hardly be satisfied with a secondary position at the end of a Northern Pacific branch line. Indeed there was every possibility that they would encourage the construction of other overland railway connections. Union Pacific, for example, might well be induced to build northwestward on the line of the Oregon Trail and descend upon Portland along the left bank of the Columbia River.

Rivals could not be excluded from Portland without forfeiting a valuable part of the land grant. No such obstacle, however, prevented pre-emption of the southern approach to Puget Sound. On April 13, 1869, the company's charter was therefore amended[12] to permit the extension of the Portland branch northward to the Puget Sound terminus of the main line, a move that was to keep Union Pacific out of the future Seattle-Tacoma area for another forty years. Having secured the back door to Puget Sound, the company then sought to reassure the residents of Portland. Under the terms of the charter amendment of May 26, 1870, which was primarily intended to sanction the mortgaging of the land grant, the status of the two proposed Northern Pacific lines in the Pacific Northwest was reversed, so that the Columbia Valley route and its northward extension became the main line, and the Cascade Mountain crossing was relegated to serving the role of a branch.[13]

On May 20, 1869, Jay Cooke & Co. provisionally undertook the task of financing the Northern Pacific Railroad.[14] First attempts were then made to secure a European financial alliance. During the summer of that year Jay Cooke's partner, William Moorehead, was sent to England to try to interest the Baron Rothschild and his sons in the Northern Pacific enterprise.[15] The response was disappointing. Moorehead was quickly forced to realize that his mission was impossible, for unless the United States government guaranteed the company's bond issues, conservative European financiers would not advance the huge sums required to build a second railway into the uninhabited American West. Once turned down by the Rothschilds there was little chance of receiving a favorable reception elsewhere in Europe. Moorehead, who had never been very enthusiastic about the Northern Pacific venture, therefore decided that there was no point in pursuing the matter. He wrote Jay Cooke from London recommending that the firm withdraw from the whole affair, and then left to spend the winter on the Nile!

Jay Cooke himself was not about to give up so easily. He reasoned that if part of the railroad could be built and brought into operation, Congress and the European financiers might adopt more charitable attitudes. He therefore proposed, and Northern Pacific president John Gregory Smith agreed, that construction should be started, but, for the time being, work should be restricted to about 300 miles of railway forming useful links at each end of the line. First sections would therefore be built from Duluth to the Red River, and from a point on the lower Columbia River below Portland to the still undefined terminus on Puget Sound.

On January 1, 1870, a final agreement was concluded between the Northern Pacific Railroad Co. and Jay Cooke & Co. setting out the terms under which the bankers would finance construction of the railroad.[16] Northern Pacific was to issue bonds with a total face value of $100 million, to mature in thirty years and yield 7.3 percent interest. Both the prinicipal and interest were to be payable in gold, and the bonds were to be secured by a mortgage upon the railroad and all its land and other property. Jay Cooke & Co., as sole financial agents, would sell the bonds at par and credit Northern Pacific with 88 percent of the proceeds, thus earning 12 percent commission. The company was to have an authorized capital stock of $100 million, 80 percent of which would be made available to the owners of the proprietary shares in installments coming due as 25-mile sections of the line were completed and brought into operation. The remaining 20 percent of the stock was to be issued, fully paid up, to Jay Cooke & Co. at a rate of $200 for each $1000 sale of bonds. The twelve proprietary shares distributed at the time of the Original Interests Agreement of 1867 were supplemented by twelve more, which were immediately assigned to Jay Cooke & Co. In return Jay Cooke agreed to raise a first $5 million for construction purposes within thirty days. This he did by selling $5 million Northern Pacific bonds at par to a pool of eastern investors, who were then allowed to purchase the new proprietary shares at a price of $50,000 each.

The risks undertaken by Jay Cooke & Co. as financial agents for the Northern Pacific Railroad Co. appeared to be minimal. At any given time, advances to the railroad company were to be restricted to $500,000 over and above proceeds available from the sale of bonds. And, with the exception of the first $5 million, bond sales were not guaranteed. One feature of the agreement, however, bode ill for the future. The bankers' control of the company's affairs was far from commensurate with their potential claim to ownership. They were only allowed to choose two of the thirteen directors, and two of the eight members of the executive committee.[17]

Once the agreement with Northern Pacific had been signed, Jay Cooke swept energetically through the various eastern business communities soliciting subscriptions to the $5 million pool. By January 24, 1870, largely as a result of exerting personal influence upon friends and business associates, he had fulfilled his task.[18] Some of the money, it was true, was to be paid later in installments, but enough had been made available to allow the work to begin at the earliest opportunity.

During the spring of 1870 surveys were carried out in Minnesota to locate a line from Thomson's Junction, 20 miles west of Duluth on the existing Lake Superior & Mississippi Railroad, to a point later known as Brainerd, on the Mississippi River. Contracts for building this first section of the main line were let in June 1870 and work began a month later. Thereafter, progress was rapid. By December of the same year the first objective had been reached and the graders were already pushing on westward towards the Red River.[19] Meanwhile, in April 1870, the Northern Pacific board instructed Richard D. Rice, George W. Cass, and William B. Ogden to proceed to the Pacific Coast for the purpose of locating the company's main and branch lines and selecting new townsites.[20] Soon, they too had work well under way.[21] Grading of the initial part of the line from the lower Columbia River to Puget Sound began in the Cowlitz Valley later in the year and the first 25 miles of track was laid there in the spring of 1871.

As the pace of construction quickened the procurement of more funds became urgent. In spite of Moorehead's failure to interest the Rothschilds, Jay Cooke still thought in terms of raising much of the money in Europe. Unfortunately, an alliance with German bankers,[22] formed in March 1870, was brought to an untimely end later that year by the outbreak of the Franco-Prussian War. Cooke was therefore obliged to fall back upon American sources of capital. Using methods previously developed to sell United States war bonds, he launched a high pressure sales campaign at home.[23] The results, however, were disappointing, for the patriotic emotions which had induced people to make wartime purchases of government bonds could not be regenerated to finance construction of a transcontinental railroad. To persist in trying to dispose of Northern Pacific securities on the same terms as United States war bonds was self-defeating. Although the Northern Pacific securities bore quite a high rate of interest, few people could be expected to buy them at par when securities of other more profitable railroads were being offered at a considerable discount. Had it not been for Jay Cooke's personal prestige the bonds would hardly have sold at all.

Elaborate preparations were made to take advantage of the land grant, but awards of land were only made to the company as adjacent 25-mile sections of the railway were completed and approved. Between Duluth and the Red River the line passed through heavily wooded country unsuitable for farming. Not until the Red River Valley was reached would any good agricultural land become available. For the time being, therefore, bond sales were the only remaining source of income. The subscriptions, however, failed to offset Northern Pacific Railroad Co. spending. By July 1, 1871, only $2.5 million had been subscribed over and above the original $5 million pool. Sales improved during the summer but the completion of a considerable length of railway demanded the purchase of locomotives and rolling stock. By August 23, 1871, the Northern Pacific overdraft upon Jay Cooke & Co. had reached $600,000 and was growing steadily.

Inadequate income apparently caused little concern among the officers of the Northern Pacific Railroad Co., who continued to award contracts and purchase large quantities of materials without pausing to consider where the money was to come from.[24] Jay Cooke & Co. was simply expected to provide the funds as required whether bonds had been sold or not. The blame for this state of affairs rested largely with the Northern Pacific president, John Gregory Smith, who drew a salary of $20,000 per year but spent very little time looking after the company's affairs. Construction work on the line was allowed to proceed without meaningful supervision by Northern Pacific personnel. The contractors were simply given a free hand and allowed to take maximum advantage of it!

As the Northern Pacific Railroad was extended westward bond sales followed fluctuations in the money market, rising to over $1 million in some months and falling to less than $400,000 in others.[25] Jay Cooke was between "the devil and deep sea." He was a banker with a responsibility to his depositors, but he was also a trustee for the railroad bondholders. He could have stopped further advances to Northern Pacific, but if he had done so construction would have been halted in the middle of nowhere. The ability of the railroad to earn revenues, either by hauling traffic or selling land, would then have been delayed indefinitely. Having failed to hold Smith to his promise to pause at the Red River, Cooke was practically obliged to underwrite construction of the railway to the next logical stopping place, on the Missouri.[26] He therefore had to commit the entire resources of Jay Cooke & Co. to the Northern Pacific enterprise and try as best he could to bring about some degree of cost control. Cooke had complained time and again to Smith about unrestrained spending, but to no avail. As matters got worse it became more and more clear that Smith would have to go. Finally, in May 1872, Cooke was presented with an $800,000 bill for rails purchased a year before they were needed.[27] That was the last straw! In June, Smith was induced to resign and in September the presidency of the company passed to George W. Cass.[28]

In the spring of 1872 the Northern Pacific directors turned their attention westward with the threefold purpose of selecting the best route from the Rocky Mountains to the Columbia River, securing the Columbia Gateway, and locating the terminus on Puget Sound.

There were several possible ways of getting from the Rocky Mountains to the lower Columbia Valley.[29] One was to head southwestward from the Three Forks of the Missouri over the mountains to the Salmon River basin, and then follow the Salmon and Snake rivers to the confluence with the Columbia. Another was to follow the Clark Fork River to Missoula, proceed south by west over the Lolo Pass to the valley of the Middle Fork Clearwater, and then descend with the Clearwater to meet the Snake at Lewiston. The third, and by far the easiest route, was to follow the incised valley of the Clark Fork all the way through the Bitterroot Range to Lake Pend d'Oreille and then pursue a southwesterly course across the Interior Plain. The survey parties had been trying for two years to find suitable passes through the mountains and had not succeeded. After a third attempt in 1872 they concluded that in the 300 miles to the south of Lake Pend d'Oreille the Bitterroots could not be crossed at any elevation less than 5,400 feet above sea level. The Clark Fork River route appeared to detour a long way to the north but was in fact found to be only 5 miles longer than a line crossing the Lolo Pass and following the hundred or more contorted miles of the Middle Fork Clearwater. The Clark Fork-Lake Pend d'Oreille line would be easier and less costly to build and operate, and there would be less risk of train services being disrupted by heavy falls of snow. By the end of 1872 all the arguments in its favor were already well developed and could not be denied.

Early in 1872 Northern Pacific was presented with an opportunity to gain control of the Columbia Gateway. The directors of the Oregon Steam Navigation Co., which had by then achieved an almost total monopoly of traffic on the Columbia River, became alarmed by the prospect of railroad competition and suddenly offered to sell out. Their proposition was too tempting to turn down, for the acquisition of the river fleet and the two existing portage railways could greatly facilitate construction of the Northern Pacific line from Portland to the Wallula Gap and might also be used to impede others. And if the present owners retained a minority interest, their powerful local influence could be used to strengthen the Northern Pacific position in Portland. Ignoring Jay Cooke's objections, Northern Pacific therefore purchased three-quarters of the Oregon Steam Navigation Co. stock.[30] The price was $1.5 million, of which $750,000 was remitted in the form of Northern Pacific bonds, $250,000 was to come from ongoing OSN earnings, and the remainder was to be paid in gold over the next nine months. The transaction was strategically sound. The only problem with it was that Jay Cooke, somehow or other, had to find the $500,000 worth of gold!

North of the Columbia, on the Pacific Division, work had been proceeding steadily. Another 50 miles of track were to be laid in the summer of 1872, and the line was expected to reach the southern end of Puget Sound in 1873. Definition of an ultimate destination was urgently needed. While Jay Cooke faced the coming financial storm, Messrs Cass, Ogden, Canfield, Billings, Wright, and Windom cruised the placid waters of the Sound in search of a site for the western terminus. On board the steamer *North Pacific*, W. Milnor

Roberts, who by then had been made chief engineer of the company, pointed out the salient features of various locations on the shore and discussed the many factors involved in the choice. A good harbor was most important but there also had to be enough flat land to accommodate railway yards. Of great concern to some of the directors, moreover, was the availability of a townsite with good potential for real estate promotion. Olympia was too far up a muddy tidal creek, Steilacoom was not an ideal harbor, and Seattle had no level ground. Points further north would require a longer railway, so were out of the question. All things considered, Tacoma, on Commencement Bay, appeared to be the most suitable choice. This finding was confirmed by a more detailed study carried out soon afterward by Richard D. Rice, who was ably assisted by Captain J. C. Ainsworth of the Oregon Steam Navigation Co. A final recommendation was sent to New York in July 1872, and an executive committee decision to adopt Tacoma as terminus was ratified by the board on September 10, 1872.[31]

On the Great Plains, meanwhile, progress was also being made. At the close of 1871 the railroad had reached the Red River, and during 1872 it was pushed rapidly toward the Missouri. In a report to the United States secretary of the interior, written on September 30, 1872, Samuel Wilkeson stated that over 2 miles of track were being laid each day, and predicted that the road would reach the Missouri River in less than five weeks. Wilkeson, however, seemed to be trying to maintain a climate of optimism. As usual, he waxed enthusiastic about the country through which the railroad passed, noting "the directors of the Company have been most happily disappointed in finding that their entire line in Dakota ran through an agricultural region adapted equally to grain and grazing and of an average excellence equal to the lands in Illinois."[32] If the line could only be completed all might yet be well. The realities of the financial situation, however, were far from reassuring.

In February 1873 confidence in large railway ventures was completely undermined by the disturbing revelations of a congressional investigation into the fraudulent relationship between the Union Pacific Railroad Co. and its auxiliary "construction" company, Credit Mobilier of America.[33] Sales of Northern Pacific bonds, which had reached a very low level the year before, practically ceased. In April 1873 Jay Cooke decided to close the 7.3 percent bond issue at $30 million.[34] Up to that time $21 million had been placed. The remaining $9 million, which he hoped would be enough to complete the sections of line under construction and repay the amounts overdrawn, were offered to a syndicate at a price of 83-plus-interest. Money, however, was still tight and the market was flooded with railroad bonds. Consequently, less than $2 million was subscribed.

During the summer of 1873 matters improved a little, and there were some encouraging indications of Northern Pacific's future potential. The railroad was completed to the Missouri River at a point named Bismarck, 450 miles west of Duluth, on June 3.[35] Work on the Pacific Division meanwhile proceeded rapidly. With a total of over 500 miles of road completed, the company was already entitled to 10 million acres of land. Moreover, as a result of enterprising efforts by European-based agents of the company's immigration department, first settlers were beginning to arrive. In the year ending June 30, 1873, railway traffic revenues amounted to more than $500,000.

Unfortunately the summer respite was overshadowed by apprehension about the fall. The burden of supporting the railroad and paying for its subsidiaries told heavily upon the bankers. By August 15, 1873, $5.1 million had been advanced to Northern Pacific and another $1.8 million to Lake Superior & Mississippi, which had been leased by Northern Pacific.[36] Jay Cooke & Co. was in poor condition to weather another financial storm, and many other firms, ominously, were no better off. There was an early harvest in 1873 and the financial stringency of the previous winter re-asserted itself sooner than expected.[37] Serious trouble began on September 8, when the New York Warehouse & Securities Company, which had been financing the Missouri Kansas & Texas Railroad, declared itself insolvent. On September 13 Kenyon Cox & Company, who had been acting in a similar manner for the Canada Southern Railway, also went under. Thereafter, matters went from bad to worse. Shortly before 11:00 a.m. on Thursday, September 18, 1873, Jay Cooke & Co., New York, was obliged to close its doors, and within the hour the Philadelphia and Washington houses did likewise.[38] The failure of Jay Cooke & Co. was followed immediately by suspension of business at the First National Bank of Washington D.C., and precipitated panic on the New York stock market. There was a rush to sell bonds, depositors withdrew their money, loans were called, and financial collapse ensued. Worst hit were the bankers and brokers who had invested heavily in railroads or made large advances to sustain their construction. On Friday, September 14 alone, thirty major financial houses failed, and during the following month more and more went under. Credit dried up overnight, railway construction ground to a halt, and iron mills and other factories closed down. Several hundred thousand persons were thrown out of work and suddenly found themselves "distressed to obtain means of life."[39] Destitution, hunger, and crime stalked the land.

At the time of Jay Cooke's downfall the rails of the Pacific Division were still 22 miles from Tacoma. For some time the work went on without interruption and another 10 miles of railway were completed, but at that point the company ran out of money. Angry workmen demanding $73,300 arrears in wages seized the Clover Creek trestle bridge and prevented any further progress. Their action created a desperate situation that was relieved only when Captain J. C. Ainsworth, who had joined the Northern Pacific board in September 1872 and was acting as Pacific Coast managing director, came to the rescue with his own money and credit. The work got under way again and the line was completed to Tacoma just 24 hours before the charter deadline at the end of the year.[40]

Once the Kalama-Tacoma line had been completed, construction of the Northern Pacific Railroad came to a complete halt. Financially *in extremis,* the company was obliged to part with its subsidiaries and, unfortunately, lost control of the Columbia Gateway. The depression that followed the financial collapse of 1873 was long and severe. Northern Pacific was barely able to meet its operating expenses and could no longer pay the interest on its bonded debt. The creditors were nevertheless held at bay for more than a year.

During this period, and for some time afterward, the pace of the company's railway operations remained stagnant. In 1876 the Pacific Division was reported to have a staff of 114 persons employed at " . . . salaries and wages as low as can be maintained in that country."[41] Of these employees sixty were Chinese who were paid $27 per month. The service between Kalama and Tacoma was limited to a single mixed train each way daily. The line, however, was operated on a year-round basis, which was more than could be said for the Dakota Division. Beyond the Red River the railroad was completely shut down every winter until 1876-77[42] when the United States Army asked that it be kept open for troop movements. For several years the company had been using threat of Indian attack and lack of military protection as excuses for deferring work.[43] The Army's request, therefore, could hardly be denied, and the trains were at last obliged to venture forth into the prairie snows.

The lack of construction activity left the Northern Pacific Railroad Co. vulnerable to political attacks upon the land grant. In 1875 citizens of Seattle and residents of new communities in Eastern Washington, acting in concert, proposed to build a Seattle & Walla Walla Railroad through Snoqualmie Pass,[44] and demanded that the land which had been promised to Northern Pacific for building the Cascade branch be awarded to their enterprise instead. This threat to the land grant forced the Northern Pacific directors to devise a method of canceling the company's debt and restoring freedom of action. For this purpose Frederick Billings put forward a bold plan of reorganization.[45] Preferred shares in a new Northern Pacific Railroad Co. would be issued in return for bonds of the old company. Every $1,000 worth of bonds would be replaced by $1,400 worth of preferred stock. Thus, the bondholders would become part owners of the company and the debt would disappear. Common stock was to be exchanged on a share-for-share basis, but in any particular year no dividends would be paid on the common until the preferred had received 8 percent. On April 16, 1875, the old company was declared bankrupt and General Cass was appointed receiver. Then, on August 12, 1875, the mortgage was foreclosed, the rights and property were sold to the reorganization committee, and a new Northern Pacific Railroad Co. came into being. By the end of 1875 the bonds had been exchanged for preferred stock and the debt was eliminated.

Northern Pacific was still in a poor position to resume construction, but if the land grant was to be preserved in its entirety some action had to be taken. Fortunately, just at that time, coal was discovered on the western flank of the Cascade Mountains. Most of the coal then used in Portland and San Francisco arrived as ballast in ships coming from England to load grain. The supply was somewhat limited, and in Portland the prevailing price was $11 per ton. In the summer of 1875 Benjamin Fallows, an experienced mining engineer from Pennsylvania, examined the Washington deposits and reported them to consist of bituminous coal of excellent quality, that could be mined and sold in Portland for $7 per ton. Later that year surveys were made for a railway extending southeastward from Tacoma, by way of Puyallup to the mines, and on May 6, 1876, a finalized right-of-way plan was filed with the Department of the Interior. The company then diverted the net earnings of the Minnesota and Dakota Divisions into a fund to be used for construction purposes and began work on the roadbed between Tacoma and the new colliery town of Wilkeson. Charles B. Wright of Philadelphia, the president of the reorganized Northern Pacific Railroad Co., meanwhile, used his personal credit to obtain a cargo of rails and had it shipped around Cape Horn to Puget Sound. Grading was completed in the summer of 1877 and by September of that year 17 miles of track had been laid. The whole 31 miles of railway was finished shortly afterward,[46] at a total cost of $552,732.17. The output of the Wilkeson colliery was unfortunately limited by serious flooding problems, but the railway had been built and Northern Pacific had gained a foothold in the Cascades.

The very incorporation of the Seattle & Walla Walla Railroad suggested that settlement on the Interior Plain was becoming an increasingly important factor in the development of the Northwest. That the Northern Pacific directors realized this was demonstrated in the 1877 *Report to Stockholders*, which noted that "a rapid agricultural settlement is now being made upon that part of our unconstructed line, extending eastwards from the Columbia River. . . ." The report drew attention to the land there, saying that "the high rolling plains of this region have, from the time of their first exploration, been considered wonders of pasture land, but the fact of their possessing also enormous grain producing capacity has but lately been determined." A contemporary article by the Rev. George H. Atkinson, Home Missionary for the Congregational Churches of Oregon and Washington Territory, which was also quoted, intimated that "these high table lands, under the plow, exhibit the finest tilth, from one to twenty feet or more deep, and alike through the whole mass."[47]

In October 1872, Northern Pacific's chief engineer, W. Milnor Roberts, summarized the relative merits of the company's main and branch lines to Puget Sound, noting that the Columbia River route would have easier grades, suffer less from falls of snow, give direct access to Portland, and allow the company to use the river transportation system to leap-frog rapidly into " . . . a region which admits of settlement."[48] By 1878 it had become clear that Northern Pacific's next priority would be to occupy the Interior Plain. As Milnor Roberts had suggested, construction of the railway along the Columbia River from Kalama to Portland and Wallula was to be deferred until later.

During 1879, preparations were made for construction of the so-called Lake Pend d'Oreille Division, which was to extend 225 miles from the confluence of the Snake and Columbia rivers to Lake Pend d'Oreille in Northern Idaho. To finance the work the company issued $4.5 million 6 percent first mortgage bonds and offered a gratuity of $70 worth of preferred stock for every $100 worth of bonds subscribed. While these financial arrangements were being made, survey parties were sent into the field to locate the line, tenders were called for bridge timbers and ties, and a first consignment of 2,500 tons of iron rails was dispatched from the East Coast to the Columbia River by ocean freight.

In the annual *Report to Stockholders*, issued on September 24, 1879, the company announced that it had " . . . been enabled through a full and complete adjustment of its affairs, to avail itself of the favorable circumstances of the times and resume its work of extending the main line of the road."[49] Construction of the Lake Pend d'Oreille Division would be started as soon as possible. Everything appeared to be going along according to plan, but just as Northern Pacific started to build their line northeastward the newly formed Oregon Railway & Navigation Co. moved into the gap behind them and thirty years of bitter railroad rivalry commenced.

2

OREGON STEAM NAVIGATION

The Columbia River provided the Oregon country with a great highway to the Interior. For thirty years or more before the advent of overland railroads the steamboats probed the hinterland and brought its wealth downstream to Portland. The waterway, however, was not continuous, for the impassable rapids at the Cascades, and falls between The Dalles and Celilo, divided the Columbia and Snake river system into three separate navigable reaches, known individually as the Lower, Middle and Upper rivers. Each section had its own captive steamers, and between sections there were quite long portages. Every ton of freight proceeding up or down the river therefore had to be loaded onto and taken off three different steamboats and two portage railways. The system was cumbersome, but one powerful company, gaining control of the portages, secured a monopoly of all the traffic on the river and carried on a very profitable business for almost twenty years.

The first steamboat to ply the waters of the Columbia River, and indeed the first such vessel on the entire Pacific Coast of North America, was the Hudson's Bay Company's diminutive side-wheeler *Beaver*, built on the Thames in 1835 and brought to Fort Vancouver by way of Cape Horn and Honolulu in 1836.[1] The earliest regular steamboat service was provided by the *Columbia*, which was built at Astoria in 1850 and spent the next two or three years making round trips between Astoria, Portland, Oregon City, and Vancouver.[2]

Columbia was quickly followed by the much larger *Lot Whitcomb* built by S. S. White, Berryman Jennings, and Lot Whitcomb at Milwaukie on the Willamette River in 1850, and placed in service in 1851.[3] *Lot Whitcomb* was a significant venture, and the more so because two men brought to Oregon to run her were later to play a vital part in the development of navigation on the Columbia River. Whitcomb procured the steamer's machinery in San Francisco, where it had originally been sent for use on a Sacramento River vessel. At the same time he also persuaded the mechanic who was to have erected the engines, and a young Upper Mississippi riverboatman who had migrated to California to act as pilot, to return with him to Oregon. The one became chief engineer of the *Lot Whitcomb*, and the other took command of the vessel and became its part owner. The two men were Jacob Kamm and J. C. Ainsworth.

In 1850 the opening of a United States Army post at The Dalles[4] appeared to offer prospects of up-river traffic. The brothers Daniel F. and Putnam T. Bradford, who had established themselves at the Lower Cascades Landing, therefore, got together with Captain J. O. Van Bergen and built a small side-wheel steamer called the *James P. Flint*, which they hauled over the rapids and put into service on the Middle River.[5] The expected business, however, failed to materialize, and during the following season the *James P. Flint* was returned to the Lower River, where she was only operated for a short time before striking a rock and sinking. In 1853 she was raised and taken to Vancouver, where the hull was repaired and fitted out with the engines of the *Columbia*, thus producing a "new" steamboat called *Fashion*.[6]

For two years traffic between Portland and the Cascades was very light, and *Fashion* was apparently the only steamboat working on the route. In 1855, however, Governor Isaac Stevens of the newly formed Washington Territory initiated moves designed to concentrate the Interior Indians in reservations and free the remainder of Eastern Washington for settlement. This policy inevitably led to trouble and there were armed clashes between Indians and whites.[7] Military forces were sent up-country to quell the disturbances and traffic on the Columbia River increased. At about the same time the Bradfords sold the *Fashion*, replacing her first with *Belle* and later with *Senorita*. They also opened a boat-building yard at the Upper Cascades Landing, and joining forces with Lawrence W. Coe, built the *Mary* for use on the Middle River. *Fashion*, meanwhile, changed hands several times and was eventually bought by Captain J. O. Van Bergen and Colonel Joseph Ruckel.[8] These gentlemen then formed an alliance with Captain McFarland of The Dalles and built the *Wasco* to serve as their own Middle River connection.[9] By the end of 1855 two rival groups of steamboat owners were thus established on the river and both of them sought to secure portages at the Cascades.

A first attempt to ease the difficulty of handling freight at the Cascades was made in 1851 when Francis A. Chenoweth, a young lawyer from Ohio, built a primitive wooden tramway on the Washington side of the river.[10] Chenoweth used a single mule-hauled vehicle to transfer goods from the steamer *James P. Flint* on the Middle River to the old brig *Henry* on the Lower River and charged 75 cents per cwt. for his trouble. For some time business was fairly brisk but after the *Flint* left for the Lower River traffic dwindled, and Chenoweth, becoming discouraged, sold out to the Bradfords. When activity increased again in 1855, the old tramway had to be rebuilt. This work was still in progress when the Klickitat and Yakima Indians attempted to beseige the Upper Landing in March 1856, and was completed shortly afterward. The line did not, however, extend below the Middle Landing. Ascending steamers, therefore, had to breast the lower Cascades rapids to reach it.

In 1857 Colonel Ruckel and Captain Van Bergen replaced the *Fashion* with a larger steamer called *Mountain Buck*.[11] Until that time goods exchanged with the *Wasco* moved over a wagon road operated on the Oregon side of the river by W. R. Kilborn.[12] Increased traffic, however, dictated that better facilities be provided, and in 1858 a start was made on a new portage railroad.[13] The work was at first directed by Captain Van Bergen but he soon withdrew and Colonel Ruckel was obliged to take the job over. The project suffered from a chronic lack of money, and when a section of the partly completed line was washed away in the spring flood of 1859 work was temporarily abandoned.

All the early steamboats were side-wheelers but a new type of vessel was soon introduced. With the benefit of several years of local experience Jacob Kamm and J. C. Ainsworth concluded that stern-wheelers would be better suited to the narrow Willamette waterway. With cleaner lines such vessels might also consume less fuel, a factor increasing in importance as the Columbia River operations were extended into the open treeless country of the Interior. In 1854 they built *Jennie Clark*, the first stern-wheeler in the Northwest, and brought about a regional revolution in the naval architecture of riverboats.[14] *Jennie Clark* was employed on the Willamette River between Portland and Oregon City, but in 1857 the Bradfords placed a similar vessel called *Hassaloe*[15] in service on the Middle River, thus helping *Mary* compete more effectively with *Wasco*.

As the Indian wars progressed there was a growing demand from the Army for transportation on the Upper River. Lawrence W. Coe therefore sold his interest in the *Mary* and joined R. R. Thompson in contracting with the government to carry supplies for Fort Walla Walla. In 1858 these gentlemen constructed two new stern-wheelers to handle the up-river traffic. *Venture*[16] was completed at Five Mile

Creek, near the Upper Cascades Landing for service on the Middle River, and *Colonel Wright*[17] was launched at the mouth of the Deschutes for work above Celilo. The *Venture*, unfortunately, was swept stern-first over the Cascades on her first trial trip and, although only slightly damaged, was sold. *Colonel Wright* compensated for her wayward sister. She ran a maiden trip to Wallula in the spring of 1859, and being the first steamer to work above The Dalles, was an immediate commercial success. Passengers who traveled with her on the downstream journey arrived in Portland just 30 hours after leaving Walla Walla! Commanded by Captain Leonard White, she made three round-trips to Wallula each week, and, although the freight rate was reduced to $80 per ton, her owners rapidly made a fortune.

On October 29, 1858, General W. S. Harney, commanding the military district of Oregon and Washington, proclaimed the Indian wars to be over and without further formality threw the Interior open to settlement. In anticipation, perhaps, of the burden that this edict would impose upon their facilities, the steamboat owners soon moved to place their operations on a sounder organizational footing. In 1859 J. C. Ainsworth, Jacob Kamm, and the Portland banker, W. S. Ladd, formed an association with the Bradfords, Joseph Ruckel, and others for the purpose of coordinating steamboat services on the Lower and Middle Rivers. The vessels *Jennie Clark, Carrie Ladd, Express, Multnomah, Mountain Buck, Senorita, Wasco,* and *Hassaloe* were thus brought under loosely unified control. The association, which was known as the Union Transportation Line,[18] was found to work well. A year later, therefore, matters were taken further. An understanding was reached with R. R. Thompson and Lawrence Coe concerning the *Colonel Wright*. Then, on May 12, 1860, after a great deal of argument over the relative value of their respective assets, the riverboat owners agreed to pool resources. Formal incorporation followed. On December 19, 1860, the Washington Territorial Legislature passed a special enabling Act and ten days later the Oregon Steam Navigation Co. was formed.[19]

OSN had no sooner been organized than it was overwhelmed with traffic. Gold was found on the Clearwater in the summer of 1860, and there was a first rush to the Interior in the spring of 1861. More discoveries were then made and an even greater rush developed in 1862. Unfortunately, the Cascades portages presented a serious bottleneck. The company had agreed to pay the portage owners one-quarter of the tariff charged for moving goods from Portland to The Dalles, $5 per ton out of a total $20 per ton, seven-twelfths of which accrued to the Bradfords and five-twelfths to Ruckel, regardless of which portage was actually used.[20] The settlement was generous but the portage owners persisted in using their position as OSN directors to fend off claims for theft and damages sustained at the Cascades. Morever, mutual jealousy between the Bradfords and the Ruckel group impeded work on improvements needed to facilitate the flow of traffic. Inevitably, the other OSN directors concluded that the portages would have to be taken over.

When OSN was first formed, most of the Lower River traffic was carried on Ainsworth's powerful stern-wheeler *Carrie Ladd,* which was able to run the lower Cascades rapids and turn freight over to the Bradfords' railroad at the Middle Landing.[21] As the loads increased, however, this procedure was frequently found to be impossible. Completion of the full-length portage railway on the Oregon side of the river therefore became a matter of urgency. Ruckel, however, lacked the necessary funds and had to borrow money from Ladd & Tilton, who appointed Harrison Olmstead to look after their interests.[22] In November 1859 the title to Ruckel's land at the Cascades was transferred to Olmstead in trust. A civil engineer named John W. Brazee was engaged to supervise completion of the 4-1/2-mile-long portage railway line. The work was finished in May 1861. All the traffic was then concentrated on the Oregon side of the river.

During the first year of operation Ruckel and Olmstead used horses and mules to haul the freight, but in the spring of 1862 they obtained a small steam locomotive. *Pony,* later referred to as the *Oregon Pony,* was an 0-4-0 tank engine of grotesque appearance, designed and built by Charles W. Stevens at the Vulcan Iron Works in San Francisco. It cost $4,000, which was covered by an advance from Ladd & Tilton. The little engine was put in working order by a manufacturer's representative named Theodore A. Goffe and first ran in steam on May 10, 1862.[23] Strap-iron had to be added to the face of the 6 X 6 ft. timber rails to carry it.

Meanwhile, on the Washington side of the river a group of local residents obtained a territorial charter to build a Cascades railroad, which was to extend all the way to the Lower Landing and thus bypass the rapids completely.[24] In October 1861 this charter was sold to the Bradfords who then had surveys made to locate a suitable line. In May 1862, however, OSN stepped in and bought both charter and survey. Then, to Joseph Ruckel's consternation, they began to build a first-class railroad on the opposite bank of the river.[25] And, as if all that were not enough, the Bradfords retained ownership of their now disused tramway and continued to claim seven-twelfths of all the revenues earned by the railway on the Oregon side![26]

It was an intolerable situation. On October 24, 1862, Harrison Olmstead, in desperation, proposed that OSN take over the Oregon portage. That, of course, was exactly what Ainsworth wanted. There was some haggling over its value but on November 6, 1862, the property was conveyed.[27] The price was $155,000, of which $49,000 was paid to Harrison Olmstead for disbursement to Ruckel and associates, and the remaining $106,000 went to Ladd & Tilton to cover outstanding debts. Control of the portages thus became vested in the one single organization and a monopoly of the river traffic was virtually secured.

In anticipation of a final settlement with the portage owners OSN was reincorporated in the state of Oregon on October 18, 1862.[28] The reorganized Oregon Steam Navigation Co. had a capital of $2 million in 4,000 shares. The principal shareholders were: the Bradfords and their associates (758 shares), R. R. Thompson (672 shares), Harrison Olmstead (558 shares), Jacob Kamm (254 shares), Lawrence W. Coe (336 shares), T. W. Lyles (210 shares), J. C. Ainsworth (188 shares), A. Barker (260 shares), and Simeon G. Reed (128 shares). Captain J. C. Ainsworth was president, and D. F. Bradford, vice president. George W. Murray was company secretary. The directors were J. C. Ainsworth, D. F. Bradford, L. W. Coe, S. G. Reed, and J. S. Ruckel. By 1867 ownership of the company was concentrated in the hands of J. C. Ainsworth, R. R. Thompson, and S. G. Reed.[29] In 1872 a three-quarters interest was sold to Northern Pacific Railroad Co., but when that company encountered financial difficulty following the collapse of Jay Cooke & Co. in 1873 some of the shares reverted to the "big three" in Portland and the remainder were dispersed among Northern Pacific creditors. Fortunately the stock was unfamiliar to eastern investors and its price fell. Ainsworth, Thompson, and Reed were therefore able to buy it back at very low prices and soon regained complete working control of the company.

OSN's first priority was to bring more steamers into service on the Upper River. Before the 1860 incorporation the stern-wheeler *Tenino* had been laid down by Coe and Thompson at the mouth of the Deschutes River. *Okanogan* followed in 1861 and both were ready for the great rush to the Interior in 1862.[30] These vessels were to make their owners wealthy men! Traffic increased rapidly from 10,500 passengers and 6,290 tons of freight in 1861, to 24,500 passengers and 14,500 tons of freight in 1862. Altogether in the years 1861 to

1864 the company's steamers carried 93,000 passengers and 60,000 tons of freight. In April and May 1862 upstream passenger fares collected at The Dalles alone averaged over $4,000 per departure and reached a maximum of $10,945. For freight, fares, meals, and berths *Tenino* brought in a record $18,000 in one single trip![31]

Golden days, indeed, but the system was strained to the very limit. With the arrival of every ship from San Francisco a fresh multitude clamored for passage to the Interior. On the Lower River J. C. Ainsworth's fine *Carrie Ladd* was helped out by *Mountain Buck* and the decrepit steeple-engined side-wheeler *Wilson G. Hunt*. Some passengers also traveled on the Bradfords' big stern-wheeler *Julia*.[32] On the Middle River, where the old *Mary* and *Wasco* were almost life-expired and the *Hassaloe* underpowered, Colonel Joseph Ruckel's new side-wheeler *Idaho* bore the brunt of the traffic. Fortunately the passage from Upper Cascades Landing to The Dalles was only about 38 miles and a relatively rapid turnaround could be made. Freight, however, piled up at the portages!

The portage railways[33] were put into order as quickly as possible, but the Cascades railroad especially involved a great deal of trestle work, and progress was slow. The new line from The Dalles to Celilo, which took the place of Orlando Humason's old wagon road over the high ground, was easier to build, but suffered perennially from burial by drifting sand. Both lines used iron rails laid to 5-ft. gauge. At the terminals floating landing stages for the steamers were reached by inclines over which the railway vehicles were moved by rope haulage. At The Dalles and Celilo the ropes were activated by steam-driven winding engines. In 1862 *Pony* and two other small locomotives called *Anne* and *Betsy* were the only mechanical motive power available. *Anne* and *Betsy* were merely enlarged versions of *Pony*, each one being combined with a flatcar to form an odd-looking, self-propelled utility vehicle.[34] Something more sophisticated was obviously required! Lawrence W. Coe, who had been appointed OSN resident manager at The Dalles, was therefore sent east to buy larger locomotives and standard railway rolling stock.[35] The result was a pair of Danforth & Cooke 4-2-4 tank engines named *D. F. Bradford* and *J. C. Ainsworth*, and a relatively respectable ensemble of twin truck passenger coaches and boxcars. The locomotives must have been more picturesque than powerful and for that reason, perhaps, four American standard type 4-4-0 engines were procured later.[36] Coe's shopping spree was his last assignment for OSN. Shortly afterward he sold his holding in the company and retired to San Francisco a wealthy man. He was thirty-two years of age! The two new portage railways were opened on April 20, 1863.[37] Olmstead's Oregon portage railroad at the Cascades was then left disused.

In 1863 OSN's difficulties on the Columbia River were eased by an agreement with the People's Transportation Company, whereby OSN withdrew from the Willamette and the PTC abandoned the Columbia.[38] OSN was then able to concentrate more vessels between Portland and the Cascades and stabilize the freight rates and passenger fares as follows:

Portland to	Freight (per ton)	Passengers (per person)
The Dalles	$15	$ 6
Umatilla	$45	$10
Wallula	$50	$12
Lewiston	$90	$22

Three new steamers were placed in service that same year.[39] The *Oneonta,* a large side-wheeler sporting high twin smokestacks, Mississippi style, was put on the Middle River. She was a fine looking vessel but very expensive to operate and therefore the last of her type to be taken into the OSN fleet. *Nez Perce Chief* and *Webfoot,* meanwhile, were built for the Upper River. They too suffered from disadvantages. *Nez Perce Chief* lacked cargo space, while the larger *Webfoot* was poorly constructed and constantly gave trouble. Fortunately, they were supplemented in 1864 by *Yakima* and *Owyhee.*[40] *Yakima* was one of the fastest boats ever to ply the waters of the Columbia. In June 1867 she ran the 279 miles from Celilo to Lewiston, against a strong current, in 41 hours 35 minutes, thus averaging 6.7 mph upstream.

As the mining excitement ran its course and the diggings were extended to ever-remoter areas, the steamboat men tried their best to follow. Few went farther than Captain Leonard White,[41] R. R. Thompson's erstwhile commander of the *Colonel Wright,* who had resigned from OSN because J. C. Ainsworth wanted to reduce his salary. White pioneered navigation on the far upper reaches of the Columbia. In 1865 he set up a boat-building yard at the Little Dalles, 16 miles south of the international boundary, and using engines salvaged from the *Jennie Clark* built a small stern-wheeler called *Forty-Nine.*[42] On December 9 of that year he set off northward, cutting wood as he went, and reached the head of the Lower Arrow Lake before winter compelled him to retreat. Next spring he was back, going as far north as Arrow Head. He then ran an irregular service on that 175-mile-long route for the next four successive seasons. Leonard White was a gifted pathfinder. Tragically, the hardships of life in the wilderness undermined his health. He died at Portland in 1870.

OSN attempted to cover as much of the routes to Boise, Idaho, and Helena, Montana, as they possibly could. At great expense *Shoshone* was built at Old Fort Boise in 1866 for service between there and Old's Ferry on the Upper Snake River.[43] Before she could be completed, however, the teamsters found a better route to the mines and she was left with little work to do. Eventually Ainsworth decided to recover her for use elsewhere. In April 1870, Captain Sebastian Miller, chief engineer Daniel E. Buchanan, and three men, Livingston, Smith, and Hedges, brought her down the Hell's Canyon of the Snake River to Lewiston, the first of but few vessels ever to make that hair-raising trip. She was later taken over both the Tumwater Falls and the Cascades and delivered to Portland, thus traveling a greater continuous length of the Snake and Columbia rivers than any other vessel ever to grace those waters.

While *Shoshone* was being put together at Boise, an OSN subsidiary called Oregon & Montana Transportation Co., set up in Northern Idaho, built the *Mary Moody* for service on Lake Pend d'Oreille and the Clark Fork River. Others, meanwhile, constructed *Cabinet* and *Missoula* for use on the separate navigable reaches of the Clark Fork between Cabinet Rapids, Thompson's Falls, and the mouth of the Jocko. These endeavors were intended to ease the rigors of the journey to Last Chance Gulch, but they too were a commercial fiasco.[44] In June 1870 the service was withdrawn and the intrepid Captain Miller, fresh from his exploits on the Snake River, brought the *Cabinet* and *Missoula* through the rapids to be laid up on the lake. Portland's tenuous bid to influence events in the remote Interior thus ended in failure.

During the depression years of the early 1870s few new steamers were added to the OSN fleet. In 1871 *Dixie Thompson* and *Emma Hayward* were built for the Portland-Astoria run,[45] and in 1873 the *Daisy Ainsworth* was put on the Middle River.[46] No significant changes took place until two unfortunate mishaps occurred several years later. In 1875 *Yakima* sank after striking a rock at the John Day Rapids, and then, one foggy night in November 1876, *Daisy*

Ainsworth was wrecked on the rocks near the Upper Cascades Landing. These disasters inconveniently coincided with returning prosperity and growth of grain shipments from the Interior, and resulted in an acute shortage of vessels. A series of new steamers was therefore laid down.

The magnificent *Wide West*,[47] described as "the perfect stern-wheeler," was placed in service on the Lower River in 1877 and joined by the *S. G. Reed* in 1878.[48]

Mountain Queen[49] was built in 1877 to fill the gap left in the Middle River fleet by the loss of the *Daisy Ainsworth*. *Oneonta* was then retired to make way for the luxurious *R. R. Thompson*.[50] On the Upper River *New Tenino*[51] replaced *Tenino* in 1876; *Almota* and *Annie Faxon*[52] got under way in 1877; *Spokane,*[53] *John Gates*, and the elegant *Harvest Queen*[54] appeared in 1878; and the fleet was rounded out by *D. S. Baker* in 1879.

Fine new vessels all, but their days were numbered, for quite apart from imminent construction of an overland railroad along the Columbia Valley, significant changes were beginning to take place in the pattern of Portland's trade with the Interior. The stern-wheelers were well able to cope with passengers and general cargo, but they were hard-pressed to handle steadily increasing quantities of grain. During the Gold Rush of the 1860s the steamers carried an average 15,000 tons of freight per year up-river from Celilo, and in 1864 six vessels totaling about 2,455 net tons register moved a peak 21,834 tons.[55] In 1878 27,000 tons of grain had to be moved down-river from Wallula.[56] In each case the freight-handling capacity of the Upper River transportation system seems to have been about nine tons per available vessel-net-ton per year, which suggests that during the late 1870s the rate of expansion of grain shipments from the Interior may well have been limited by the productive capacity of the boat-building yard at Celilo.[57]

Utilization of available vessels was severely restricted by seasonal conditions on the river.[58] The water was generally high in the summer and low in the winter, so that just when the harvest was ready to be moved the river level fell and the steamers began to run aground. During the winter months navigation on the Snake River was out of the question and the company tried to turn its vessels around at Wallula. During periods of very low water, however, the service had to be terminated below the rapids at Umatilla. And, as if that were not bad enough, freezing weather could bring everything to a halt for as much as sixty days a year.[59]

As the Interior was opened the effect of all these disadvantages became more and more acute. It now seems likely that even if the overland railroad companies had not wanted to use the Columbia Valley to reach tidewater a railway would, in any case, have been built from The Dalles to Wallula and beyond to bypass the Upper River navigation and facilitate the flow of export grain. That the ability of the riverboats to handle grain became critical just as efforts to complete the Northern Pacific Railroad were renewed was to have a significant influence on the immediate course of events.

OSN had been a fabulous success. In less than seventeen years between its incorporation with $2 million capital in 1862 and its final sale for $5 million in 1879, $2.7 million were paid out in dividends and $3 million were put back into the company.[60] When the property was turned over to the newly formed Oregon Railway & Navigation Co. on July 1, 1879, the Columbia River fleet[61] consisted of fourteen vessels, all but four of which were less than three years old. There were also the two portage railways and the recently acquired Walla Walla Columbia River Railroad. And at the same time the subsidiary Willamette Locks & Transportation Company provided another fourteen steamers.

The Oregon Steam Navigation Co. had served the Northwest well enough, but by 1879 the days when the riverboats could keep pace with the development of the Interior were over. Ainsworth's successor intended not only to preserve the established regional influence of Portland but also to secure a monopoly of railway transportation and economic activity throughout the Pacific Northwest.

3

HENRY VILLARD'S DEBUT

The Oregon Steam Navigation Co. earned such handsome profits that its owners had no incentive to build a railway along the Columbia Valley.[1] The early history of railways in Oregon therefore is that of lines on either side of the Willamette River.[2]

On July 25, 1866 the United States Congress made provision for two companies to be formed under the laws of California and Oregon, and set aside land to encourage the construction of a railway linking the two states. The same Act gave the state legislators power to administer the land grant. Four months later, a group of Portland businessmen formed the Oregon Central Railroad Co. and duly claimed both the franchise and the land.[3] Although the promoters of this "west side road" included the OSN "big three" and other wealthy men, little money was subscribed. Construction was delayed and the land grant placed in jeopardy.

Others quickly took advantage of the situation. An unscrupulous Californian promoter named S. G. Elliot persuaded Governor Woods and other influential Oregonians to join him in promoting a rival Oregon Central Railroad Co. of Salem, or "east side road," incorporated on April 22, 1867. During the following year Elliot was ousted by Ben Holladay, a former stage coach and freight line operator, who had grown rich by questionable means. Holladay, quickly persuaded the legislature to revoke the franchise granted to the original Oregon Central Railroad and transfer it to his own company. On March 16, 1870 he formed the Oregon & California Railroad Co., which took over the assets of the east side road and provided an advantageous legal framework for raising further funds. The west side company, deprived of the land grant, then sold out to Holladay on his terms.

The Oregon & California Railroad was financed by extensive issues of first mortgage bonds, sold mainly in Germany.[4] Advancing southward the railway reached Roseburg in 1872. Construction had proceeded rapidly, but the venture was not very successful. The associated European & Oregon Land Company, with offices in New

York and San Francisco, offered the land at reasonable prices, but the country was covered in dense forest and there was no existing market for the lumber that would have been produced by clearing it. Few settlers bought land, the country remained undeveloped, and the promised railway traffic and revenues failed to materialize. In 1873 the company failed to meet its financial obligations, and the German investors were obliged to appoint a special agent to protect their interests.[5] The name of this envoy extraordinary was Henry Villard.

Henry Villard (Ferdinand Heinrich Gustav Hilgard)[6] was born the son of a distinguished jurist at Speyer, in Rhenish Bavaria, on April 10, 1835. He was educated in schools at Zweibrucken and at Pfalzbourg in Lorraine, and briefly attended the universities at Munich and Wurzburg. As a result of the revolutionary upheavals of 1848 he was exposed to liberal ideas that conflicted with his father's conservative opinions and led to dissension within the family. In 1853, therefore, he emigrated to America, where he adopted the name by which he was later well known. He established a reputation as a journalist, formed a personal acquaintance with Abraham Lincoln, and became a successful Washington press correspondent. During the early part of the Civil War he accompanied the Union Army in both Virginia and Tennessee and reported directly from the battlefields. In 1863 he contracted malaria and was forced to retire to Germany for a prolonged period of convalescence. He returned to the United States in 1865 and married Helen Frances "Fanny" Garrison, daughter of the abolitionist William Lloyd Garrison, early in 1866. After a period of almost two years as secretary of the American Social Science Institution in Boston, he accepted a newspaper assignment to cover the Franco-Prussian War, and when that was over he settled down to live at Wiesbaden, near Frankfurt am Main in Germany. He then became interested in the negotiation of American railroad securities and began to play an active part in the work of several committees formed for the protection of German investors. His extensive knowledge of the United States was recognized as a valuable asset in the conduct of such affairs and in 1874 the Oregon & California bondholders asked him to travel to Oregon on their behalf.

Henry Villard's negotiations with Ben Holladay resulted in a so-called General Compromise Contract, the terms of which gave the bondholders the right to nominate three of the Oregon & California directors.[7] It also allowed them to appoint a resident financial agent empowered to collect all revenues, make disbursments for expenses, and oversee the land business. In return, the rate of interest on the bonds was substantially reduced. The contract could have gone a long way toward solving the company's problems, but Ben Holladay also controlled the Oregon Central Railroad Co. and the Oregon Steamship Co., the one running trains on the west side road and the other operating steamboats on the Willamette. To circumvent the bondholders' control of the Oregon & California Railroad and retain the revenues, he simply diverted the traffic to his other carriers. The bondholders were therefore forced to conclude that the only way to improve the Oregon & California's financial position was to buy up all three companies. On February 26, 1876, the creditors forced Holladay to sell out and in May of the same year Henry Villard was elected president of both the Oregon & California Railroad and the Oregon Steamship Co.[8] Indirectly he was also placed in control of the Oregon Central Railroad.

Unified management of these various enterprises worked fairly well, but within two years the marine operations ran into difficulties. The Oregon & California Railroad helped the Oregon Steamship Co. to update its fleet,[9] but no sooner had it done so than newcomers entered the coastal trade and a disastrous rate war followed.[10] Returns diminished rapidly, and the Oregon & California bondholders, anxious to minimize their losses, demanded that the steamship company be sold. For anyone wanting to gain a foothold in the transportation business it was an opportunity not to be missed!

In addition to handling the affairs of the Oregon companies, Henry Villard had also been acting as receiver for the bankrupt Kansas Pacific Railroad.[11] His successful efforts to revive that company not only enhanced his financial reputation but also brought him into personal contact with Jay Gould and Sidney Dillon of the Union Pacific Railroad. In 1867 General Grenville Dodge, then Union Pacific's chief engineer, had proposed that surveys be made to see if the Snake River would provide a feasible route to the Pacific Northwest. Vice President Thomas Durant agreed, and in 1868 and 1869 J. O. Hudnutt carried out an extensive reconnaissance. Hudnutt was greatly impressed by the volume of freight brought overland from the Columbia Valley to Boise, Idaho, and by the rates paid to the teamsters for handling it. In his report he noted, moreover, that because of the two portages the movement of goods on the Columbia River was a very inefficient and costly process. If a railroad was to be built it would allow the entire traffic to flow smoothly and cheaply all the way from Portland to points beyond the Blue Mountains. A Union

Pacific extension to the northwest was, in many ways, an attractive proposition, but a subsidy would have been required to build it. The main line from Omaha to Ogden had only just been completed and Congress was in no mood to grant further concessions to railroad promoters. The project was therefore allowed to lapse. It was not, however, entirely forgotten. General Dodge said at the time, "I shall always think that the mission of the Union Pacific Railroad is not fulfilled until it builds this branch to the Pacific Ocean."[12] Ten years later Henry Villard resurrected the idea.

Villard had been able to study the Hudnutt survey reports and was impressed by them.[13] Early in 1879 he approached Gould and Dillon with a proposal for joint construction of a railway on the line of the Oregon Trail. The Union Pacific officials were initially receptive to the idea,[14] and agreed to subscribe to an Oregon Construction & Improvement Co., organized to bring the project to fruition. Thus encouraged, Villard formed a syndicate that was soon to blossom as the Oregon Railway & Navigation Co. He then left for Oregon, where he promptly bought up the Oregon Steamship Co. and opened negotiations for the purchase of the Oregon Steam Navigation Co.

Between 1875 and 1878 there had been a threefold increase in wheat shipments from the Columbia Interior. OSN was well equipped with a fleet of new riverboats and was doing a roaring trade. Captain Ainsworth and his partners therefore declined to sell their holdings at anything less than par. The company's operations, however, brought in a return of 12 percent on the $5 million invested, and strategic advantages were to be gained. Villard therefore agreed to pay the price. For a sum of $100,000 in cash he secured an option to purchase 40,320 of the 50,000 Oregon Steam Navigation Co. shares at par. These were to be paid for 50 percent in cash, 20 percent in the bonds of the new Oregon Railway & Navigation Co., and 30 percent in its stock. For an additional $10,000 he obtained an option to purchase the Walla Walla & Columbia River Railroad at "a satisfactory price." Both options were valid until October 1, 1879.[15]

Arriving in New York on June 9, 1879, Villard immediately " . . . reported his doings to the Union Pacific parties, and, true to his understanding with them, offered them half an interest . . . in the new company." To his great surprise, however, Jay Gould and Sidney Dillon, in a sudden reversal of previously agreed policy, declined the offer. What had happened, apparently, was that Collis P. Huntington and the California group controlling the Central Pacific Railroad, who were just then building the Southern Pacific Railroad eastward toward El Paso as part of a through route from San Francisco to New Orleans, had objected to the proposal for a Union Pacific extension to the Northwest. Huntington and other members of the "Big Four" threatened that unless the partnership with Villard was dissolved they would divert traffic from the Overland Route to their new Sunset Route and thus effectively cut off the Union Pacific at Ogden, Utah. At that time Union Pacific was in the process of buying up Kansas Pacific and could ill afford to lose the San Francisco traffic. Dillon and Gould were thus obliged to forego any immediate participation in OR&N. Their temporary withdrawal from the project, however, involved little risk, for Northern Pacific remained relatively impecunious and was not expected to able to buy Villard out. For the time being, therefore, Villard was left free to go ahead alone, and on June 13, 1879, the Oregon Railway & Navigation Co. was formed as an independent enterprise.

4

WALLA WALLA & COLUMBIA RIVER

The earliest American settlement in the Walla Walla Valley was Marcus Whitman's ill-fated mission to the Cayuse Indians, founded in 1836 when the Columbia Interior was still part of the Hudson's Bay Company's vast trading empire. The present city of Walla Walla, however, had its origins in a military post established there by Colonel Edward Steptoe in 1856. Fort Walla Walla was only briefly used as a base from which campaigns were mounted to drive the Indians into reservations, but the adjacent trading facilities remained to form a useful staging point on the route from Portland and The Dalles to the far Interior. In the early 1860s, therefore, Walla Walla became the center of a tributary farming area supplying provisions for itinerant miners on their way to the gold camps along the Clearwater and Salmon rivers.

The agricultural settlement of the Interior began in the valleys of the Walla Walla and Touchet rivers and gradually spread to the northeast. At first the homesteaders cultivated oats for their own use, but soon they began to grow wheat to satisfy the miners' demand for flour. By 1865 the placer mining boom was over, but as more and more land was brought under the plough, wheat production increased. The grain was then hauled to Wallula Landing and shipped down the Columbia River. Most of the flour required in Portland and any shortfall in San Francisco, however, was milled from wheat grown in the Willamette Valley. Portland merchants therefore offered the Interior wheat for export and in 1869 the British ship *Adeline Elwood*, chartered by Corbett & Mcleay, sailed from the Columbia River with a first cargo of grain bound for Liverpool and the world market.[1]

Thereafter, wheat production and grain-handling problems increased steadily. The citizens of Walla Walla first convened to consider building a railway to Wallula Landing in 1861. A Washington Territory charter[2] for a Walla Walla Railroad Co. was granted on January 28, 1862, but the promoters were unable to raise enough money to undertake construction. The scheme consequently lapsed.

Within five years, however, the grain transportation problem assumed more serious proportions and the need for a railway became acute. Thirty local residents decided to try again and on March 23, 1868, their endeavors resulted in the formation of the Walla Walla & Columbia River Railroad Co.[3]

For a while there was some hope that the new company might receive financial help from the community. In 1869 Washington Territory adopted general legislation authorizing the issue of county bonds to finance works of public benefit. Such bonds were subject to two-thirds majority approval by local electorates, and normally had to be secured by a first mortgage on any real property involved. To take advantage of this legislation the Walla Walla & Columbia River Railroad Co. (WW&CR) sought a $300,000 Walla Walla County bond issue for construction of the railway to the landing.[4] On September 18, 1871, however, the proposition was defeated at the polls and the company was obliged to proceed without public help. Many of the participants then gave up in despair, but the local banker, Dr. Dorsey S. Baker, steadfastly refused to be discouraged. Buying up many of the shares, he began to build a 3 ft. gauge railroad with his own resources. On December 4, 1871, he left Walla Walla by stage for Kelton, Utah, and then traveled by train to Pittsburgh, Pennsylvania, where as a first great act of faith in the railway's future he placed a $4,400 order for a 7-1/2-ton saddle tank locomotive.[5]

Dr. Dorsey Syng Baker[6] was born in Wabash County, Illinois, on October 18, 1823. Educated as a physician, he graduated from Jefferson Medical College, Philadelphia, in 1845. Three years later he migrated to Oregon and, tiring of medical practice, became a businessman. A variety of commercial adventures followed but by 1858 he had successfully established himself as a general merchant in Portland. When the Clearwater gold rush stimulated trade with the Interior, Baker joined a group of Portland capitalists and Columbia riverboat men in building and operating the independent Upper River steamer *Spray*. In 1861 he removed to Walla Walla and, entering into partnership with his brother-in-law, founded the mercantile firm of Baker & Boyer. The venture flourished to the extent that within ten years enough capital had been accumulated to establish one of the first banks in Washington Territory.[7] By January 1, 1870, the institution that was to become the Baker-Boyer National Bank of Walla Walla had a capital of $120,008.46 and held deposits totaling $17,223.57. Dr. Baker still lacked the resources to build a railroad, even of limited length, but he proceeded undaunted.

Under an agreement worked out with Northern Pacific the survey for the railroad was undertaken by General James Tilton, whose report was delivered to WW&CR directors on May 20,1871.[8] The railway was to climb 559 ft. in 31-2/3 miles between Wallula and Walla Walla, with a maximum grade of 59 ft. to the mile occurring on a one-mile long section just west of Walla Walla. In the first ten miles above Wallula the line was to cross the Walla Walla River no less than six times. Including other bridges across the Touchet River and the Dry and Mill Creeks, the total length of trestling added up to nearly a mile. The cost of the railroad, including rolling stock, buildings, and other amenities was estimated at $673,367, or $21,275 per mile.

During the summer of 1871 reconnaissance parties were sent to the headwaters of the Clearwater and Yakima rivers to seek out and claim suitable timber for bridges and track.[9] D. W. Small and other contractors then undertook to supply the raw timber required, and for several successive winters their men and teams went to the bush to bring it out. The first logs were cut early in 1872 and floated down the Yakima later in the year. A sawmill, meanwhile, was set up 1-1/2 miles north of Wallula at a place named Slabtown,[10] where a convenient eddy in the Columbia River helped bring the booms of logs inshore. Ties were first sawn there on November 11, 1872. When construction finally got under way the line was built from Slabtown eastward, a spur being put in to reach the freight wharf at Wallula.

Due to the acute shortage of capital the first track was constructed almost entirely of timber, with 16 ft. long, 4-1/2 in. X 6 in. section rails[11] faced with 3/8 in. thick X 2 in. wide strap iron. The iron was spiked down to the wood and taken right around the rail ends to prevent it from curling upward under the loads imposed by the train wheels. In practice, however, it often broke and quickly rolled up into "snake-heads," which penetrated the floors of the cars, posing a hazard for passengers. The iron-faced timber rails placed a severe restriction on the speed of trains, but their interim use allowed a minimal cost railway to begin earning the money needed to pay for more conventional permanent track. In 1873 it was estimated that $100,000 would be needed to provide the railway with "T-iron" rails, whereas, in the meantime, $40,000 would suffice to lay it with timber and strap-iron.

During 1873 the river levels remained low and further supplies of timber were stranded. By October of that year, therefore, only 6 miles of wooden track had been laid.[12] Another year elapsed before the railway reached the half-way point at Touchet, 16 miles from

Wallula. In the next three months, however, 4,000 tons of grain were
taken down by train to the Columbia River and the company's financial position was much improved. Dr. Baker was then able to order
enough 26-lb Welsh iron rail to lay 20 miles of track.[13] Including
the ocean and river freight charges, this material was to cost $65,000
and the whole amount was to be paid either upon delivery at Wallula
or within five months of shipment from Great Britain. The residents
of Walla Walla clamored for early completion of the railway but were
reluctant to help out financially. Asked in January 1875 to subscribe
$75,000 to finish the job, their committee offered only $20,000. After
further negotiation, however, Dr. Baker received $25,000 and three
acres of land for a terminal site within half a mile of the intersection
of Main and Third streets.[14] A further order was then placed for
the balance of the rails required and the work was pressed ahead to
a satisfactory conclusion. The first train steamed into Walla Walla
on October 23, 1875.[15]

When the railway was brought into operation Baker established
a freight rate of $5 per ton, to which a charge of 50 cents was added
for wharfage at Wallula. This tariff was lower than those previously
levied by the teamsters, but some local shippers were less than satisfied
and conspired to force the rates down.[16] In the late summer of 1876
they reverted to using the wagon road. Baker attempted to retaliate
by persuading the Oregon Steam Navigation Co. to give shipping
preference to "fast freight" originating on the Walla Walla & Columbia River Railroad. Since payment was not made for grain until
it was delivered in Portland, and prices were then high, this strategy
temporarily sustained the rates. By September 1877, however, grain,
flour, bacon, and lard were being carried down to Wallula for $1
per ton, and shipping charges for incoming merchandize had fallen
to $4 per ton. With the establishment of more reasonable rates the
railroad became accepted as the cornerstone of the community's commercial development, and leading local merchants including Rees
& Winans, Hawley Dodds & Co., Adams Brothers, John Stahl, and
many more soon bought lots fronting the tracks and established
premises there.[17]

As the town grew and the surrounding country was opened up,
railway passenger traffic increased steadily. During 1877 there were
4,941 tickets sold for a total $14,824.38 in fares received,[18] a mean
$3 per passenger and seven or eight passengers per train. The first
passenger coach was a converted boxcar with a few small windows,
locally known as "the hearse."[19] This soon became inadequate, for

in the early part of 1878 there was a large influx of settlers.[20] Over 100 newcomers arrived on March 3 alone. To handle more passengers Dr. Baker bought a new car in the east and had it shipped to Wallula in pieces. It went into service early in October of that year and was reported to have " . . . all the conveniences usually found in cars of the same kind on leading railroads."[21] Twelve months later another car, built locally under the direction of Mr. Wishard, was enthusiastically received and said to be " . . . as good as could be built anywhere!"[22]

Each year more and more freight was also carried, as the following statistics[23] make clear.

Year	1874	1875	1876	1877	1878
Grain and flour (tons)	4021	9155	15266	28807	27365
Merchandize (tons)	1126	2192	4034	8368	10454

In the fall of 1877 the railroad appeared to have been overwhelmed by the harvest. All the warehouses in the vicinity of the Walla Walla depot were full, and sacks of grain were piled eight and ten deep in the surrounding open lots. On September 15 of that year no less than 15,000 tons still awaited shipment and there were fears that not all of it would be moved before low water closed the Columbia to navigation.[24] The steamboats were cited as being the limiting factor, for only two were in operation on the Upper River at the time and, although *Annie Faxon* was able to take on 268 tons per trip, only 1,000 tons were being moved downriver each week. Fortunately, heavy late-September rains[25] provided enough water to maintain navigable levels in the river, and the steamboat *Spokane* was rushed to completion at Celilo. By November 3, therefore, the Walla Walla *Weekly Statesman* was able to report that the crop was being moved with commendable rapidity and the piles of wheat were already much diminished.

Inevitably the very success of the Walla Walla & Columbia River Railroad placed a growing burden on the OSN Upper River operations. Dr. Baker was convinced that a railway would eventually have to be built all the way from Wallula to Portland. He even considered promoting such an enterprise but decided to sell out to OSN instead. The steamboat owners were said to be reluctant to acquire the railroad, but on February 18, 1878, S. G. Reed and C. E. Tilton agreed to buy a six-sevenths interest in it and to complete the purchase before January 19, 1879.[26] Dr. Baker retained one-seventh of the stock and continued to function as president. At the time of the sale the railroad property, including the locomotives and rolling stock, was valued at $356,134.85, or about $11,130 per mile.[27] Thirty-five percent of the original cost had been met from earnings, and the line had never been mortgaged.

Attempts were soon made to emulate Dr. Baker's example. In December 1877 residents of the newly settled upland area to the south of Walla Walla incorporated a Weston Pendleton & Columbia River Railroad.[28] They hoped this would provide a means of reducing the $3 tariff charged for hauling grain by wagon road from Weston, Oregon, to the intermediate station on the WW&CR Railroad at Whitman, 5 miles west of Walla Walla. Appeals for community action to build the railway failed, but early in 1879 the project was revived as a WW&CR branch line. Under Dr. Baker's supervision, construction[29] began in the spring of 1879 and by July 5 a force of 200 men was at work and 5 miles of roadbed were ready for track. However, as the graders advanced up the Dry Creek Valley into the hills the earthworks became heavier. Cuts up to 20 ft. deep slowed the work down and greatly increased its cost. To avoid the expense of crossing the height of land to join Pine Creek the steeply graded line was therefore terminated at Blue Mountain Station, 14 miles from Whitman and 2 miles short of Weston, in mid-September 1879. The railway failed to reach its objective, but for several months it nevertheless enjoyed the distinction of being part of a great trunk route. Late in 1879 and early in 1880 trains running between Walla Walla and Blue Mountain Station worked in conjunction with the Utah, Idaho, & Oregon Stage Line and carried the eastern mail![30]

With the opening of the branch line to Blue Mountain Station, WW&CR operations assumed a pattern that lasted until narrow gauge operations came to an end. The timetable effective on April 1, 1880, indicated that there were three regular round-trip trains working each day.[31] The service consisted of a freight train from Walla Walla to Blue Mountain Station and back in the morning, a mixed train from Walla Walla to Wallula and back to meet the steamer in the late afternoon, and a daily freight train coming up from Wallula in the morning and returning early in the afternoon. The entire schedule could have been maintained by two locomotives, one based in Walla Walla and the other at Wallula, thus allowing for the operation of extras and work trains and for engines being out of service for repairs. Trains were not allowed to exceed 20 mph anywhere on the system and had to slow down to 4 mph when passing over bridges and trestles. The latter precaution was the result of bitter experience, for early in September 1877 a 35-ft.-high trestle about 10 miles from Wallula collapsed under a down train running at excessive speed.[32] The engine managed to reach the far side but six freight cars fell to the footings and were wrecked. Fortunately no one was hurt. Train crews were also given strict instructions to avoid collisions with livestock wandering at large upon the right-of-way. If necessary the trains were to stop. The object seems to have been to reduce the number of claims made by local farmers for animals killed along the line.

The Walla Walla & Columbia River Railroad employed 125 men regularly and took on up to 200 more for construction work as required.[33] The numbers seem to have reached a maximum in 1879, for after the branch line had been graded the main line was extensively relocated. The laborers were paid $30 for working twenty-six days per month and received "board of high quality." Skilled men, including locomotive engineers such as "that prince of good fellows H. D. Chase,"[34] who drove the engine *Blue Mountain*, received up to three times that amount.

As time went on and the traffic increased, more powerful engines were obtained. Eventually there were six locomotives, one of which was bought after the railway had been sold to OSN. All were built by Porter Bell & Co. of Pittsburgh, Pennsylvania. Two of these were described as "light-weight" and the remaining four as " . . . up to date construction passenger and freight locomotives for the period."[35] These engines may be listed as follows:[36]

Name	Type	Built
Walla Walla	O-4-OST	1872
Wallula	O-4-OST	?
Columbia	O-6-O	1876
Blue Mountain	2-6-O	1878
Mountain Queen	2-4-O	1878
J. W. Ladd	2-6-O	1879

On May 4, 1879, Dr. Baker agreed to surrender his remaining interest in the Walla Walla & Columbia River Railroad to Henry Villard, who was about to buy OSN and form the Oregon Railway & Navigation Co.[37] This transaction was completed on October 1, 1879. Baker continued to handle WW&CR affairs until early in 1880 when he resigned and was replaced by H. W. Fairweather, who acted as local general manager for OR&N.

After being temporarily adorned with short-lived narrow gauge extensions to Umatilla[38] and South Ainsworth,[39] the main line of the Walla Walla & Columbia River Railroad was relaid to standard gauge in May 1881. It then became an integral part of the growing OR&N network south of the Snake River. The branch line from Whitman to Blue Mountain Station survived as a narrow gauge remnant for nearly another two years. Late in 1882, however, OR&N began to build a direct line from Walla Walla to Pendleton, Oregon, and opened a new section of standard gauge railway from Walla Walla through Milton to Barrett, where it joined the existing narrow gauge alignment. In February 1883 the narrow gauge railroad between Barrett and Blue Mountain Station was rebuilt with wider cuts and fills and changed over to standard gauge.[40] The narrow gauge Whitman to Barrett section was then abandoned.

Dr. Baker did not rest for very long after leaving "the Bobtail" to the tender mercies of OR&N . In 1881 he built another 3-ft.-gauge railway 6 miles long from Walla Walla eastward to the foot of his Blue Mountain timber flume at Dudley, on Mill Creek. A committee of local farmers then asked him to construct a diverging extension northeastward to the settlement of Dixie, which lay at the forks of that other Dry Creek which flows to the north of Walla Walla. This he agreed to do, and another 8 miles of railway were opened in September 1882. In addition to serving the timber flume and carrying grain down from the hill country, the Mill Creek Flume & Manufacturing Co. railroad[41] also carried summer excursion traffic to picnic grounds at Dudley. For several years the line was operated at a bucolic pace matching the seasonal requirements of local trade. The establishment of the Washington Penitentiary at Walla Walla, however, created a demand for strong and durable building materials and provided the railway with a new source of traffic. A good quality clay,[42] discovered near Dixie when the line was being built, was used to make bricks for the penitentiary buildings.[43] Moreover, when the institution was opened, in 1887, the commissioners decided to set up a brick yard to provide employment for the inmates.[44] Clay was then hauled over the railroad to furnish a steady supply of raw material. The promise of increased traffic inevitably made the railway more attractive to potential buyers. In September 1887, therefore, Dr. Baker was able to sell it to OR&N for $165,000.[45]

Dr. Baker died at Walla Walla on July 5, 1888. Many stories later told about the Walla Walla & Columbia River Railroad tended to belittle his achievements, but the historical record confirms that, pre-eminent among his contemporaries, he laid the foundations of commerce in the area south of the Snake River. Even before his death the so-called "Rawhide Era" of railroading was a thing of the past. The development of the railroad system in the Pacific Northwest was henceforth to be controlled to an ever greater extent by the policies of large companies based in New York. Inevitably Walla Walla was bypassed by their great trunk lines, and grew but slowly. That the city survived and prospered was due in no small measure to the solid commercial cornerstone laid by the man who built the first railroad in the Interior.

5

OREGON RAILWAY & NAVIGATION

The Oregon Railway & Navigation Co., incorporated in the state of Oregon on June 13, 1879, was authorized to acquire the holdings of the Oregon Steamship and Oregon Steam Navigation companies and build a narrow gauge railway along the left bank of the Columbia River. It was further empowered to extend this line over the Blue Mountains to the Oregon-Idaho boundary and purchase, lease, or consolidate with any other railroad in Oregon, Washington, Idaho, or Utah. This generous franchise to build and operate railroads was supplemented by almost total freedom of commercial navigation upon the rivers and coastal waters of the entire Pacific Northwest. The venture was first financed by a $6 million issue of 6 percent, thirty-year, first mortgage bonds, placed by Farmers Loan & Trust Co. of New York. Capital stock consisted of sixty thousand $100 shares, 70 percent of which were distributed as a free bonus to encourage bond sales.[1]

Villard's objectives in forming OR&N were to secure control of the Columbia Gateway and its eastern approaches, perpetuate the monopoly previously enjoyed by the Oregon Steam Navigation Co., and funnel all the traffic of the northern transcontinental railroads into Portland on his own terms. He expressed relief that Union Pacific had withdrawn from the scheme, admitting that his preference all along had been to " . . . proceed upon an independent basis until the Oregon Railway & Navigation Co. had secured absolute control of the Columbia Valley and of the approaches thereto, so that it could command its own terms of connection with any through line coming either from south or north. . . . "[2] Despite the fact that construction of an OR&N line along the Columbia Valley would quite clearly conflict with the provisions of the federal charter for the Northern Pacific Railroad, Villard's enterprise was supported by Portland merchants and Oregon legislators, all of whom saw it as a means of preserving their own established regional influence. OR&N was, in fact, an alliance between eastern capitalists and Portland businessmen.

Joining Henry Villard on the first board of directors were James B. Fry, Artemus H. Holmes, and William H. Starbuck of New York, and J. C. Ainsworth, H. W. Corbett, J. N. Dolph, C. H. Lewis, S. G. Reed, Paul W. Schulze, and George W. Weidler, all of Portland. Henry Villard was elected president and J. N. Dolph, vice president. Hans Thielsen was appointed chief engineer, and G. H. Andrew undertook the duties of company secretary.[3]

Once Union Pacific had declined to participate in OR&N and had been released from their pledge to subscribe to the auxiliary Oregon Construction & Improvement Company, Villard was left free to make his own arrangements for financial support.[4] To bring money in quickly, cash subscriptions to the bond issue were rewarded with a 10 percent discount and a 70 percent bonus in stock. On these terms Villard had no difficulty persuading his financial acquaintances and friends to rally around him. Within ten days sufficient funds had been raised to complete the purchase of OSN stock. He was then able to telegraph J. C. Ainsworth, asking him to be prepared to complete the transaction on July 1, 1879. Before Villard sailed for Europe on July 10, 1879, the majority interest in OSN had been bought and paid for, the European creditors of the Oregon Steamship Co. had been reimbursed, and there was enough money left over to start work on the Columbia Valley railway and place an order for a new and luxurious steamship for the Portland to San Francisco service!

Despite the Union Pacific withdrawal, Jay Gould assured Villard on June 19, 1879, that a branch of the subsidiary Utah & Northern Railroad would eventually be built westward to meet the OR&N Blue Mountain extension.[5] Utah & Northern was a 3-ft. gauge road, and an ultimate connection with it required that OR&N also be laid to that gauge. Villard's initial plans[6] for OR&N were therefore made upon that basis, and for a period of six months or more there was a real prospect that the narrow gauge tracks of the two companies would eventually extend all the way from Ogden to Portland. The first OR&N capital appropriation[7] was made for a narrow gauge railroad along the left bank of the Columbia River from the Lower Cascades Landing to a connection with the existing Walla Walla & Columbia River Railroad at Wallula. The importance of forestalling the Northern Pacific and facilitating the movement of grain from the Interior, however, dictated that first priority be given to completing the section between Celilo and Wallula.[8] Immediate preparations were therefore made to start work at both of those points.

Other strategic considerations, meanwhile, were not neglected. In addition to securing the Columbia Gateway, Villard also intended to occupy the southern part of the Interior Plain and planned to perfect a system of narrow gauge railways there.[9] On July 25, 1879, Thielsen went a step further and suggested that two lines also be built north of the Snake River. A month later an alarm was raised by renewed reports that Northern Pacific might still attempt to build over the Lolo Pass and descend the Clearwater and Snake River valleys. Thielsen therefore reiterated his ideas, stressing the urgency of making surveys, procuring land, and starting work on a railroad from the Snake River northeastward along Union Flat Creek into the Clearwater country.[10]

Sharing Thielsen's concern, Villard authorized preliminary work north of the Snake. Then, to shield OR&N from any unexpected move by Union Pacific, he also ordered that steps be taken to survey and occupy the Meacham Pass route over the Blue Mountains.[11]

Taking advantage of the summer weather, Thielsen immediately sent his surveyors up-country, and by late August 1879 four parties were in the field.[12] Campbell was running a line from Walla Walla northward, Hale was locating an extension up the Pataha, Kennedy was on the north side of the Snake River working his way up Alkali Flat Creek to Union Flat, and Symons was on the flats of Cabin Creek somewhere beyond the Blue Mountains. With the onset of winter, however, these crews came out of the hills and work was again concentrated in the Columbia Valley.[13] By January 17, 1880, Thielsen was able to report that the line from Celilo to Wallula had been located and construction would begin as soon as men became available.

Villard evidently believed that the only good natural route from the Interior to tidewater lay along the left bank of the Columbia. He hoped that prior occupation would enable him to persuade any approaching transcontinental railroad to use OR&N facilities to reach both Portland and Puget Sound. Having secured a monopoly of coastal shipping, OR&N would be in a position to control the commerce of the entire Pacific Northwest. In the case of Union Pacific there was little doubt that such an outcome could be achieved. The Northern Pacific directors, however, were far less likely to cooperate. Northern Pacific had been granted a federal charter to complete an overland railroad to Puget Sound and was thereby entitled not only to construct a main line along the Columbia River Valley but also to build a branch through the Cascade Mountains. If the OR&N monopoly was to be preserved, Villard had to persuade Northern Pacific to abandon both of these schemes, and this he set out to do.

The task of reaching an understanding with Northern Pacific was clearly going to be difficult and perhaps impossible. Frederick Billings and his colleagues were angry about recent events in Oregon, and not without reason. J. C. Ainsworth, himself a Northern Pacific director, had recommended that work on the company's Columbia River line be deferred in favor of prior construction on the Lake Pend d'Oreille Division farther to the east. Ainsworth had promised that his steamboats would provide connecting services on the Columbia River. He had then suddenly turned around and sold the controlling interest in OSN to the Villard syndicate, which had promptly formed a rival railway company and pre-empted the Wallula Gap. It was hardly surprising, therefore, that the tone of Villard's overture to Northern Pacific was conciliatory. The initial press releases indeed were almost apologetic. On January 2, 1880, *Railroad Gazette* carried an article commenting on the difficulties of operating steamboats on the river and describing the Celilo-Wallula railway as a necessity. The report stated that while OR&N was quite prepared to build the line, negotiations would nevertheless be opened with Northern Pacific for joint construction and operation.[14] When Northern Pacific failed to respond to this approach Villard was forced to adopt a more bellicose attitude. A few weeks later he issued a circular which asserted that the Celilo to Wallula line would " . . . strengthen our hold on, and exclusive control of the Columbia River, which may be termed the back bone of our enterprise. . . ." He announced that OR&N had made all the arrangements needed to build the line that very year, and also proposed to " . . . commence the construction of an independent railway from a point on the Snake River to, and through, what is called the Palouse country. . . ."[15] Villard spoke from a strong position but because the Northern Pacific charter still offered alternative courses of action, Billings and his associates declined to make any immediate concessions. It was agreed, however, that Northern Pacific director Joseph D. Potts of Philadelphia would visit Portland during the coming summer to discuss matters of mutual concern.

Villard hastened to consolidate his position. Upon his return to Oregon in April 1880 he immediately traveled to the Interior, accompanied by Boston financiers George M. Pullman and William Endicott Jr., to review railway construction plans and progress.[16] He then made two important decisions. The original concept of a narrow gauge system was abandoned in favor of using standard gauge throughout, and approval was given to Thielsen's proposal to build a line from Texas Ferry, on the north bank of the Snake River opposite Grange City, northeastward to Colfax and other points in the Palouse country.[17] As the year went on, it became clear that this line would divide at Colfax, with one branch proceeding northeastward to Farmington and another finding its way southeastward to Moscow, a settlement described by the Walla Walla *Weekly Statesman* as being "a place on the very top of the mountains!"[18]

During the summer of 1880 the graders working on the left bank of the Columbia River made rapid progress and by early August the roadbed between Celilo and Wallula was almost complete.[19] On August 20 *Railroad Gazette* stated that the entire grading force would soon be moved from the Columbia Valley to the north side of the Snake River to work on the 33 miles of line between Texas Ferry and Union Flat in Whitman County. Having completed that task they would then proceed to the other side of the Snake River to begin work on a railway from Grange City, at the mouth of the Tucannon River, southward to Walla Walla. Although *Railroad Gazette* failed to mention it, work had already begun at the Walla Walla end of the Grange City line, and was proceeding rapidly.[20]

With railway construction well under way, Henry Villard turned his attention to affairs that promised to generate traffic and provide the basis for an industrial empire in the Northwest. As a first step he asked his cousin E. W. Hilgard, who was professor of geology at the University of California, to undertake a survey of regional coal and iron resources.[21] Hilgard inspected both the Puyallup-Carbon River coal-field east of Tacoma and the Newcastle-Cedar River deposits near Seattle and reported that, although the Carbon River coal was of better quality, larger and more economic operations could be carried on at Newcastle. His report was so enthusiastic that Villard decided to form another company, " . . . the object of which should be the development of the natural resources, mineral, agricultural, and otherwise of Oregon and Washington and the North Pacific coast in general."[22] This decision soon resulted in the organization of the Oregon Improvement Company, which was set up with a capital stock of $5 million and authorized to solicit subscriptions for the same amount in bonds. Once again Villard's appeal had a magnetic effect on the financial community. Before the subscription lists closed, the bonds were selling at premiums of 40 and 50 percent, and within a few months the price of the shares reached 91-1/2!

By early October 1880 the Oregon Improvement Company was able to purchase the Newcastle colliery and the 21-mile-long narrow gauge Seattle & Walla Walla Railroad over which the coal was brought down to Puget Sound.[23] The Seattle & Walla Walla Railroad was soon reincorporated as the Columbia & Puget Sound Railway. A branch line 7 miles long was then built from Renton to the McAllister mine at Cedar Mountain, and an order was placed for three new steam colliers to ply the route between Seattle and both Portland and San Francisco.

The Columbia & Puget Sound Railway was primarily a coal hauler, but it also possessed inherited powers to build a line through Snoqualmie Pass to the Interior. It therefore provided Villard with a means of countering the threat posed by Northern Pacific's projected Cascade branch and may have been purchased primarily to secure that particular strategic advantage.[24]

As part of the bargain driven in Seattle, Villard also obtained a large interest in the Pacific Coast Steamship Company and acquired waterfront properties in Seattle, San Francisco, and Alaska, all of which were important to his marine enterprises.[25]

The Ocean Division of OR&N, meanwhile, received a new flagship. Under the command of Captain Fred Bolles, the magnificent screw steamer *Columbia* arrived in Portland from the East Coast, by way of Cape Horn, on July 22, 1880.[26] *Columbia* joined *Oregon* and the PCSS Co. *State of California* on the Portland to San Francisco "Five Day" service, where she made an unsurpassed record for reliability. In common with the *Oregon* and the two other former Oregon Steamship Company vessels, *George W. Elder* and *City of Chester*, *Columbia* was built by the John Roach shipyard at Chester, Pennsylvania. At Villard's insistence she was fitted out with Edison electric lighting and was said to have been the first ship in the world to be so equipped.[27] Later on, one of her dynamos found its way, somewhat mysteriously, to the far Interior, where it provided nothing less than a catalytic impulse for the growth of that region's principal center of commerce.

During 1880 Henry Villard rapidly became the Northwest's prime purveyor of transportation and fuel. His ambitions were not, however, confined to those fields. Seeing himself as the patron of a West Coast steel industry, he encouraged Simeon G. Reed's efforts to establish the Oregon Iron & Steel Company, an enterprise that exploited iron ore deposits and operated a blast furnace at Lake Oswego in Clackamas County, Oregon.[28] Villard, no doubt, had visions of an industrial

empire in the Northwest and was, for that very reason, doubly determined to bring potential competitors to terms.

Negotiations between OR&N and Northern Pacific went on
spasmodically throughout the summer of 1880 and although Billings
and his associates refused to abandon their ultimate objective of
building a Northern Pacific line to Puget Sound, some progress was
nevertheless made. The Northern Pacific *Report to Stockholders* issued
prior to the annual meeting on September 29 stated that, following
Mr. Potts's meetings with Mr. Villard in Portland, there was every
reason to believe that the current "harmonious relations" between
the two companies would continue.[29] Negotiations for joint use of
the OR&N line along the left bank of the Columbia River re-opened
in September, and an accord was reached in mid-October.

The traffic agreement signed on October 20, 1880,[30] provided that
Northern Pacific would recognize both the OR&N right-of-way along
the left bank of the Columbia from Wallula to Portland and title to
station grounds, and would waive all claims for damages resulting
from the building of the OR&N line. The two companies further
agreed to divide the Interior plain into separate zones of influence,
so that OR&N would control the country to the south of the Snake
River and Northern Pacific would retain the area to the north. Northern Pacific, however, consented to the completion of the OR&N extensions then supposed to be under construction in the Palouse country. OR&N, for their part, agreed to complete a standard gauge railway
from Wallula to Portland within three years and to grant Northern
Pacific the right, without the obligation, to run their trains over it
at a fixed charge per train mile. The Oregon company was to give
the transcontinental road a 66-mile advantage on all freight interchanged and carry its construction materials at reasonable fixed rates.
A final proviso was that the Oregon Improvement Company would
contract to sell 300,000 acres of Northern Pacific land in the Palouse
country at a price of $2.50 per acre.

The agreement was a satisfactory interim measure but it failed to
provide OR&N with any guarantee of future security. Northern
Pacific would only use the OR&N line until a railway of their own
could be completed, either along the right bank of the Columbia or
over the Cascade Mountains. For the time being the Northern Pacific
trains would pass through Portland, but their true objective would
be to reach the natural deep-water harbor at Tacoma. Given the
navigational difficulties of reaching Portland, ocean-going shipping
would inevitably concentrate on Puget Sound, and Portland and

OR&N would lose business to Tacoma and Northern Pacific. Villard, however, was not immediately perturbed, for Northern Pacific still lacked access to the vast amounts of money required to complete the transcontinental line east of Ainsworth.[31] While negotiating the traffic agreement, he had offered to form a syndicate that would raise $10 million to assist ongoing Northern Pacific construction.[32] If Billings accepted this offer, and it seemed likely that he would, the conditions attached to it could be designed to provide enough say in Northern Pacific affairs to guarantee ample protection for OR&N interests.

The news of the October traffic agreement was generally well received, and there was an immediate increase in the market price of OR&N stock. Mr. Villard and his friends were therefore "exultant."[33] Their rejoicing, however, was short-lived, for less than a month later it was learned that the Northern Pacific Railroad Co. had succeeded in making independent arrangements with New York financial houses for an unprecedentedly large issue of first mortgage bonds, and had suddenly secured the $40 million required to complete their entire line. Villard's advantage had disappeared overnight and the future of OR&N lay in jeopardy.

6

THE LAKE PEND D'OREILLE DIVISION

Construction of the western part of the Northern Pacific Railroad was resumed late in 1879 when work began on a line that would enable the company to occupy the northern part of the Interior Plain and secure the western approach to the defile of the Clark Fork River. The Lake Pend d'Oreille Division was to extend more than 200 miles from the mouth of the Snake River to Lake Pend d'Oreille and provide a basis for eastward extension to an eventual meeting with the railroad from Duluth.

Early in the summer of 1879, Thomas Doane, a consulting engineer engaged by Northern Pacific to oversee location of the Lake Pend d'Oreille Division, went over the ground with the men chosen to lead the survey parties.[1] This reconnaissance completed, the detailed locating work[2] began. A first party led by D. D. Clark started at the mouth of the Snake River and progressed northeastward along a route first examined by Eastwick in 1872. Two other groups, meanwhile, set out in each direction from the small but growing town of Spokane Falls. I. S. P. Weeks conducted an examination of alternative crossings of Hangman Creek and then proceeded westward to meet the Clark party, while Jack Scurry blazed a more difficult trail to Lake Pend d'Oreille.

The Clark and Weeks expeditions met near Big Lake on the headwaters of the Cow Creek in August, and by mid-September the cross-sections and estimates for the first 150 miles of railroad were substantially complete. Shortly afterward, H. M. McCartney, "an accomplished civil engineer," who had just returned from leading yet another attempt to find a feasible route up the Middle Fork Clearwater to the Lolo Pass,[3] took charge of construction work.[4] A supply base was set up at a point named Ainsworth, just north of the Snake River's confluence with the Columbia, bids were called for the supply of ties and timbers,[5] and a force of graders was assembled. Then, at 1:00 p.m. on October 2, 1879, General J. W. Sprague, Northern Pacific general agent and manager in the Pacific Northwest, ceremonially turned the first sod and work at last got under way.[6]

The gradient profile of the original 216-mile-long Northern Pacific route from Ainsworth to Lake Pend d'Oreille presented a somewhat roller-coaster-like aspect.[7] The line first climbed a progressively steepening grade for 59 miles, ascending from an elevation of about 350 ft. at Ainsworth to a summit 1,534 ft. above sea level at Providence. It then descended for 7 miles to an elevation of 1,337 ft. in the Lind Coulee and climbed again through Paha and Ritzville to reach a second summit approximately 1,950 ft. above sea level near the 95th mile. There was then a slight dip to just below 1,900 ft. on the north shore of Sprague Lake, a short level stretch beside the lake, and a 23-mile climb from Sprague to a third summit almost 2,400 ft. above sea level at the 131st mile. From that point the road descended 16 miles, by way of Cheney and the Marshall Canyon, to cross Hangman Creek at an elevation of about 1,800 ft. just 3 miles west of Spokane Falls. After a short, sharp climb to 1,907 ft. at the 150th mile it followed a gentler grade eastward. Traversing the Spokane Valley and the Rathdrum Prairie it ascended gradually for 40 miles to reach a summit 2,460 ft. above sea level at a point about 14 miles beyond Rathdrum and several miles to the east of the present alignment. There was then a steep and tortuous 6-mile-long descent from the height of land into the area of broken relief lying to the north. Reaching an elevation of 2,215 ft. at Granite, 196 miles from Ainsworth, the road traversed undulating country to Cocolalla and finally descended to a shoreline elevation of 2,056 ft. on the west arm of Lake Pend d'Oreille.

Stations and distances in miles from Ainsworth were: Eltopia, 21; Bluff Wells, 29; Twin Wells, 47; Providence, 59; Well No. 7, 67; Ritzville, 84; Sprague, 108; Cheney, 133; Marshall, 140; Spokane Falls, 149; Westwood (soon to be called Rathdrum), 176; Dry Lake (soon to be called Lake Prescott), 195; Cocolalla, 205; Lake Pend d'Oreille (south shore of West Arm), 216. Note that after 1881 distances were given from Wallula, 12 miles being added to the above figures.

This first railway route across the Interior Plain was less than ideal. Eastbound trains faced long, unbroken upgrades, while westbound trains were forced to contend with three shorter, but nevertheless, difficult hills. The railroad had to be built quickly and economically through sparsely settled and almost totally unsurveyed country, using only the primitive methods of the time. The builders, moreover, had to wrestle with lack of surface water and standing timber, and depend upon supplies of rails and equipment brought all the way from the East Coast by sea. To the extent that local landforms allowed, rock excavations and major structures had to be avoided. The wonder then was, not that there were some rather steep grades, but that there were so few of them and their maximum severity did not exceed about 1.3 percent. Under the circumstances prevailing in 1879, indeed, the route was well enough chosen.

Construction commenced with a force of about 100 Chinese, sent up from Portland on September 26, 1879.[8] More such laborers followed and by October 19, when the grade was 8 miles out from Ainsworth, there were 300 Chinese on the job, along with 50 whites and 20 scraper teams.[9] In the easily graded terrain rapid progress was made and by mid-November 1879, 17 miles of roadbed had been completed. Difficulties, however, were encountered, for as the grade was extended northward across the sagebrush desert and into the Esquatzel Coulee, water was found to occur only at the 26th and 40th miles. An intensive program of well sinking was undertaken and led to the discovery of an aquifer 128 ft. below surface at the 21st mile. The water, however, still had to be drawn up in buckets and hauled several miles to supply the entire grading force.[10] Despite this inconvenience, and the cold weather, which caused nighttime suffering among the animals working on the grade,[11] construction went on, and by Christmas 1879 some 25 miles of roadbed lay ready for track.[12]

Grading proceeded well enough but from the very outset the delivery of rails, ties, and timber presented problems. The first two shiploads of iron rails, amounting to 2,500 tons, or about enough for 32 miles of track, left the East Coast in April and May 1879 and reached San Francisco in September.[13] At the end of October some of this iron had been shipped onwards to Portland, and by November 15 enough for 2 miles had been landed at Ainsworth. The remainder was said to be on the Columbia River and expected within ten days. Unfortunately the level of the river then fell, and by December 25, 1879, only enough rails for about 5 or 6 miles of track had been brought up.[14] The rest lay stranded at Wallula and other points downstream and could not be delivered until early in February 1880. Out along the line, meanwhile, ties were also in short supply, and lumber was said to be "worth its weight in silver."[15] William Harkness of Lewiston, the prime tie and timber contractor, brought out some ties from the Blue Mountains in November and December,[16] but the great mass of material then being cut on the headwaters of the Clearwater and Yakima rivers could not be floated downstream until spring. During the winter of 1879-80 the delay in the delivery of rails prevented the laying of more than about half a dozen miles of track, and when the level of the Columbia River rose again and the remainder of the iron became available, there were only enough ties to complete the railway to the 16th mile.[17] By March 25, 1880, therefore, tracklaying operations once more ground to a halt and remained stalled pending the arrival of rafts of ties and timber from the high country.

The graders, meanwhile, pushed on as best they could. For men with horses there was money to be made. A two-horse team brought in $4 per day and made a profit of $50 per month, while four- and six-horse outfits doubled and tripled that rate of return. For those working on foot, however, the remuneration was less. White laborers earned $1.75 per day and paid $4.50 per week for full board, while the Chinese had to be content with 85 cents per day and survive on simpler fare.[18] Since no other large-scale railway construction projects were yet under way in the Interior, the contractors, J. B. Harris & Co., temporarily found these labor rates to be adequate. In the first six months of 1880 fair progress was made and, although it was not possible to build the trestles or finish excavating the rock cut at Providence summit, grading was substantially completed to the 62nd mile.

In April 1880 a contract was let to Coulter McBean & Co. of Portland for grading the 16 miles of line immediately west of Spokane Falls,[19] and by May 29, 1880, mobilization was well under way. Clarence Coulter was reported to be at Palouse Landing on the Snake River, receiving and forwarding horses, implements, wagons, and supplies, while D. D. McBean made on-site preparations for the excavation of 1,250,000 cu. yds. of earth and 50,000 cu. yds. of basaltic rock. "A herd of over 40 chinamen . . . " had just arrived, 260 more were on their way, and another 700 were expected within a month. M. Smyth and a small force of men, meanwhile, had already begun to clear the right-of-way below Marshall.[20] Two weeks later John G. Steel, the third partner in Coulter McBean & Co. had set up an office at the mouth of Lake Creek,[21] and the fiery D. D. McBean himself was said to be ruthlessly destroying barrels of gin consigned to the Chinese![22]

At intermediate points others also buckled in to work on the grade. During the month of May, Phillip Ritz returned to Ritzville from

Portland with grading equipment. His, however, was the easiest of all sections of the line. He was said to have such light work that he " . . . could sweep the track with a broom to grade were it not for grass roots."[23]

With construction in progress all the way along the line Northern Pacific hoped to complete the entire grade between Ainsworth and Spokane Falls by late summer 1880 and have the trains running shortly afterward. The early opening of the railway, however, depended not only on completion of the roadbed but also on the prompt delivery of rails, ties, and timber. Steps had been taken to ensure that the rails, and the locomotives and rolling stock required to bring them up to the front, were on hand when needed. On December 16, 1879, Northern Pacific president Frederick Billings advised General Sprague of shipments soon to leave the East Coast,[24] including 17,000 tons of steel rails; six locomotives; hardware for 150 cars; and a full outfit for a machine shop. Since the cars could not be completed until wheels, axles, and springs arrived, this hardware was given first priority and shipped to the Pacific Coast on the mail steamers, one of which left New York carrying half of the total shipment on December 30, 1879. The workshops at Tacoma were thus able to assemble 125 flatcars and twenty-five boxcars and send them off to Ainsworth early in May. Shipment of the other materials and equipment began when the vessels *Chandos* and *Belle of Bath* sailed from the East Coast on January 10 and 15, 1880, each carrying two locomotives and a thousand tons of rails. Other consignments soon followed and by the end of May 1880 the whole great quantity of supplies for the Lake Pend d'Oreille Division had been shipped and was beginning to arrive in the Columbia River. No chances, however, were taken on late arrival of the vessels bearing locomotives.

When track was first laid at Ainsworth in December 1879, the little saddle tank engine *Otter Tail*, which had first been used on construction of the line from Duluth to the Missouri River,[25] was sent up from Kalama to handle supply trains. Journeys beyond the 16th mile, however, demanded more sophisticated motive power. Arrangements were therefore made to have two bigger engines shipped to Ainsworth before ties once more became available. The new 30-ton Baldwin locomotive No. 25 was hauled over the Union Pacific and Central Pacific railroads to Sacramento, California, and promptly sent onward by sea to the Columbia River. There it was joined by the 25-ton Pittsburgh locomotive No. 13, previously used on the Tacoma-Kalama line of the Pacific Division. Both of these engines were brought upriver together in mid-May, accompanied by Mr. Thomas E. Roberts of the Baldwin Locomotive Works, who had personally shepherded No. 25 all the way across the continent from Philadelphia. By early June 1880 locomotives and cars were thus available for use, and when the first 10,000 ties arrived from the Clearwater a daily supply train began to run to the front.[26]

Harkness & Co., meanwhile, got ready to receive the logs expected to arrive shortly at Ainsworth from the headwaters of the Yakima. A two-and-a-half-story sawmill[27] building, 150 ft. long and 40 ft. wide, was erected on the left bank of the Columbia River about a mile west of the main railway line, to which it was later connected by a spur. The sawmill machinery, made by the Willamette Iron Works at a cost of $16,000, was brought upriver from Portland early in May and installed by Leroy Shipley, who had previously served as millwright at Grant's Mill near the Upper Cascades. The new sawmill had a daily capacity of 60,000 board feet and was equipped with " . . . a double 54 inch circular saw, a 48 inch pony saw, a niggar for turning logs on the carriage, and a bull wheel which hauls logs 400 ft. from the Columbia River." Power was provided by a 160 HP 18 X 24 single cylinder stationary steam engine with a 14-ft.-diameter flywheel weighing 7 tons. The engine was supplied with steam by three single flue cylindrical boilers with shells 42 in. in diameter by 16 ft. long. Due to the late arrival of the machinery, and the time required to install it, the sawmill was not ready for operation until about the third week in June 1880. By that time, however, the Yakima drive had been overtaken by disaster and the saw logs that were to have provided all the bridge timber, along with most of the ties required for the first 100 miles of track, had largely been lost.

The woodcutters had been hard at work in the Cascade Mountain forests above Ellensburg throughout the winter, and by the spring of 1880 a great mass of logs and ties lay ready to be carried down the Yakima River. When the drive to Ainsworth finally got under way,[28] however, things went wrong. According to some reports there was a flash flood on the river; other accounts averred that a logjam suddenly broke up; but whatever the cause of the resulting deluge the rafts were carried away, completely out of control. The booms at the mouth of the Yakima River were broken, and the whole winter's cut went floating away down the Columbia. Some of the material was later recovered between Umatilla and Celilo and taken to a temporary sawmill at Blalock's, Oregon,[29] but much of it was never seen again.

The unfortunate outcome of the Harkness drive brought tracklaying to a complete halt. Grading continued throughout the summer of 1880, but curiously, for many months, there was no news of the steel advancing farther. On September 11, 1880, the *Spokan Times* remarked, "We fear that the railroad track will not be laid this side of the summit, 60 miles from Ainsworth, before the white flakes of winter are upon us."[30] The Northern Pacific Railroad Co. *Annual Report to Stockholders*, issued on September 29, 1880, noted that "the grading is complete to Spokane Falls, 150 miles, and the track is laid 25 miles." It went on to say, evasively, that "the rapidity with which the track is laid depends upon the promptness with which the OR&N Co. forwards rails and fastenings up the river, and the success of contractors in floating timbers and ties down to Ainsworth." The report wishfully concluded, "There is every reason to believe that the track will reach Spokane Falls this season."[31] The true facts were withheld for several months, and not until Christmas Day 1880 did the Walla Walla *Weekly Statesman* carry a coherent account of the whole affair.[32] By that time, however, the sawmill was well supplied with logs and work was once more under way.

William Harkness & Co., meanwhile, was reduced to insolvency. In November 1880 their employees went on strike demanding payment of wages and seized control of the mill and all the logs on hand. Northern Pacific was then forced to pay the men off, take over the plant, and run it as part ot its own operations.[33] During the following winter more timber was cut in the Cascade Mountains, but contractors such as George Smith, who undertook to supply 3 million board feet at $5 per thousand, insisted on being paid as soon as their men "banked" logs on the Yakima River. Northern Pacific was thus forced to assume the entire responsibility for getting the rafts safely downstream.[34]

During 1880 Ainsworth briefly became a thriving town, for in addition to the sawmill the railway divisional facilities were also established there.[35] By February 1881 these installations consisted of a ten-stall roundhouse, a large machine shop, a car shop 300 ft. long X 50 ft. wide, a blacksmith shop, a carpenter shop, an office building, boarding and bunkhouses, and stables. The machine shop was equipped with a variety of heavy machine tools, including a driving wheel lathe, an axle lathe, a wheel borer, a 500-ton hydraulic press, two compound planers, an automatic bolt and screw machine, a 5-ton plate shear, and numerous devices for punching and drilling holes. Taken together, the sawmill and the workshop complex provided employment for 350 men and " . . . an equal amount of heathens" (the latter term apparently being a derogatory reference to the Chinese). John E. Stone was superintendent overall, and Thomas E. Roberts, "late of the Baldwin Locomotive Works in Philadelphia," had charge of the shops. The social amenities enjoyed by the work force included a good, clean, commodious hospital (supported by $1 per month employee insurance contributions), a post office, a Wells Fargo express office, and various stores, hotels, and restaurants. Despite these blessings, however, Ainsworth remained a wild and woolly place, where fights, it was said, broke out " . . . three to twenty . . ." times nightly.[36]

Throughout the summer of 1880 very little steel was laid on the Lake Pend d'Oreille Division. The few ties arriving from the Clearwater late in May were set out at more than twice the normal spacing to allow the track to be extended, somewhat flimsily, to the 26th mile. When more ties became available, later in the year, first priority was given to building a railway from a point on the south bank of the Snake River, nearly opposite Ainsworth, 12 miles across the sandy sagebrush flats to Wallula.[37] Initially laid to narrow gauge, the line from South Ainsworth to Wallula was completed late in November 1880 and temporarily operated by OR&N as an extension of the Walla Walla & Columbia River Railroad. In conjunction with that company's other line from Wallula to Umatilla, completed at about the same time, it reduced the risk of being unable to bring up rails during the winter low water period.

With the problems of tie and timber supply resolved and the connecting line to Wallula completed, work on the main line was resumed.[38] By Christmas 1880 the steel had been extended to the 37th mile (just south of the present town of Connell), where construction of 2,000 ft. of trestlework delayed further advance until early in January 1881. Between Ainsworth and the 54th mile (Beatrice) there were only three trestles, but in the next 12 miles over the height of land no less than twenty more had to be built.[39] As the steel gang advanced up the narrow valley of the seasonal watercourse leading northward from the 40th mile, they were inevitably impeded by the bridge builders working ahead of them. The pace of tracklaying slackened and the construction train did not negotiate the 1,000-ft.-long, 35-ft.-deep rock cut at Providence Summit until 5:30 p.m. on Wednesday, March 23, 1881.

Passing through the cut in a northwesterly direction, the railway swung immediately northeastward to emerge high on the hillside

overlooking the Providence Coulee (now called the Lind Coulee).
From that point there is an exhilarating view to the north and west
that inspired a grandiloquent description written by the first newspaper correspondent to see it.[40] In the spring of 1881 the rolling hills,
in their pristine state, formed a continuous green sward of bunchgrass
prairie, as yet unbroken by the plough. Between Ainsworth and Ritzville the country was still entirely uninhabited. Settlers, however,
were already moving into areas with easier access to standing timber
farther east, and the demand for land was growing. Late in 1879
Northern Pacific opened a branch land office at Colfax[41] and made
preparations to dispose of the 5,350,400 acres of land to be granted
to the company when the Lake Pend d'Oreille Division had been
completed and duly approved by the United States Government.
Lands within 40 miles of the railway line were to be offered at $3
per acre cash, or $4 per acre and 7 percent interest on deferred pay-
ment. The Colfax office was staffed by Messrs. D. C. Lewis and
W. H. Cushman. Since land sales depended upon the number of settlers attracted to the country, Northern Pacific simultaneously opened
an emigration office in the great seaport city of Liverpool, England,
and placed Mr. George Sheppard in charge of affairs there.[42]

On April 9, 1881, the trestles on the descent from Providence had
all been completed and a hundred bridge carpenters, working under
the direction of Mr. J. B. McLain, moved on to undertake other tasks
in the vicinity of Spokane Falls.[43] The track, meanwhile, was laid to
Well No. 7 at the 67th mile (later Lind), and eight gangs of Chinese
laborers, eighty in a gang, were sent out along the line ahead to repair
winter-damaged parts of the roadbed. At Ainsworth enough ties were
on hand to lay track to the 120th mile and there were sufficient rails
to reach the 100th mile. By mid-April, therefore, everything was ready
for Mr. S. V. Stevens and the steel gang to begin laying track at an
accelerated pace.[44] From the 67th mile the rate of advance increased
to almost 2 miles per day, and by April 24 the railway had been extended all the way up the Paha Coulee to the nascent settlement of
Ritzville.[45] Hardly allowing his men to pause at William McKay's
solitary eight-room home and hostelry,[46] Stevens relentlessly urged
them onward across the open country to reach and pass the 100th mile.

As the railway increased in length the journeys of the supply trains
became longer and longer, and stops were made at more and more
watering points: Bluff Wells, Twin Wells, and Well No. 7 (Mesa,
Hatton, and Lind), each with its windmill pump, elevated water tank,
and section house – and the well at the 21st mile named Eltopia,

because when a train arrived there late one winter night, short of both wood and water, and the crew found none available, the exasperated engineer angrily shouted out that there would be "hell to pay." Railroad men thereafter called the place "El-to-pai," but the company, being obliged to make concession to polite society, reversed the last two letters.[47]

Hell to pay or not, steam engines soon replaced the windmills as motive power for the well pumps and by the end of 1882 occurrences such as the episode at Eltopia became a thing of the past. Or nearly so, for when a settlement first developed at Ritzville the local residents all drew water from the Northern Pacific tank and made no effort to sink wells of their own. This convenient state of affairs was said to have lasted for several years until, inevitably, there came a day when the locomotive department was no longer able to share the water supply with the local populace. The company then lowered the boom and there was a panic rush to drill private wells. Water, however, was not immediately discovered at a readily accessible depth and plans were hastily made to move the entire settlement bodily eastward to the vicinity of a flowing well a mile away. Municipal confusion ensued but water was eventually found and a more self-reliant community survived to flourish *in situ*.[48]

Ritzville was only one of several incipient towns[49] appearing along the projected Northern Pacific line in the spring of 1880. Others included Sprague, Augusta, Depot Lake and Marshalltown. Augusta, apparently, was stillborn, Depot Lake (also referred to as Depot Springs, and nearly called Billings) matured as Cheney, while Marshalltown survived, but hardly flourished, without its suffix.

Sprague[50] lay at the intersection between the Northern Pacific line and the old military wagon road from Walla Walla to Fort Colville. Originally called Hoodooville, after a local resident rejoicing in the name of "Hoodoo Billy" Burrow, it was not a particularly attractive spot for settlement. Anticipating railroad construction, however, several enterprising characters moved into the area and made preparations to relieve the graders of their wages. To circumvent a Northern Pacific decree that liquor should not be sold within a mile of the proposed right-of-way, E. M. Kinnear and Patrick Wallace opened a saloon at Whiskey Rock, exactly one mile north of the surveyed line. The location was inconvenient but trade was brisk, and by July 1880 both gentlemen had accumulated enough capital to found other more respectable institutions adjacent to the railway. Kinnear went into general merchandizing and soon developed a business of "mammoth proportions," while Wallace set up a lucrative livery stable. Other people and enterprises followed and in December 1880 a town site was formally platted and named in honor of General Sprague.

As the tracklayers approached Sprague early in May 1881, work was briefly interrupted by labor trouble.[51] Five months earlier wages had been increased from $2 to $2.25 per day to prevent the loss of men to other railway construction projects. The steel gang now struck for an additional 50 cents per day, and several days were lost before a compromise agreement was reached for a 25-cent increase. Celebration of this victory then resulted in even more delay. Sprague was the first approximation to civilization encountered since leaving Ainsworth and the men felt entitled to a break there. The town boasted two boardinghouses, two general stores, a livery stable, a blacksmith shop, and, by that time, two saloons. Both of the latter refused to close, and for several days drunkenness prevailed. Fearing that these events would be repeated at Cheney later in the month, Stevens forcefully requested that the saloons there be kept closed while track was laid through town.[52] Surviving records, however, give no indication that his plea was successful.

In St. Paul, meanwhile, the new general manager of the Northern Pacific Railroad sternly confronted the twin threats of alcoholism and labor unrest. In a classic message to company employees, issued in the spring of 1881, General Herman Haupt gave notice that "vicious habits of any kind, profanity, or the use of alcoholic drinks will be an obstacle to promotion when others who are free from such disqualification can be found." Addressing the problem of labor's relationship with management, General Haupt recommended that " . . . brotherhoods, combinations, and unions, be avoided." He promised that efforts would " . . . be made to secure the beneficial objects proposed in such organizations by (providing) substitutes less liable to be controlled by designing leaders for mischievous purposes." The general manager concluded, "Loyalty should be the duty of every employee."[53]

The tracklayers appear to have reached Sprague, 108 miles from Ainsworth, no later than about May 8, 1881,[54] for on May 9 an unfortunate Charles Evans had both legs broken by an engine cowcatcher while attempting to couple up to a car there.[55] A regular service of trains carrying passengers between Ainsworth and Sprague was probably established on Monday, May 16, 1881. Five days later the Walla Walla *Weekly Statesman* noted departure times of 10:30 p.m. from Ainsworth and 3:30 a.m. from Sprague and added that the trains left

Ainsworth with " . . . that beautiful irregularity incident to new-ness."[56]

The steel gang's pause for liquid refreshment at Sprague apparently had but little eventual effect upon progress eastward. Indeed it may have helped for, as the Reverend Dr. H. G. Atkinson confirmed to *Spokan Times*, the railway reached Cheney, 133 miles from Ains-worth, on Wednesday May 25, 1881.[57] No less than 25 miles of track must have been laid in twelve or thirteen days. This rapid advance should, however, be qualified, for the construction train proceeded on a skeleton track and more than half of the ties were brought up on supply trains and inserted afterward. The overall progress was, nevertheless, impressive, for by the end of the first week in June the steel had been extended all the way down the Lake Creek Valley and the Marshall canyon to the crossing of Hangman Creek, and regular trains were running to Cheney.

Construction of the 16 miles of railway between Cheney and Spokane Falls was a relatively difficult proposition. Two routes had been surveyed, based respectively on high and low level crossings of Hangman Creek.[58] A high level crossing offered much easier grades but would have required a bridge 165 ft. high and 3,000 ft. long. Materials for such a structure were not locally available, nor was there any existing railroad on which they could be brought up beforehand. The only immediately feasible solution, therefore, was to descend almost to the floor of the Hangman Creek Valley, cross that stream on a much smaller bridge, and climb out again to reach the benchlike town site at Spokane Falls.

By October 1880 Coulter, McBean & Co. had finished the road-bed,[59] but all the pile driving and bridge building remained to be carried out by Northern Pacific's own forces in the spring. Three main tasks were involved: piling had to be driven to carry the railway across 300 ft. of boggy ground near Cheney; extensive trestlework was needed in the Lake Creek Valley; and a single-span Howe-truss bridge had to be built to cross Hangman Creek 3 miles from Spokane Falls. Most of the material required for this work was cut locally and sawn by the Pioneer Mill Co. of Spokane Falls,[60] who contracted with Northern Pacific to supply 2.5 million board feet of lumber and 175,000 ties, all to be delivered by December 31, 1880. Early in 1881 a mess house and a blacksmith shop were established near the existing Hangman Creek wagon road bridge,[61] and work on the railway bridges and trestles slowly got under way. During the month of January, when the water level was low, a gang of stonemasons, directed by Mr. Hays of the Northern Pacific bridge construction department, built the piers upon which the main span of the Hangman Creek bridge was to rest.[62] Completing this job early in February, they then moved on to construct the abutments for the larger bridge across the Spokane River 9 miles east of the falls. Meanwhile, in mid-December 1880, the first piles for the bog section were hauled to Cheney from Spokane Falls by George F. Graves.[63]

A pile driver, locally built by Mr. Hays,[64] was completed early in March and began driving piles into the bog shortly afterward.[65] When J. B. McLain and his hundred carpenters arrived from Well No. 7 in mid-April, sixty men were at first put to work capping the piles. That done, the entire force was then concentrated on the trestlework in the Lake Creek Valley.[66] All of these structures were thus completed by the end of May 1881, and the steel gang was immediately able to lay track right through to the site of the Hangman Creek bridge, which awaited its main span. As there was obviously going to be some delay while the bridge was completed, the "great terminus tent" was brought to the end of track and set up[67] on or about June 6, 1881, to receive and forward goods for Spokane Falls and vicinity.

The Hangman Creek bridge was to consist of a single 180-ft.-long Howe-truss span with trestle approaches.[68] The heavy timbers required for the trusses were cut and sawn to size on the coast, and cast iron spacers with an aggregate weight of 30 tons were made in the foundry at Northern Pacific's Tacoma shops. The lumber was not checked until the whole shipment arrived at Ainsworth early in June, and only then were the actual dimensions found to be at variance with the sizes specified on the bill of material. To the consternation of the bridge builders, the main members could not be mated with the iron spacers. Timbers for the Spokane River bridge, however, formed part of the same consignment and were fortunately found to be large enough to be modified for use at Hangman Creek. This material was therefore sent up from Ainsworth and cut to the correct dimensions on site. Mr. A. J. McLellan, the Northern Pacific superintendent of bridge construction, " . . . proceeded with energy . . ." and within ten days the span had been completed and lifted into place on the piers. The structure was then tested by running a locomotive and several flatcars, heavily laden with rails, backward and forward across it. No sign of collapse having been discerned, the finished bridge was declared safe, and the tracklayers resumed work on the far side of the creek.[69]

The growing city of Spokane Falls, planted on gently sloping ground just south of the great cataracts on the Spokane River, was already well enough established for residents of Walla Walla to recognize it as a threat to their own city's pre-eminence in the Interior. Writing from Spokane in May 1881, a correspondent for the Walla Walla *Weekly Statesman* acidly remarked that "it really is amazing how warm the advocates of a one stove and one tavern town can become." And a month later the same paper, noting that the railroad was within 3 miles of Spokane Falls, alerted its readers to the fact that the first locomotive was about to enter " . . . the sacred precincts."[70] The founding fathers of the new city, however, were not to be diverted from their purpose by disparaging remarks. Sensing that Spokane Falls would be the key to rich areas farther to the north and east, these enterprising men were already making plans for the development and domination of a vast hinterland of their own.[71] Northern Pacific was now about to place the new metropolis indelibly upon the map. The opening of the railroad was a cardinally important event.

The first issue of the Spokane Falls *Chronicle*, published four days after the first train arrived, reported that throughout Saturday, June 25, 1881, there was " . . . an unusual degree of excitement among the people." It was, the *Chronicle* said, " . . . of that nature which manifested itself in the fervour of greetings and enthusiastic expressions of pleasure." Early in the afternoon the steel gang spiked down the rails of the 149th mile and came to a halt near the intersection with Howard Street. At about half past six in the evening Graham's Band assembled at the Depot Grounds and striking up " . . . a lively tune," summoned the entire populace to welcome the city's first railway passengers. At 7:14 p.m. a train consisting of a locomotive and six boxcars came into view, making " . . . a rapid run of the splendid curve below town." Then as it rolled up to the Mill Street crossing " . . . the crowd cheered, ladies waved their handkerchiefs, the band played, and the most enthusiastic greetings were extended to those who came to Spokane by rail." For posterity the *Chronicle* added that " . . . the train was in charge of Len Curtis, conductor. Nelse Bellinger held the throttle, and James Black fired up."[72]

With the completion of the railway across the Interior Plain, Northern Pacific was able to establish title to a vast area of potentially good agricultural land. The first objective sought by building the Lake Pend d'Oreille Division was thus attained. Frederick Billings and his associates, however, were denied the personal satisfaction of bringing their enterprise to fruition, for when the first train arrived in Spokane Falls, the Northern Pacific Railroad Co. had already fallen into other hands.

7

THE BLIND POOL

In the fall of 1880 negotiations between Northern Pacific and a group of leading New York bankers resulted in an agreement to finance completion of the company's entire main line.[1] Formally announced to the board by Charles B. Wright on November 19, 1880, the transaction was one of unprecedented magnitude. A syndicate headed by Drexel Morgan & Co., Winslow Lanier & Co., and August Belmont & Co. contracted to purchase $40 million worth of Northern Pacific forty-year, 6 percent, first mortgage gold bonds. Ten million dollars' worth of these bonds were taken firm at a price of 90 on January 1, 1881, and the remainder on $10 million options available at a price of 92-1/2 during each of the three succeeding years, all of which promised to provide Northern Pacific, over a four-year period, with more than $36 million, a sum then considered ample for all the purposes contemplated.

Given the state of Northern Pacific's credit at the time, the directors were probably entitled to congratulate themselves on the conclusion of such an agreement. In the long term, however, there were difficulties.[2] The mortgage applied not only to the railroad, but also to the land grant, and for that reason the bonds were only to be issued at a rate of $25,000 per mile as completed lengths of railway were duly inspected and approved by the United States government. In other words, Northern Pacific would only get the money to build the railway as the government granted the land, and the government would only grant the land as the company completed significant lengths of railway. Just how serious a problem this was to be was not apparently appreciated at the time the agreement was signed. In retrospect, the bankers got the better part of the bargain, for they not only bought the bonds at 7-1/2 and 10 percent discount and sold them at prices above par, but they also received a bonus in preferred stock equal to 5 percent of the total amount.

The news of the Northern Pacific financing agreement came as a complete surprise to the directors of the Oregon Railway & Navigation and Union Pacific Railway companies. Henry Villard, in particular, was thunderstruck, for until that time he had considered Northern Pacific to be a relatively impecunious company that could eventually and inevitably be molded to fit his own plans for domination of the Pacific Northwest. Now, however, the whole pattern was suddenly disrupted. In his own words:

> He perceived at once distinctly what damaging consequences the great financial strength thus secured to the other company might have for the interests represented by him. The fear, indeed, was justified that his company would be struck in its vital part by the continuation of the Northern Pacific main line down the Columbia. He knew that the mere threat of this would greatly affect the market value of his company's securities, and much impede the raising of additional capital for it.[3]

Faced with a resurgent Northern Pacific Railroad Co., Villard had to choose between two alternative courses of action.[4] He could either sell out to one of the two transcontinental roads (i.e. Northern Pacific or Union Pacific) or boldly attempt to purchase a controlling interest in Northern Pacific. William Endicott Jr., Villard's principal financial associate, evidently believed that rivalry between the two transcontinentals would allow OR&N to be sold at a high price. He therefore advised Villard to sell. Villard, however, was determined to cling to his unfolding dreams of empire and took the opposite course. He quietly began to buy up as much Northern Pacific stock as his private means and credit permitted.[5]

By December 4, 1880, he had already been successful enough to sense that what he was attempting to achieve might perhaps be within the realm of possibility.[6] Throughout December 1880 and January 1881 he continued to buy more stock, but by early February 1881 he realized that he had gone as far as his own resources would take him. He therefore decided to appeal for help from friends and business associates. This he did by sending out a circular letter to about fifty persons inviting them to participate to the extent of $8 million in a potentially very profitable venture, the details of which he was not yet able to disclose. In short, he asked them to buy a pig in a poke! OR&N, however, had paid dividends of 8 percent on stock and the promise of participation in another such venture brought the investors scrambling in. The rush to subscribe was so great, in fact, that rights had to be allocated, and within a few days these traded at premiums of up to 50 percent. The money was called for in three installments, due between February 15 and April 2, 1881, and without exception all the payments were promptly made. This syndicate was afterward called "The Blind Pool" and provided Villard with the additional funds required to buy a controlling interest in the Northern Pacific.[7]

Before the end of February 1881 the financial community was already well aware of what was going on. On February 25 *Railroad Gazette* noted that " . . . the OR&N Co. is engaged in an effort to secure control of this company (i.e., NPRR), its chief object being to prevent the building of lines which will compete with its own."[8] Within the next two weeks Villard sensed that control was practically within his grasp and decided to confront Billings in person.[9] At a meeting held in Northern Pacific's New York office on March 11, 1881, he offered to buy all of Billings's own considerable holdings in the company. Billings, however, refused to cooperate. In a reply to Villard, written on March 14, 1881, and made public shortly afterward, he eloquently explained the Northern Pacific position. Defending his company's right to build a railway directly through the Cascade Mountains to Puget Sound, Billings wrote:

> I am so certain a road will be built there by some company I think it would be almost a crime if the Northern Pacific should lose its right to build there, and its land grant. And it certainly will if it should not go to work and keep at work on that line.

and

> . . . the Northern Pacific is chartered to go to Puget Sound, both by the Columbia River and by the Cascade Range. Certainly by at least one route or the other it should go there. It will not be a complete trans-continental line from the Great Lakes to the Pacific Ocean unless it does so. On the Sound I believe commerce will in time do its chief work instead of on the Columbia River. The dangers and difficulties of entering the river and its navigation will tell against it, as soon as the Sound is easily accessible from the interior.

Billings concluded as follows:

> Excuse my long letter, I had no notion of any such length, but I want you to get hold of my views of the situation and the spirit in which I am ready to deal with it. I recognize the fact that you are president of a corporation in which you have money and reputation. I do not complain that you seek to develop and strengthen your enterprise. But you have a large field for development in the roads you have planned. You will have plenty of business to do in your own field. Why, virtually, put a pistol at the breast of Northern Pacific at Ainsworth or Wallula, and say thus far and no farther. It is of this I complain. The Northern Pacific has a field in eastern Oregon and Washington Territory to develop north of your contemplated system of roads. It will soon have its line across

the continent. With a right to go to the Sound by two ways, ought it to let your company build the river line and somebody else the mountain line, and itself never go there at all? You may say you do not mean this. But this is what will happen if this company postpones work on the road to the Sound. It will take time to build the line. Meanwhile you will have all the business. By the time it is completed and the road is finished across the continent there will be business for both lines, and then the two lines can be worked in harmony as if owned in common.[10]

Billings's appeal was eminently reasonable but Villard was no longer in a position to compromise, even if he wanted to. As leader of an advancing army of expectant investors he could hardly turn back. Northern Pacific's policies had to be rendered compatible with Oregon Railway & Navigation Co. plans for economic control of the Pacific Northwest.

By mid-March 1881 Villard's syndicate had purchased 60 percent of the available common stock of the company.[11] Billings and his associates, however, still had a last card to play. Under the 1875 plan of reorganization, originally conceived and implemented by Billings himself, the company issued $51 million worth of preferred stock to former bondholders. At the same time the total value of common stock, to be made available to holders of proprietary rights, was set at $49 million. Of the latter, $26 million was issued immediately and the remainder held back to be distributed in installments as various sections of the railroad were completed.[12] By March 1881 a further $5 million common stock had been issued but $18 million still remained in reserve. Most of the holders of proprietary rights, being parties to the Original Interests Agreement or its subsequent amendments, either belonged to or sympathized with the existing management. If the residue of the common stock could be distributed, forthwith, to this select group, Villard's plan might yet be thwarted. On March 18, 1881, therefore, the executive committee decided to issue the reserve shares, without delay, to the 240 persons who would eventually have been entitled to them.[13] Control of the company was thus wrenched from Villard's grasp.

Villard reacted quickly. On March 25, 1881, his attorney asked the Superior Court of the City of New York to grant an injunction prohibiting distribution of the reserved shares.[14] The basis of Villard's complaint was that since the amount of Northern Pacific preferred stock had been reduced to $43 million by exchanges for land, the issue of 180,000 common shares would transfer control of the company, not only to holders of common stock but to the recipients of those particular shares. The court granted a temporary injunction, and ordered the Billings group to show why it should not be made permanent. Other actions, launched to dispute the sufficiency of dividends paid on preferred stock, served to multiply the legal difficulties. After suffering almost two months of tiresome litigation and the added strain of trying to persuade his own intransigent colleagues to accept a compromise, Billings capitulated.[15] Confiding only in two close friends, he concluded a secret and personally rewarding agreement with Villard and presented the other members of the board with a *fait accompli*.

The terms of the compromise agreement, as published in the Portland *Daily Oregonian* on June 8, 1881, were as follows:

1. The recognition of Mr. Villard by admitting two of his friends to the directory.
2. The building of the Cascade branch as soon as the surveys were completed.
3. That Mr. Villard should cast his vote and proxies at the September election for a majority of the present board of directors.
4. That the road from Tacoma to Portland, which was already finished to Kalama, be finished as soon as possible.
5. That Mr. Villard withdraw suits and place no further obstacles in the way of issuing the 180,000 shares of new stock.
6. That Mr. Billings transfer to Mr. Villard $9 million stock at $50.

The crux of this "compromise" lay in the last of its terms. By handing over $9 million worth of common stock Billings and his confidants in effect canceled the advantage previously gained by issuing the $18 million worth of reserve shares. To make up the $9 million common stock required, Billings put forward his own holdings of $5 million and obtained a further $1 million on the market. His two friends, meanwhile, provided the remaining $3 million in a similar manner. Billings's $5 million worth of common stock was said to have cost him, as a holder of proprietary rights, approximately $75,000. He now conveyed this holding to Villard for $50 per share, or a total of $2,500,000, and after paying perhaps $500,000 for the shares purchased on the market, probably made a net profit of something like $1,925,000. The "compromise" could, therefore, have been more accurately termed a "sell out." The *Daily Oregonian* reported that when the board met on May 19, 1881:

> . . . no one knew of the arrangement of the proposed compromise and when it was announced Mr. Billings excused his action on the score of ill health. The actual sense of the Board in agreement was not taken as Mr. Villard already had control.[16]

It is of interest to note that J. C. Ainsworth was said to have played a large part in arranging this "compromise."

Henry Villard's control of the Northern Pacific Railroad Co. could no longer be denied, and at the May 19 meeting he was granted immediate representation on the board.[17] Johnston Livingston and Joseph Dilworth therefore resigned to make way for Thomas F. Oakes and Artemus H. Holmes, both of whom were associated with Villard in OR&N. On June 9, 1881 Frederick Billings ceded the presidency of the company to A. H. Barney, a signatory of the Original Interests Agreement. There was no doubt, however, that Barney's appointment was only temporary and that Villard would formally take over as president at the annual general meeting in September. On June 10, 1881, a correspondent for the St. Paul *Pioneer Express* interviewed the principal participants in the upheaval and forwarded a revealing dispatch to his paper. Mr. Billings, he wrote

> . . . looks more serene and happy than at any time before since surrendering to Villard. He is glad to get away on account of his health and that of his daughter, and because his relations with some of the directors are no longer pleasant.[18]

Mr. Barney, who was also managing director of the United States Express Company, was quoted as saying that he would not go to the Northern Pacific office more than once a week as he considered himself merely a temporary functionary. And Henry Villard, in turn, was said to have confirmed that Mr. Barney was "president pro-tem" whose only functions would be to sign the company's documents and preside at meetings.

On June 24, 1881, Henry Villard called the members of his syndicate together for the meeting originally promised for May 15.[19] His object, he now explained, was to form a corporation that would hold a controlling interest in both the Northern Pacific Railroad and Oregon Railway & Navigation companies. The new organization, to be called the Oregon & Transcontinental Co. would coordinate the policies and actions of the two older concerns and provide them with financial assistance as required.[20] In the intoxicating atmosphere of triumph, the members of the syndicate not only endorsed the plan but also enthusiastically agreed to subscribe yet another $12 million to finance it. Thus encouraged, Villard took immediate steps to obtain legal sanction for his imperial ambitions. Articles incorporating the Oregon & Transcontinental Co. were filed with the clerk of Multhomah County in the state of Oregon on June 28, 1881.[21] The promoters were Henry Villard, Artemus H. Holmes, J. N. Dolph, R. Koehler, C. H. Prescott, Paul Schulze, George J. Ainsworth, and Joseph Simon. The company had an authorized capital stock of $50 million, of which $30 million was distributed among the members of Villard's syndicate in return for their $20 million cash contributions. The Oregon & Transcontinental Co. was granted sweeping powers to develop a comprehensive network of transportation and auxiliary facilities in the Pacific Northwest. Every conceivable strategic route was pre-empted, and authority was obtained to finance, construct, or operate railways, riverboat and ocean steamship lines, and all related facilities. The first board of directors consisted of J. C. Ainsworth, E. F. Adams, J. N. Dolph, William Endicott Jr., R. R. Fay, Henry Failing, R. Koehler, C. H. Prescott, Thomas F. Oakes, Paul Schulze, and not least, Henry Villard himself.

Less than three months later Villard secured the third crown and his ascendancy was complete. At the annual meeting of the Northern Pacific Railroad Co., held in New York on September 15, 1881, the voting power of the Oregon & Transcontinental Co. interest returned a new board of directors, consisting of Ashbel H. Barney, Frederick Billings, John W. Ellis, Robert Harris, Artemus H. Holmes, Thomas F. Oakes, Rosewell G. Rolston, and Henry Villard, of New York; Benjamin P. Cheney, Elijah Smith, and J. L. Stackpole, of Boston; John C. Bullitt of Philadelphia; and Henry E. Johnston of Baltimore. Henry Villard was elected president; Thomas F. Oakes, first vice president; Anthony J. Thomas, second vice president; Samuel Wilkeson, secretary; and Robert L. Belknap, treasurer.[22]

Henry Villard was at last president of the Oregon Railway & Navigation Co., the Northern Pacific Railroad Co., and the Oregon & Transcontinental Co. In his own words " . . . he assumed the burden of forging a new rail chain across the continent, twenty-seven hundred miles long, by connecting the existing links."[23]

8

THE UPPER RIVER AND
THE SOUTHERN INTERIOR

The Oregon Railway & Navigation Co. plan to occupy the Columbia River Valley matured slowly. Thielsen's construction superintendent, John L. Hallett, had the advantage of being able to use the riverboats to bring up supplies to various points along the line. Grading and bridge building therefore proceeded apace, but completion was delayed by an unexpected shortage of rails. Construction of the 112-mile section between Celilo and Wallula began early in 1880, and although there was little rock work the road was not entirely opened and the whole Upper River navigation superceded until the middle of April 1881.

As a first step toward construction of the Columbia Valley line, the 14-mile long, 5-ft. gauge portage railway from The Dalles to Celilo was changed over to standard gauge in February 1880.[1] Work on the new road began shortly afterward and within three months 1,200 men were at work,[2] 30 miles of the line had been graded, and all the bridge piers built. By early July 1880, 45 miles of roadbed were ready, and the iron Howe-truss bridge across the Deschutes River had been finished.[3] Rails, however, had not yet been delivered, and very little track was laid. Two ships carrying railroad iron from Cardiff had run into trouble at sea. One had been forced to put into Rio de Janeiro for repairs and discharge its cargo there, and the other was feared to be a total loss.[4] Consequently, no rails were brought up to the front until after July 22, 1880, when the new OR&N Co. ocean steamer *Columbia* arrived in Portland on her maiden voyage from the East Coast.[5] The cargo of rails discharged from the *Columbia* was promptly sent upriver to The Dalles and tracklaying began, but by then it was quite evident that the railway would not be completed until the following spring.

To avoid repetition of the annual inconvenience caused by low water in the river, priority was given to building enough of the upper part of the railway to bypass the Umatilla Rapids. For the time being this line was to be laid to narrow gauge and operated as an extension of the Walla Walla & Columbia River Railroad. The original quite modest plan, published in *Railroad Gazette* as early as May 21, 1880, was to run trains from Walla Walla to Grande Ronde Landing, 8 miles below Umatilla.[6] Later in the year, however, a more ambitious proposal was put forward whereby the narrow gauge would have been extended to the mouth of Willow Creek, 34 miles below Umatilla. Grain cargoes could then have been increased to 300 tons on *Annie Faxon* and *D. S. Baker* and 350 tons on *Harvest Queen*, and, although *Spokane* and *John Gates* had been chartered to Northern Pacific, 600 tons could have been brought down daily. Shortage of ties, however, frustrated this plan. Track was laid to Coyote, 44 miles below Wallula, but the 17 miles beyond Umatilla remained unballasted and were not used. The narrow gauge line from Wallula to Umatilla was opened at the end of November 1880.

Standard gauge track, meanwhile, was laid from Celilo to Blalock's Landing, 46 miles above The Dalles, and completed on Saturday, November 13, 1880.[7] The hull of *Tenino* was brought up to Blalock's to act as a wharf boat, while the steamer *Northwest* served as a station building and provided accommodation for thirteen company employees working there. A "Y" track and double incline were put in to bring railway cars down to the waterfront, and a 20-ft. Eclipse windmill was installed to pump water into a 200-barrel tank for the locomotives.[8] For the next five months trains left The Dalles for Blalock's at 7:00 a.m. daily, and others running on the narrow gauge line made round-trips three times a week between Walla Walla and Umatilla. The stern-wheelers *D. S. Baker* and *Harvest Queen* continued to ply the 53 miles of river between Blalock's and Umatilla, thus providing a connection between the two railway systems.

For OR&N, the winter of 1880-81 was an ordeal indeed. At The Dalles the temperature fell to 17 degrees F on the night of November 16 and within a week the navigation was practically closed by ice on the river.[9] By December 13, 27 inches of snow had fallen at The Dalles and 8 to 10 inches up-country. A week later a sudden thaw caused the ground to heave, and on Tuesday, December 21, 1880, the Walla Walla train was overturned by a landslide 9 miles above Umatilla.[10] Nobody was injured but the line was blocked for almost a week. In mid-January 1881 part of the John Day River bridge was carried away in a flood and the train service between The Dalles and Blalock's was disrupted.[11] Worse was yet to come, for during the first week in February the weather again moderated rapidly and the rivers became raging torrents full of ice floes and drift timber.[12]

Damage to the railway was extensive. The new bridge just west of Wallula was swept away, as were two others between Wallula and Walla Walla. The Deschutes River bridge, meanwhile, was damaged and could not be repaired until the water level fell. Several stretches of roadbed up to 350 ft. long were badly washed out. At a point about 1-1/2 miles east of the Des Chutes siding (now called Miller) Engine No. 5 and four flatcars plunged into one of the resulting gaps in the railway, thus presenting The Dalles shopmen with a major recovery job. Despite these misfortunes some progress was made. Throughout the winter two trains brought up gravel needed to fill the timber trestles on the former portage line, while a third carried ice down from Celilo to the company's ice house at The Dalles.[13] Rails, meanwhile, were sent up to the front and held in readiness for the resumption of work in the spring.

Tracklaying recommenced at Blalock's on Monday, March 7, 1881, and proceeded at a rate of more than a mile per day.[14] By April 4, 1881, the 36-mile gap between Blalock's and Coyote had been closed and the engineers were preparing to standardize the railway gauge between Umatilla and Wallula.[15] During the next ten days large forces of men took up positions along the line, and on Sunday, April 17, 1881, the gauge was changed.[16] Two locomotives borrowed from the Oregon & California Railroad were brought upriver,[17] and within five days standard gauge trains were running through the Wallula Gap. Connections at the junction then enabled passengers from Walla Walla to travel the 157 miles to The Dalles in 11 hours and reach Portland in 19 hours. The fare was $9 to The Dalles and $14 to Portland. The schedule was as follows:[18]

6:30 p.m. Dep.	The Dalles	Arr. 4:30 a.m.
5:30 a.m. Arr.	Walla Walla	Dep. 5:30 p.m.

Further improvement soon followed, for within six weeks the gauge of the WW&CR line from Wallula to Walla Walla was also changed.[19] The first standard gauge locomotive arrived in Walla Walla at 6:15 p.m. on Wednesday, May 25, 1881, and a through service to The Dalles was inaugurated on the following Saturday night.

Stations and distances in miles westward from Wallula were: Umatilla, 27; Coyote, 44; Castle Rock, 52; Willows, 63; Alkali, 72; Blalock's, 80; Quinn's, 87; John Day's, 96; Grant's, 103; Des Chutes, 110; Celilo, 113; and The Dalles, 126.

Once the railway had been opened, refinements soon followed. During the first week of July 1881 four Pullman palace cars were placed

in service between The Dalles and Walla Walla.[20] Owned by the
Pullman company, these luxurious sleeping cars were fitted out with
berths for forty-eight passengers. They had glass doors tastefully
decorated with etched designs, ornamental chandeliers, and a
multiplicity of mirrors set in highly finished wainscotting. Built at
a cost of $12,000 each, the cars were heated with hot water and
equipped with air brakes. The supplemental charge for traveling in
them was $2. Pullman company business in the Columbia Valley
was conducted from an office established at The Dalles and run by
Mr. H. F. Shield. When the Walla Walla sleeping car service was
inaugurated, the trains were hauled by the two new Baldwin 36-ton
locomotives nos. 14 and 15, which arrived at The Dalles from
Philadelphia at about the same time as the cars.[21]

The main line of the Walla Walla & Columbia River Railroad was
converted to standard gauge without incident, but two weeks later
there was a sad accident.[22] On the evening of Friday, June 10, 1881,
a mixed train with one passenger car was returning to Walla Walla
from South Ainsworth, and as it began to slow down for Nine Mile
Tank several persons accustomed to traveling on the narrow gauge
put their heads out of the windows. Conductor D. J. McKinney heard
a sound that he assumed to be the car striking an obstruction.
Brakeman Jimmy Walsh was leaning out of a window, and McKinney
asked him what had happened. Receiving no reply the conductor
tapped the brakeman on the shoulder, but he once more failed to
respond. McKinney then drew Walsh into the car and found to his
horror that the man's face was covered in blood. Four seats back,
two women were sitting side by side, and the one nearest the aisle,
seeing what had happened to the brakeman, suddenly became concerned for her companion who was also leaning out of the window.
Quickly she drew the other girl's head back into the car, only to find
that she too had been terribly injured. A telegraph message was sent
out from Touchet and by the time the train arrived in Walla Walla,
Superintendent Buckley had carriages waiting to take the victims to
hospital. The *Weekly Statesman* reported that the unfortunate female
was Minnie Wells, better known in Walla Walla as "Dutch Minnie."
She was not expected to live. The standard gauge railway rolling stock,
unfortunately, was just too tight a fit on parts of the old narrow gauge
line.

Once the road from Celilo to Wallula had been graded, forces
became available for railway construction in the Interior. Thielsen's
first plan was to begin work at Texas Ferry on the Snake River and

build a railway northward up the Alkali Flat Creek to Union Flat in Whitman County.[23] Having secured an OR&N foothold in the Palouse country, the force would then be moved across the river to construct a road southward to Walla Walla. This scheme depended upon the company's ability to procure timber on the Clearwater and float it down the Snake River. Early in April 1880, therefore, H. C. Hale was sent up-country to make the necessary arrangements, and within three weeks a party of carpenters had been landed at Texas Ferry to build a sawmill.[24] It soon became clear, however, that more reliable sources of timber could be developed in the Blue Mountains. Construction of a railway from Walla Walla to Dayton then became a matter of urgency.

Fortunately, during the summer of 1880 Henry Villard met with Joseph Potts and prepared the way for the traffic agreement with Northern Pacific. The need to use the Palouse road as a threat therefore diminished and OR&N was able to modify its strategy. In August 1880 it was announced that the graders would start work at Walla Walla and proceed directly to Dayton,[25] then return to a point just west of Waitsburg and build a line northward to Grange City at the mouth of the Tucannon River. The company would bridge the Snake River at a point about half a mile above Grange City and construct 4 miles of railway along the north bank to Texas Ferry. The road to Union Flat and Colfax would then follow.

The OR&N line into the Interior started out from an elevation of 906 ft. at Walla Walla, passed over higher ground north of the city, and descended to a crossing of the Dry Creek at Valley Grove. It then climbed northward through the hills to mile 17 and dropped abruptly into the Touchet Valley. Bridging the river just west of Prescott, the railway to Dayton proceeded eastward through Bolles Junction to the established town of Waitsburg. It then recrossed the river and wended its way up the southeast side of the valley to Dayton, where it reached an elevation of 1,660 ft. Swinging away northward from Bolles Junction, 1,166 ft. above sea level, the Palouse line crossed Whetstone Hollow on a huge trestle bridge and climbed with McKay Creek up to the Alto summit, 1,906 ft. above sea level. From that point it made a steep 11-mile descent down the Kellogg Creek Valley to meet and cross the Tucannon River at Starbuck, 645 ft. above sea level. Turning northwestward, the road followed the Tucannon to Grange City and finally swung eastward onto the left bank of the Snake River.

Stations and distances in miles from Wallula were: on the Palouse line—Walla Walla, 32; Prescott (established in 1883), 53; Bolles Junction, 57; Alto, 69; Starbuck, 80; Grange City, 84; and South Texas (soon to be called Riparia), 88; and on the branch—Waitsburg, 61; and Dayton, 71.

As soon as the decision had been made to build the Interior line northward from Walla Walla, work quickly got off to a good start. By October 9, 1880, the graders had already completed the roadbed between Walla Walla and Dayton and returned to Bolles Junction to begin work on the line to the Snake River. As winter approached, however, the rate of advance diminished. The Chinese laborers complained of the cold nights and many of them left for more temperate zones.[26] Then a violent dispute between a Chinese timekeeper and a white foreman precipitated a more general exodus. The men were soon replaced and by January 6, 1881, 400 whites and 750 Chinese were again hard at work north of the Alto summit.[27] In the Palouse soils on the high ground rapid progress was made, and by the end of January grading was practically complete.[28] On the approach to the Snake River, however, rock work went on for several more months, and in the vicinity of Grange City winter's tranquility was intermittently shattered by the roar of blasting.[29]

During the last week of February 1881 there was a spectacular blasting accident in which two workmen, as a result of their own foolishness, were "sent to eternity."[30] C. W. Colburn and G. W. Conkling were working on a rock bluff on the south side of the Snake River and, having drilled an 18-ft.-long hole into the volcanic rock, inserted and ignited two sticks of Giant Powder. Instead of breaking the rock out to surface, the explosion opened a large blind cavity within the formation. Frustrated, the men decided to go on loading until the void was filled, no matter how much explosive was required. Bringing up twenty-five kegs of black powder, they earnestly began to ram it down the hole, using, of all things, an iron rod. Somehow or other they managed to insert eighteen kegsfull before their luck ran out. The tamping rod then produced the inevitable spark, and there was an earth-shaking explosion. Colburn was hurled 350 ft. and killed on shore, while Conkling was shot far out into the river and never seen again.

By spring 1881 the OR&N lines to Dayton and Grange City had been graded, but before the track could be laid a lot of bridges and trestles had to be built. Between Walla Walla and Dayton there was a 50-ft. Queen-truss bridge at Dry Creek, five or more single and double tier trestles on the descent from mile 17, two 110-ft.-span Howe-truss bridges across the Touchet River, and many other lesser structures.[31] Enormous quantities of lumber were required, but a shortage of draft horses limited the rate at which it could be brought down from the Blue Mountains.[32] Tracklaying was started as soon as rails became available late in May,[33] but the steel gang was repeatedly held up by the bridge carpenters and failed to reach Dayton by the Fourth of July as predicted.

When some appreciable progress had been made, Thielsen invited the press to inspect the first 20 miles of the road. A special train, consisting of "one of the NPRR large engines . . . and a fine passenger car," steamed out of Walla Walla on the morning of Sunday, June 26, 1881, carrying journalists bound for the front.[34] The party noted that sidings had been put in at Dry Creek, mile 17, and mile 11 for the convenience of farmers. Track had been laid almost to the first crossing of the Touchet River, where seventy-five men were busily putting finishing touches to the bridge. The forces engaged on this work were living under canvas down in the valley. One camp had been set up for the carpenters and another, consisting of tents "laid out with military precision," was occupied by Chinese laborers. One onlooker, admiring this encampment, remarked that it reminded him of ". . . those exceptionally fine camps we Feds used to strike occasionally in the south." The steel gang, it was noted, ate and slept aboard the construction train. On the day after the press visit, the bridge just west of Prescott was completed and O. H. Kimball and his tracklayers were able to press on eastward at a rate of over a mile per day. Passing through Bolles Junction and Waitsburg, they arrived in Dayton at about noon on Thursday, July 14, 1881.

Few railways can have achieved the dubious distinction of the OR&N line to Dayton, which was the scene of one fatal accident on the very day of completion[35] and another within two weeks.[36] The stage was set for the initial calamity when the conductor in charge of the construction train agreed to take residents of Waitsburg on an unofficial inaugural trip to Dayton. Despite the newness of the track all went well until the return trip, when the engine had to propel the train from the rear. A dust storm had blown up and visibility was poor, but an air of festivity prevailed and caution was thrown to the wind. The train was bowling along at a fair speed, about 2 miles from Waitsburg, when it suddenly ran into a herd of cattle and nine flatcars were thrown off the track. Of the thirty passengers on board, one was killed instantly, another died the following morning, and three more suffered serious injuries. Several days later misfortune struck again when a brakeman who had been stooping over the end of a platform car to insert a coupling pin was thrown to the ground by a sudden movement of the train. Several cars ran over him, and he too was killed. His name was J. S. Murray, and he was said to have been a sober, hard-working man.

A regular train service to Dayton began on July 24, 1881,[37] and a grand inaugural excursion was announced for Sunday, August 7, 1881. Alarmed perhaps by the recent tragedies, the public displayed a marked reluctance to travel. Five hundred persons were expected to join the excursion from Walla Walla to Dayton, but when the great day came only about fifty determined trippers turned out. Nevertheless it was a memorable event![38] A heavy rain had spent itself during the night and the morning was crisp and clear. Arriving in Dayton at about 10:00 a.m., the excursion party emerged from the cars just as local residents were about to congregate at their accustomed places of worship. Forming up on the depot grounds with the Washington Guards band in the lead, the excursionists immediately set out on a noisy parade through the quiet streets. In the words of a correspondent reporting to the Pendleton *East Oregonian,*

> The church bells rang out in opposition, calling the worshippers of the Most High to repair to church and not to be contaminated by the un-godly which had just arrived. It was about a stand-off between the christians and the infedelic and free thinkers, the latter following the Washington Guards as they marched and marched along . . .

Reaching the picnic grounds, a little way from the main street, the party passed out the lager beer and, ignoring the icy demeanor of the staid and respectable citizens of Dayton, gaily danced the day away to festive tunes rendered by Professor Boulong and the Guard's ensemble. All too soon it was 4:00 p.m. and the revellers found themselves obliged to return to the depot, where the train

> . . . took back all there was left of the Walla-Wallans that was worth taking home.

After the inaugural excursion the citizens of Dayton may well have concluded that the railroad was a very mixed blessing. The branch line, however, was not primarily built to carry passengers but to bring out the Blue Mountain timber required for railway construction in the vast expanses of open country to the north. It was, moreover, only one part of a more extensive transportation system set up for that specific purpose. High in the mountains to the southeast of Dayton, the Oregon Improvement Company secured 2,000 acres of prime timberland and set up a large sawmill. They then constructed a flume 23 miles long to deliver timber to the railhead. Designed and built by J. E. Palmer, the flume consisted of a triangular section trough, made of 2-in. plank and supported on trestles. Laid on a continuous and uniform downgrade, it carried 20 in. of water flowing at a speed of 10 mph and was capable of delivering about 100,000 board feet of lumber daily.[39] The Dayton flume was completed early in August 1881, and whenever enough water was available it was a great success. Prodigious amounts of material were brought out.[40] In 1881, the Oregon Improvement Company cut 1,500,000 board feet from one tract of 160 acres alone. This and other timber was promptly sent down the flume to Dayton and delivered to the site of a huge trestle viaduct then being built to carry the Grange City railway across Whetstone Hollow.[41] Completion of this immense structure, 900 ft. long and up to 90 ft. high, was thus expedited, and by mid-September 1881 the tracklayers were able to press on rapidly northward. Just as they approached Grange City, however, the railway was deprived of its prime purpose.

In February 1881 R. M. Steel & Co. was awarded a contract to grade the line to Colfax, and undertook to start work north of the Snake River just as soon as satisfactory arrangements could be made for " . . . chinamen, tools, etc."[42] Mr. Steel, who hailed from St. John's, Michigan, arrived on site early in April and within a month grading was well under way.[43] Although *Railroad Gazette* of March 11, 1881, stated that the road to Colfax would start " . . . from a suitable point opposite Grange City, about 4 miles below Texas Ferry,"[44] it is not known whether a roadbed was in fact graded along the north bank of the river at that time. Contracts for building " . . . the bridge across the Snake River at Grange City" were to have been let on June 15, 1881,[45] but after considering the bids submitted for construction of the piers, OR&N decided to execute the work themselves.[46] The bridge was to consist of piers in the form of ". . . cribs, filled with stone, iron faced, and heavily braced throughout," supporting a superstructure made up of nine timber Howe-truss spans and a centrally pivoted iron drawspan. Seven of the Howe-truss spans were to be 110 ft. long and the other two, 154 ft., 6 in. The drawspan, to be manufactured in the east, was to be 336 ft. long and allow 150 ft. clear passage for river vessels. The total cost of the bridge was estimated at about $310,000. Its completion was optimistically scheduled for the end of the year.

Despite the announcement of specific plans for the bridge, curiously little progress was made toward building it. Late in June 1881 a diver named Spencer was said to be examining the river bottom near Grange City.[47] By early August the decision not to use contractors had apparently been reversed,[48] and on October 11 D. D. McBean was reported to have fifty men quarrying stone at Granite Point near Wawawai.[49] The same report, however, referred to a bridge with seven piers, located at Texas Ferry, and added that the OR&N was ". . . also putting a cable and ferry boat across the river at this point for their own use." R. M. Steel & Co., meanwhile, pressed on with work on the Palouse line. By mid-September the roadbed had been completed to the mouth of Rebel Flat Creek (i.e., Winona), and less than a month later the contractor was reported to have moved his base camp to a new site within about 3 miles of Colfax.[50] Evidently there was still a commitment to opening the Palouse country, but each day there was more doubt about the bridge.

At long last, in mid-October, Villard himself arrived on the scene[51] and a decision was made. Since the Oregon & Transcontinental Co. now controlled Northern Pacific Railroad, and that company was going to build a bridge across the Snake River at Ainsworth, there was no longer any need for OR&N to erect a similar structure at Grange City. A branch could be built from the Northern Pacific main line, eastward along the Washtucna Coulee to intersect the OR&N Palouse line at some point on Union Flat. Construction of the OR&N bridge at Grange City could therefore be suspended and a steam ferry used instead.[52] A ferry, however, required railway terminals on both sides of the river and dictated that the crossing be moved upstream to Texas Ferry where there was flat land on each bank. The railroad from Walla Walla was therefore extended eastward to a point opposite Texas Ferry and was not completed and opened until early in December 1881.[53] The roadbed up the Alkali Flat Creek was then left without track and passengers were obliged to take the stage from Texas Ferry to Colfax.[54] The trains, however, connected with steamboats for Lewiston and allowed OR&N to abandon the Lower Snake River navigation. The railway terminus and wharf on the left bank of the river was at first called South Texas but by August 1882 it was already being referred to as Riparia.[55]

9

THROUGH TO PORTLAND

The first railway on the left bank of the Columbia River was Joseph Ruckel's portage road at the Cascades. In April 1863 this line was superseded by the new Oregon Steam Navigation railway on the Washington side of the river. The Oregon portage line was left disused, but to keep out potential interlopers, such as the proposed Portland Dalles & Salt Lake Railroad, it was maintained in working order.

In 1873 the OSN, which had recently been brought under Northern Pacific Railroad Co. control, decided to rebuild the Oregon line as a first-class standard gauge railway. Work began in 1873 and was continued in 1874, but dissolution of the Northern Pacific holdings brought matters to a halt. Thereafter nothing more was done until J. C. Ainsworth and his partners regained control of OSN in 1876. A fresh start was then made, but in the spring of 1877 engineer John Brazee found that for a distance of two miles the whole hillside upon which the line had been located was sliding slowly but steadily into the Columbia River. Work was suspended, but during 1877 the river traffic increased so greatly that by year's end there was no doubt that a second portage railway would soon be required.

In December 1877 the OSN directors decided to try again. This time the line was to be laid to 3-ft. gauge and constructed to less exacting standards. Early in 1878 work was resumed under the direction of H. M. McCartney, who was later to oversee construction of the Lake Pend d'Oreille Division of the Northern Pacific Railroad. Existing trestle work was used at Tooth Rock, but new cuttings were made through lava bluffs east of Bonneville and just east of Eagle Creek. By Christmas 1878 grading and bridging had been completed and the new Oregon portage line lay ready for track. Early in 1879, however, Villard opened negotiations for the purchase of OSN, and further work was held in abeyance pending the outcome. The 30-lb. rails purchased for the road, therefore, were never laid.[1]

Villard's first priority was to complete a railroad from The Dalles to Wallula, thus phasing out the Upper River navigation. OR&N did not, therefore, begin work below The Dalles until late in 1880. In December of that year contracts were let to E. B. Sprague and Coung Le Young & Co. for clearing timber along the 66 miles of surveyed line between Sandy River and The Dalles. By mid-January 1881, 185 men were toiling away in the dense forest.[2] Initial preparations were made to drive as many as five tunnels between 300 and 900 ft. long. An order for tunneling equipment was placed with a San Francisco manufacturer, and local shipwrights laid down four large floating machinery platforms to be moored in the river near the tunnel workings.[3] At the end of February Thielsen's construction boss, John L. Hallett, announced that as the roadbed of the Walla Walla to Grange City line was nearly complete the graders working there would soon be transferred to The Dalles.[4] By April 17, 1881, 2,000 men were engaged on the Middle River section.[5] Grading of the easier parts of the line just west of The Dalles was soon completed, but further downstream the rock work presented formidable problems and progress was expected to be slower. At a score of places in the Columbia Gorge, high lava bluffs projected directly into the deep water of the river and the railway could only be accommodated by driving three tunnels and excavating numerous open cuts and slashes. Hallett, however, utilized novel equipment and methods, and accomplished the whole gargantuan task in one year.

Tunnels Nos. 1 and 2 located 9 and 12 miles below The Dalles, were respectively 325 and 265 ft. long, while Tunnel No. 3, 4 miles below Rooster Rock, was 550 ft. long. Each bore was 19 ft., 6 in. high X 16 ft. wide, and all were excavated from both ends simultaneously.[6] At Tunnel No. 1 the rock drills were driven by steam, supplied through flexible hoses from boilers mounted aboard the floating platforms moored in the river. Illumination was provided by ordinary locomotive-type headlamps. The exhaust steam from the drills raised the temperature and humidity to unbearable levels and reduced the visibility to almost nil. Consequently, the working conditions in Tunnel No. 1 were, quite literally, hellish. In one end of Tunnel No. 2, however, new and improved equipment was used and the workmen's lot became more bearable. Steam-driven air compressors and electric generators were installed aboard the floating platform and pneumatic rock drills and electric lighting were used in the heading. Telephone communications were established between the barge and the underground workings and, perhaps for the first time ever, blasting was initiated by electric detonators.[7] Tunneling was at first carried out on two shifts per day, but as the work was so arduous the company was soon forced to employ men on three 8-hour shifts. Tunnel No. 1 was started in mid-March 1881 and by early June it was two-thirds complete. Work on Tunnel No. 2 apparently began late in April or early in May 1881 and was finished on August 17. At Tunnel No. 3, meanwhile, excavations commenced on June 13 and went on for the remainder of the year.[8]

At points where the roadway had to be slashed out of the cliff faces, the proceedings were at first hair-raising and then spectacular. About 8 miles below The Dalles, a slice of rock 97 ft. high, 250 ft. long, and between 15 and 35 ft. thick had to be removed from a high bluff overhanging the river. Men were lowered down the cliff on ropes and, thus suspended, they drilled off the faces for blasting. When the charges were fired the shock was so great that the waves set up in the river water broke all the heavy ropes securing a barge moored in a cove ¼ mile away. As Hallett developed new methods of excavation his blasts became bigger and bigger. To take slices of rock off the larger bluffs, horizontal drifts and crosscuts were driven into the cliff faces to form a series of T-shaped tunnels. These were then filled with explosives that were detonated electrically to produce single enormous blasts throwing great masses of rock laterally into the river. As much as 50,000 lbs. of Giant Powder were used in a single blast. As the method was perfected, however, less and less explosive was needed to achieve more and more spectacular results, until eventually in March 1882, when the rock palisades at the east end of Tunnel No. 1 were sloped off, 23,500 lbs. of powder were required to blow off 140,000 cu. yds. of rock.[9]

In June 1881, 300 whites and 1,200 Chinese were employed on the grade, and by early August a total of 2,600 men were at work.[10] Despite the troubles at Sliding Mountain, where the OSN grade of 1878 had already sunk 5 ft., and at Shell Rock, where slides on the talus slopes were a continuous hazard, grading proceeded apace.[11] Progress was so rapid that by September 1881 the excavated parts of the roadbed were almost finished.[12] Unfortunately, there was then a great deal of timber work to be done, for in a total distance of 44-1/2 miles from The Dalles to Bonneville (as the station at the Lower Cascades was called), no less than 8-1/4 miles of trestle had to be built.[13] Skilled carpenters were in short supply and the heavy traffic on the river held up delivery of materials.[14] Tracklaying could only proceed as individual bridges were completed, and, although from December 1881 onwards steel gangs were employed on both ends of the line, progress was slow. With the completion of the Hood River bridge at the end of January 1882, a gap of 14 miles remained in which 2 miles of trestle still had to be built.[15] Hallett nevertheless pushed hard to get the job done and by March 17, 1882, exactly one year to the day after work on the Middle River section of the railway had been started, the last rail was laid.[16] Time was then taken to make a good job of ballasting and surfacing the track so that when the road was finally opened the trains were immediately able to run the 44 miles from Bonneville to The Dalles, stopping six times, in 2 hours 55 minutes.[17]

While final preparations were being made for the opening of the line, two unfortunate accidents occurred. On the morning of April 17, 1882, a handcar with six men aboard collided head-on with a construction train in Tunnel No. 1, and a bridge carpenter named Daniel Upton was killed.[18] News of this sad event, however, failed to deter Charles Hecker and Patrick Call who, eight days later, set out from Bonneville for an unauthorized joy ride on the road master's three-wheeled velocipede. At Eagle Creek bridge the machine became derailed and both men fell 40 feet onto the rocks below. Hecker died within twenty minutes and Call sustained injuries so serious that he was not expected to live.[19]

On May 20, 1882, the Middle River section of the Columbia Valley railway was at last declared complete, and early the following morning the first regular passenger train rolled into Bonneville with cars from as far away as Riparia. The steamers *S. G. Reed* and *E. N. Cooke* floated all their bunting and whistled a noisy welcome. The *Reed* then took on the passengers and mail in the normal way and proceeded downriver, arriving in Portland just before one o'clock in the afternoon. Thus, with minimal ceremony, the second part of the Columbia River navigation was phased out.[20]

First steps to complete the railway between Portland and Bonneville were taken in June 1881 when a line was located across country from the east side of the Willamette River to a meeting with the Columbia at a point nearly opposite Washougal. The line diverged from the existing Oregon & California tracks a few hundred feet above (i.e., south of) the East Side depot and swung eastward up Sullivan's Gulch. Passing to the south of Rocky Butte it turned briefly northward and then resumed an easterly course to a crossing of the Sandy River near Troutdale. Finally, from a point about 5 miles below Rooster Rock it followed the left bank of the Columbia River to Bonneville. The distance from East Portland was about 38 miles. Locating was finished on June 23, 1881, and within a week a large gang of men was already at work clearing the right-of-way.[21]

Some grading was accomplished in 1881, but due to the pressure of work upriver and the priority given to building the Northern Pacific main line, progress was slow. Moreover, there was still considerable doubt about the location of terminal facilities in Portland. Clearly there would eventually be a Union Depot on the west side of the Willamette River, but first a site had to be selected and several other difficulties resolved. For some time the railway officials talked about locating a depot and terminal facilities on 120 acres of low ground known as the Carruthers & Thomas claim, near the water works in South Portland. In May 1881, indeed, the *Oregonian* reported that the New York office of OR&N had ordered the immediate filling of 25 to 30 acres of that property to bring it to a level 18 inches above the 1876 high water mark. In September 1881 the company's *Annual Report* referred to the same site and stated that the filling of 40 acres would be commenced at once.[22] Nothing, however, was done, and the matter was not resolved until Charles F. McKim, a prominent New York architect who accompanied Villard to Oregon in the fall of 1881, returned to Portland at the end of January 1882.[23] Plans were then revised, and on March 8, 1882, the *Oregonian* announced that the "great depot" would eventually be built at Couch's Addition in North Portland.[24] The decision to build on this site, however, depended upon securing public agreement to close certain streets and required a referendum that could not be arranged immediately. There was also the question of locating and constructing a bridge over the Willamette River, which would obviously take much longer. As the Columbia Valley railway was to be opened by year's end and time was rapidly running out, it was announced that trains would initially terminate at Albina on the east bank of the Willamette River some distance north of the Oregon & California depot.

The company had recently purchased a strip of land in that vicinity extending 1-1/4 miles north to south along the Willamette riverfront and half a mile eastward and was already building a dry dock there.[25] Now they announced that their coal docks, grain elevators, warehouses, freight depot, switching yards, carsheds, roundhouse, workshops, and interim passenger facilities would all be established in the same area, beginning at once. Construction of the bridge and the Union Depot on the west side of the river would be undertaken later. As the railway from Bonneville emerged from Sullivan's Gulch it would swing around the bluff opposite the foot of F Street, turn northward to pass just to the east of the Oregon & California depot, and come alongside the river. It would then turn northeastward across

Montgomery Slough and run through Goldsmith Street to the OR&N grounds at Albina. The grain elevators, freight warehouses, and coal bins would all be built on piling along the riverside, extending into 18 ft. of water. A track was to run through the line of docks and warehouses and into the switching yard, while the roundhouse and workshops would be constructed farther back from the river, about half a mile north of the old Russell residence on the hill.

The work of leveling the grounds at Albina began immediately. On the day the announcement was made, 200 men were reported to be throwing up the grade for a semicircular railway track to be used for bringing earth fill from higher ground half a mile away to the east. Three thousand ties were loaded into scows for delivery to the site. Rails, discharged from the ships *Reporter* and *Western Belle*, berthed near the Oregon & California depot, were then taken to a stockpile a few hundred yards below I Street, where a switch had been installed in existing track to provide a lead into Sullivan's Gulch. Engine No. 13 and fifteen cars, meanwhile, were sent down-river by barge from The Dalles, and arrangements were made for the early delivery of a steam shovel.[26] By May 19, 1882, work on the OR&N docks had commenced,[27] two pile drivers were in use, and about 400 piles, extending 30 ft. from shore, had already been driven. Less than a week later construction of the Oregon Improvement Company coal dock also got under way. This was to be 250 ft. long, 40 ft. wide, and 40 ft. high, equipped with bucket elevators for unloading the colliers bringing coal from Puget Sound. The installation was to be such that although the coal would have to be shoveled into the elevator buckets within the ships' holds, no further manual labor would be required. Coal would be delivered by gravity to river steamers, railway cars, or locomotive tenders. Plans, it was said, were already being made to convert all the riverboats and railway locomotives to coal-burning just as soon as the coal dock could be brought into operation.[28]

Early in the spring of 1882 work once more got under way along the line.[29] No sooner had a start been made, however, than a serious accident occurred. To make way for railway construction a wagon road bridge spanning Sullivan's Gulch at the corner of Holladay Avenue and 16th Street had to be removed and on February 13, 1882, five men were sent to dismantle it. Unfortunately, when only 10 ft. of the planked roadway had been removed the entire 80-ft.-long bridge collapsed, throwing all the men 35 ft. to the ground and killing James G. Smith of Glencoe, Washington.[30]

Curiously, the OR&N right-of-way through Sullivan's Gulch was not approved by the City Council until mid-April 1882, when the company was ordered to erect a new truss bridge across the gulch and build a freight and passenger depot just below J Street. By that time work was well under way, both in the gulch and along the river-bank between H Street and Albina. On April 5 the *Oregonian* reported that difficulty was being experienced at the mouth of the gulch, where a large fill continued to sink as fast as earth could be dumped on it.[31] Piles were then being driven to form a retaining wall and apparently provided a solution to the problem. Widening of the gulch, mean-while, was carried out by sinking pits into the adjacent ground, charg-ing them with as much powder " . . . as thought safe . . . ," and blasting the entire hillside down. The pits were dug by hand to a considerable depth and in one case an unfortunate workman, whose name was also Smith, collapsed at the bottom and had to be hauled out unconscious. Taken to the nearby Home Hotel, however, he soon recovered.[32] In spite of such mishaps, construction of the railway proceeded rapidly and by August 18, 1882, track had been laid 17 miles to the Sandy River.[33] Rock excavations nearer to the Cascades took more time, but on October 4, 1882, a silver spike was driven to mark completion of the road.[34] The final opening was then delayed until construction of the Albina terminal facilities had advanced to a stage allowing the company to begin operations.

West of The Dalles the principal stations and distances in miles from Wallula were: The Dalles, 126; Rowena, 134; Mosier, 141; Hood River, 147; Viento, 154; Wyeth, 160; Cascade Locks, 167; Bon-neville, 172; Oneonta, 180; Rooster Rock, 189; Troutdale, 195; Clarney, 203; East Portland, 210; Albina, 212; and the proposed Portland Union Depot in Couch's Addition, 213.[35]

Rail traffic " . . . between the metropolis of Oregon and the tributary empire lying to the east of the Cascade Mountains . . . " officially began on Monday, November 20, 1882. The first train to leave Albina was the morning freight, which departed at 5:50 a.m. with fifteen cars including one loaded with furniture and carpets for the Sprague Hotel at Spokane Falls. At 4:00 p.m. the first passengers were trans-ferred across the Willamette River from Ainsworth Wharf to Albina aboard the steamer *R. R. Thompson*. Waiting for them on the incline at the east side was a train consisting of a baggage car, a mail car, three day coaches, and the Pullman sleeper *Oregon*, headed by Engine No. 3. Conductor Edward Lyons was in charge and locomotive engineer Andrew Curtis held the throttle. The train left Albina on

time at 4:45 p.m. and after stopping near the Oregon & California
depot to pick up passengers and mail from the Willamette Valley
got under way again at 5:00 p.m. As the elegant consist swung around
the curve into Sullivan's Gulch it made a fine sight, and as the *Oregonian* records, one old railroader was heard to say, "It would be a
beautiful train anywhere."[36] The Columbia Valley railroad was at
last complete and steamboat days were virtually over.

PEND D'OREILLE, CLARK'S FORK, AND THE LAST SPIKE

Early in the spring of 1881 the Northern Pacific Railroad Co. made preparations to resume construction east of Spokane Falls. During the first week of April, J. B. Harris & Co. was awarded a contract to clear and grade the remainder of the line to Lake Pend d'Oreille.[1] Grading, however, got off to a poor start, for when Mr. Harris went ahead to mile 172 to organize the resumption of the work suspended in October 1880, he was immediately faced with an acute shortage of labor.[2] "Teams they have a-plenty, but men are scarce," said the Walla Walla *Weekly Statesman* on May 21, 1881, noting that a thousand more men were needed to work on the Northern Pacific line. Large forces, however, were already engaged on the OR&N projects in the Columbia and Umatilla valleys, and fewer than 900 men were available to work in the far Interior. The contractors, therefore, remained short-handed and were unable to complete the roadbed until late in the fall.

Before the railway could be extended eastward, the Spokane River had to be bridged. Unfortunately, the 200-ft.-long main Howe-truss span of the bridge at Clifton, 9 miles east of Spokane Falls, could not be completed until the timbers used at Hangman Creek had been replaced. To allow the construction and supply trains to move ahead, a temporary trestle bridge was therefore built at a point about a hundred yards upstream[3] and placed in use on July 28, 1881.[4] During the next ten days the tracklayers advanced 16 miles, but on August 9 they were reported to be short of rails and unable to reach Westwood (later Rathdrum) until more became available.[5] Eighteen carloads of 56-lb. rails were landed from the Columbia River on August 13,[6] and the first four cars of the shipment were delivered to the front on August 17.[7] The flow of supplies then became steadier and by September 7, 1881, the track had been extended to the 188th mile.[8] It then became obvious that the steel gang would catch up with the graders before the roadbed was finished. Tracklaying was, therefore, temporarily suspended on the height of land.[9] During the next three months, progress was slow. Steel was laid downgrade to Lake Prescott (Dry Lake, later Granite), 195 miles from Ainsworth, by the end of September,[10] but almost two more months elapsed before the track was reported to be within 2 miles of the Lake Pend d'Oreille crossing.[11] By Christmas 1881 the ground was deeply covered in snow and it seemed unlikely that track would be extended beyond Hangtown before spring.[12] The last of three long trestles on the approach to the lake, however, was completed shortly afterward. The snow was then cleared from the roadbed and on January 9, 1881, rails were laid up to the south end of the projected trestle bridge across the lake, 216 miles from Ainsworth.[13]

Long before the railway reached the Lake Pend d'Oreille crossing, extensive preparations were made to start grading at various points on the north shore. Anticipating the length of time required to build a long bridge, and fearing the possibility of ice formation in the West Arm, the company's engineers decided to ferry men, animals, equipment, and supplies over open water from the far south end of the lake. In April 1881 a boat-building yard and camp were established at Steamboat Landing on what is now called Idlewilde Bay.[14] A month later shipwright James Hanahan arrived with an advance party of three carpenters and four axemen,[15] and by June 2 a force of sixty men were hard at work building a large steamboat and four barges. Named *Henry Villard*,[16] the stern-wheeler conformed to a model provided by John Gates, the OR&N naval architect and marine engineer at Celilo. The completed vessel measured 149 ft. long, 27 ft. beam, and 6 ft. hold amidships; and was propelled by 17 X 60 engines using steam at a pressure of 100 lbs. per sq. in. The machinery was installed by L. Button, who was assisted by L. C. Gray and J. M. Jones. Launched on August 17, 1881, the *Henry Villard* had fourteen staterooms for passengers and was able to carry 200 tons of freight. Commanded by Captain Pease, she steamed along at a steady 15 mph and was said to be " . . . as handsome a craft as was ever built in this Northwest." Her completion allowed supplies delivered by rail to Eight Mile Prairie (just south of Athol) and hauled over a gravel-surfaced wagon road to Steamboat Landing, to be carried with ease to the grading outfits working on the north shore. Her presence also facilitated the establishment of logging camps and sawmills at several lakeside locations remote from the railway line itself.

The railroad was carried across the West Arm of Lake Pend d'Oreille on an 8,428-ft.-long piled trestle bridge with a 94-ft. drawspan.[17] As a first step toward building this bridge, a steam pile driver

manufactured by D. Lister & Co. of New Tacoma was hauled up
from Spokane Falls by wagon train during the fourth week of July
1881.[18] Test piles up to 60 ft. long were driven early in August and
found to penetrate the lake bottom to appropriate depth without striking bedrock.[19] Two more pile drivers were then brought up and work
began in earnest shortly afterward. Piles up to 110 ft. long and 26
in. large-end diameter were required for the 600-ft.-wide channel forming the deepest part of the lake.[20] In all, the bridge was built on 1,700
piles and consisted of 1,048 8 in. X 16 in. X 32 ft. stringers and 1.5
million board feet of other lumber. Eventually, there were nine pile
drivers in operation, six of which were submersible.[21] Despite the
difficulty of working out in the middle of such a large body of water,
pile driving was completed by year's end.[22] Work on the superstructure then proceeded apace and a first locomotive was able to cross
over the bridge from Ventnor to Sand Point at 1:30 p.m. on Sunday, March 5, 1882.[23]

Proceeding eastward from Sand Point, Idaho, 218 miles from
Ainsworth and 230 miles from Wallula, the Northern Pacific Railroad
followed the north shore of Lake Pend d'Oreille to the mouth of the
Clark Fork River. The original line took what might have been called
"the scenic route" around the headland at Sunnyside. It then crossed
the mouth of the Pack River on a 6,500-ft.-long piled trestle bridge[24]
and hugged the lakeshore to Hope. The route[25] then led directly southeastward into the Clark Fork Valley. At a point 256 miles from Wallula and about a mile beyond Lightning Creek it made a first crossing of the Clark Fork River and took up an alignment on the south
side of the valley. The railroad crossed the Montana line just east of
Cabinet Landing, which was the upper limit of the Lake Pend
d'Oreille navigation. It then proceeded eastward by way of Heron,
Noxon, Trout Creek, and Belknap to a second crossing of the river
at a point 312 miles from Wallula. On the left bank of the Clark
Fork River the average eastbound upgrade was only 20 ft. to the mile.
Steeper gradients, however, were encountered at Cabinet Rock where
the railway negotiated a natural obstruction in the valley, and at Trout
Creek where there was a sharp ascent onto a long flat bench of land
set well back from the river. Returning to the north side of the valley
just below Thompson's Falls, the railway followed the Clark Fork
upstream through Weeksville and Horse Plains to the confluence with
the Flathead River at Paradise, 348 miles from Wallula. To avoid
the great bends in the Clark Fork River it then ascended the Flathead
and Jocko valleys, and passed southward to Missoula over higher

ground. Rejoining the Clark Fork River and proceeding eastward through the Hell's Gate Canyon it finally met the line from Duluth at a point between Gold Creek and Garrison. And there, 478 miles from Wallula, the last spike was driven.

Stations and distances in miles from Wallula were: Sand Point, 230; Kootenai, 234; Hope, 245; Clark Fork, 255; Cabinet, 263; Heron, 269; Noxon, 279; Trout Creek, 295; Belknap, 310; Thompson's Falls, 316; Eddy, 326; Weeksville, 333; Horse Plains, 342; Paradise, 348; Perma, 359; Jocko, 374; Ravalli, 381; and Missoula, 418.

After the Villard takeover, railway construction was organized on a new basis. All grading and tracklaying between Sand Point and Paradise were carried out by the Northern Pacific Railroad Co., and not by contractors as before.[26] Determined to show the world how a railway was built, Villard entrusted the engineering to H. Thielsen and placed all the construction forces under the supreme direction of the ambitious and energetic J. L. Hallett. The labor shortage, which had delayed construction between Spokane Falls and Lake Pend d'Oreille, was instantaneously ended by transferring large numbers of men from the Columbia Valley. With the completion, in November 1881, of the OR&N grade between The Dalles and the Cascades, the entire labor force and all the construction equipment were moved up lock, stock, and barrel to work on the Northern Pacific line beyond the lake.[27]

By early December 1881, Hallett had 2,700 men at work on the grade,[28] and enough powder, tools, and provisions on hand to keep them " . . . supplied for a winter's seige." And winter's siege it was, for the work had no sooner started than the snow began to fall. There was little news from the front until the third week of February when Thielsen returned to Portland from an arduous tour of inspection. His story was one of snow and more snow. It had lain, he said, five ft. deep on the ground, but each day 3,000 men marched out bravely to clear it from the right-of-way and pursue their appointed task. And every night the wind drifted it all back in again![29] The work nevertheless went on, and by early April 1882 enough roadbed had been graded to allow Thomas Lavoy and his steel gang to lay 11 miles of track through the mud and lingering snow to the west end of the Pack River trestle. The tracklayers reached Pack River, 241 miles from Wallula, on April 14, 1882.[30] Nearly two more weeks elapsed before William Clucas's 175 carpenters finished the bridge and the construction train was able to proceed.[31] In the meantime a wagon road was built along the south side of the Clark Fork Valley to service grading operations between the first and second river crossings, and 2,300 Chinese and 1,250 whites were put to work between the 250th and 266th miles.[32]

The gorge of the Clark Fork River was a difficult place to build a railway. First of all, a right-of-way had to be cleared through a forest so dense that the trunks of its huge coniferous trees seemed " . . . almost to form a solid rampart. . . ." Grading then presented even more formidable problems. In the constricted parts of the valley the roadbed had to be built at the foot of steep and treacherous slopes, or blasted out of high shoulders of bare rock. Elsewhere there were large unstable masses of clay which repeatedly slid across the workings and filled up the cuts. Hallett was already a master of rock excavation and resorted to the spectacular methods previously used in the Columbia Valley.[33] Horizontal drifts and crosscuts forming T-shaped tunnels were driven into the cliff faces flanking the river gorge and filled with explosives. These were then detonated electrically to produce single enormous blasts throwing great masses of rock laterally into the river. Just east of Cabinet Landing a modified version of this procedure was used to make a rock cut 800 ft. long with an average depth of 22 ft. In this case, galleries were driven from the bottom of three vertical shafts, the resulting muck being hoisted to surface by steam derricks running thirty to forty trips an hour and bringing up two-thirds of a cubic yard of broken rock per trip. Once again the tunnels so formed were loaded with explosives that produced huge blasts totally expelling about 40 percent of the surrounding rock and fracturing the rest. Giant Powder thus provided a permanent solution to the rock excavation problems, but clay slides presented ongoing difficulties of another kind. Cuttings made through unstable ground could only be kept open by building retaining walls consisting of logs laid horizontally on top of each other to a height of 6 ft., held in place by piles driven into the ground on 4 ft. spacing. Needless to say, such measures could not be regarded as permanent, nor could they be adopted to resist all the sudden and unexpected ground movements occurring in the valley. Clay slides plagued Hallett throughout the construction period and remained a problem for many years afterward.

As the work went on, prodigious amounts of material were moved. In June 1882 alone, Hallett claimed to have excavated 58,748 cu. yds. of rock and 107,372 cu. yds. of earth, and placed 173,765 cu. yds. of embankment. To do this he employed ever greater forces. On July 11, 1882, no less than 3,900 Chinese and 1,400 whites were at work between Noxon and Trout Creek, and two weeks later the total complement was said to 6,000 men and 1,600 horses.[34]

The employment of such large numbers on a single project inevitably created problems, not least of which was the risk of injury. Rock falls, blasting accidents, and railway mishaps all took their toll, and at any given time the temporary construction hospital sheltered fifteen or more badly injured men. Riotous living, moreover, added to the casualties. For example, on June 1, 1882, the patients under Dr. Littlefield's care at Cabinet Landing, and their various injuries, were listed as follows:[35]

John Larkin	Head gashed by falling tree.
George Sinclair	Broken leg sustained while at work with the pile driver crew.
W. E. Cummings	Foot cut with an axe while trimming ties.
W. C. Heater	Shoulder injuries caused by fly rock from a blast.
J. E. Eddy	Left arm injured when he was thrown from a horsedrawn vehicle and run over.
William Nichol	Head gashed by a shovel during a fight.
Antonio Fritz	Shot twice in the head by men who had been taunting him. When he lost his temper and set about them with an axe, they pulled their guns on him.

Among the laborers and camp followers lawlessness reached serious proportions, but Hallett made little or no attempt to maintain order. As the work progressed eastward, each camp was more unruly than the last. From Ellisport, Cabinet Landing, Rock Island City, Beaver Creek, Thompson's River, and Weeksville, in succession, came reports of ever-wilder goings on.[36] For example:

From Ellisport, January 1882:

A faro dealer, after winning some $250 was compelled at the muzzles of fifteen revolvers, held by his victims, to disgorge . . .

From Cabinet Landing, May 1882:

Already there are some half dozen stores and as many restaurants, and fifteen saloons.

and

Sore heads and sore eyes, as a result of running up against someone's fists, are the order of the day.

and

The vigilance committee invited six obnoxious individuals to vamoose . . .

From Cabinet Landing, June 1882:

Horse thieves are growing luxuriantly . . .

From Rock Island City, August 1882:

There are some hard cases (here) and no one ventures out at night without a trusty six shooter.

From Weeksville, December 1882:

Saloons and restaurants are thick here. One runs against them on all corners. Night is generally made hideous by . . . the concerts and dance halls. Pistol shots are heard at all times, both night and morn, giving the stranger an idea of life in old California mining towns.

And afterwards, from Heron, May 1883:

The number of graves in the vicinity of the deserted camps tell of the struggle men had with nature and the elements in forcing a passage through these mountain gorges, though several of the rough mounds mark the remains of men that died violent deaths at the hands of fellow men.

Most of the newspaper reports of insult, injury, and death referred to white men. The Chinese, however, bore the real brunt of the construction campaign and suffered far more. They were brought up to the front like cattle, as many as 135 being crammed into a single car.[37] Many were killed in rock falls and blasting accidents, and many more who ate little else but salt fish died of scurvy.[38] Of the survivors, some were robbed of their meagre earnings by gun-toting whites.[39] And when the work was finished they were all ignominiously returned to Portland in the manner of their coming, consigned in carload lots.[40]

By the beginning of June 1882 grading was well under way between the first and second crossings of the Clark Fork River. Hallett's headquarters were then situated, along with the engineers' camp and Dr. Littlefield's hospital, on the north bank of the river, opposite and aloof from the riotous precincts of Cabinet Landing.[41] Supplies for the grading and bridge-building forces were brought up on the steamer *Henry Villard* and sent ahead on the south side wagon road. Heavy rains made the going difficult, and so many more animals were needed to haul freight and forage that few were left to work on the grade.[42] High water and floating masses of timber cut from the right-of-way, meanwhile, delayed completion of the 800-ft.-long, 5-span, Howe-truss bridge at the first crossing, 7 miles below Cabinet Landing. Not until mid-June did the flood waters recede enough to allow the false-work to be completed and used as a temporary bridge.[43] Held up for almost three weeks, the construction train then crossed the river and tracklaying began on the south side of the valley. Cabinet Landing was connected into the railway system on July 1, 1882, and after a grand Fourth of July dance aboard the steamer *Henry Villard* the Lake Pend d'Oreille navigation was largely phased out.[44]

The departure of the *Villard* from Cabinet Landing on July 6, 1882, was not quite the end of Hallett's use of steamboats as an aid to construction. During the following month a smaller vessel was completed for service on the middle Clark Fork navigation between Rock Island and Thompson's Falls.[45] Named *Katie Hallett*, for the construction superintendent's daughter, who was just then visiting her father at Cabinet Landing, the diminutive steamboat was also intended for later use above Thompson's Falls. With Captain Pease once again at the helm, the *Katie Hallett* made a trial trip on or about August 20, 1882, but as the river then fell to a very low level, very little use was ever made of her.

The tracklayers paused to celebrate the Fourth of July at Cabinet Landing and then pressed on eastward, arriving at Elk Creek, just beyond Heron on Friday, July 14.[46] After a delay of several days awaiting completion of a bridge at that point they again went into high gear. Laying almost two miles of track a day they reached the site of Rock Island City, on Stevens Creek, 283 miles from Wallula, by the end of the month. Hallett then moved up everything but the hospital and by August 7, 1882, Cabinet Landing lay forlorn.[47]

Two miles beyond Stevens Creek another major rock cut had to be excavated.[48] At this point Hallett staged several spectacular blasts, at least one of which required no less than 150 cases of Giant Powder. The desired effect was achieved, but the ultimate detonation was attended by misfortune. When the blasting signal was given, some of the workmen took refuge under the construction train, which was standing near the end of track. Unfortunately, the locomotive engineer who was not aware of their presence moved the train, and one unlucky individual named Kennedy had both feet cut off.[49] During the construction period men were run over with sickening regularity. Such events were regarded as commonplace. The accident received brief notice in the press correspondence from the front, and the work went on. The rock cut at the 285th mile was duly completed during the first week of September 1882. The steel gang was then able to lay track to Beaver Creek, where the advance was again held up by both the construction of a large trestle bridge and an outbreak of labor trouble.

As the length of the railway increased and the front camps became more remote from settled areas, the cost of provisioning the work force increased continuously. Early in October 1882 the holders of the camp franchise decided to increase the charge levied upon the white laborers for their board and announced that the weekly rate would go up from $4.50 to $5.00. The men immediately went on strike and attempted to drive the Chinese from the grade. A riot ensued and peace was only restored when the increase was rescinded. A hundred alleged troublemakers, however, were discharged, and for a short time the saloons were forcibly closed. Heavy and incessant rain added to the demoralization, and many more men packed up and left voluntarily, thus creating a temporary shortage of labor.[50]

The advance was not resumed until early in November 1882. By the end of that month, however, false-work had been erected to form a temporary bridge at the second crossing and a skeleton track had been laid as far as Thompson's River,[51] where a smaller Howe-truss bridge was already under construction. Hallett had moved his camp ahead to Weeksville, and heavy rock work was going on between there and Horse Plains. Some progress was being made, but the difficulties continued to multiply. With the onset of autumn rains clay slopes began to slump into excavations at various points in the Clark Fork Valley, and the flow of materials and provisions was frequently disrupted. Thus, on the night of Sunday, November 26, 1882, Engine No. 22, hauling a mixed train of railroad iron, general freight, and passengers, bound for Trout Creek, ran into a slide about a mile beyond Rock Island.[52] The shock of the collision telescoped the locomotive tender and the flatcars carrying the rails. Fortunately, the engineer, fireman, and head end brakeman were able to jump clear before the cargo, launched like a flight of massive arrows, pierced the tender tank and wrecked the cab. Although badly shaken up, the enginemen and passengers escaped injury, but the locomotive and some of the cars were seriously damaged, and the railway was blocked for several precious days.

Winter made matters worse. In January and February 1883 there were heavy falls of snow and the railway was impassable for a week or more at a time. Then, as the weather improved and the snow melted, there were more and more landslides. Some comfort may, however, have been derived from the fact that by that time a new tool was available for clearing the line. Early in November 1882, Northern Pacific took delivery of a "mammoth excavator."[53] Manufactured by Woolcox & Stock of Toledo, Ohio, this self-propelled machine was the first of its kind to be used on the Pacific slope. It was described as having a double rotary excavator and 20 HP swinging engines, and was said to be capable of moving 1,000 to 1,500 cu. yds. of earth per day. Incorporating " . . . a patent drop crane and adjustable jack arms . . . " it could also be used for wrecking purposes. In working condition it measured 50 ft. long, 10 ft., wide, 19 ft. high, and weighed 35 tons. The steam excavator cost $10,000 and was put into operation by manufacturer's engineer F. J. Burr of Toledo, assisted by craneman L. H. Harper, who was hired in San Francisco. As the machine did not reach the front until late in 1882 there was probably very little primary excavation work left for it to do. Nevertheless, during March 1883, it was put to work clearing clay slides between Heron and Noxon, and may briefly have been quite useful. Its loading capability, however, paled to insignificance when, later in the spring, a whole forty acres of land, covered with trees, slid bodily into the river, leaving a gap in the railway 1,300 ft. long and 60 ft. deep.[54]

Despite disruptions in the flow of supplies caused by the weather and exacerbated by the uncompleted bridge at the second crossing, railway construction went on throughout the winter. The steel gang reached Weeksville during the third week of January 1883[55] and finally laid the rails to the site of the Flathead River bridge, 12 miles east of Paradise, at the end of March.[56] The bridge builders, meanwhile, completed the permanent 480-ft.-long, 3-span, Howe-truss bridge at the second crossing, and by April 7 they had erected the false-work serving as a temporary bridge over the Flathead. At that point Hallett's work came to an end, for while his forces had been pushing laboriously eastward along the Clark Fork and others had been toiling westward up the Yellowstone, Mormon contractors had taken over the middle ground. In January 1882, Northern Pacific and Union Pacific reached an interim agreement concerning access to Butte, the terms of which allowed the narrow gauge Utah & Northern Railway to serve as a third means of bringing up construction materials and supplies for the Northern Pacific Railroad.[57] Once Utah & Northern had been completed to an intersection with the projected Northern Pacific main line, the prospect of a narrow gauge extension to Helena disappeared rapidly. The contractors, Washington Dunn & Co., therefore became anxious to secure other work and readily agreed to grade the Little Blackfoot and Hell's Canyon sections of the Northern Pacific main line.[58] By September 1882 these sober and diligent people had completed a roadbed all the way from the

Utah & Northern junction (soon to be named Garrison, for Mrs. Villard's family) to a point 20 miles west of Missoula.

In the meantime, Assistant Attorney General McCammon of the United States Department of the Interior, working through an interpreter named Duncan McLoughlin, negotiated a right-of-way agreement allowing the Northern Pacific Railroad to pass through the Flathead Indian Reservation.[59] The terms were reported to be $16,000 cash to the Indian band and separate compensation to several individual farmers. Having ratified this settlement, Northern Pacific engaged Washington Dunn & Co. to grade the line through the reservation. Intentionally or not, the fragile relationship with the Indians was thus spared the strain of total exposure to Hallett's unruly mob and their undesirable camp followers. Washington Dunn's contract extended to a point 7 miles west of the third (i.e., Flathead River) crossing, but for practical reasons the work was divided at the bridge. By the end of March 1883, the railway to the west of this point had largely been completed. Hallett's supply line being overextended, he and his entire force were then summarily demobilized.

The task of putting the Clark Fork Division into operating condition was left to Northern Pacific engineer Weeks. Regular trains had been running through to the second crossing since late in February 1883,[60] and the service was extended to the third (or Flathead) crossing in mid-April. Side tracks, telegraph lines, buildings, and other amenities, meanwhile, were provided at various points along the line, including Heron, Noxon, Trout Creek, and Thompson's Falls. Heron was chosen as the division point and by May 11, 1883, a twelve-stall roundhouse had nearly been completed there.[61] Beyond the Flathead River, Washington Dunn & Co. made short work of the roadbed across the reservation, so that as soon as the Flathead River bridge was completed, Winston Brothers were able to lay track eastward. By June 1, 1883, the trains were running through to Jocko, 15 miles beyond the bridge,[62] and by June 29 the steel had been extended to Missoula.[63] After some delay due to bridge building in the Hell's Gate Canyon, the tracklayers finally met the forces advancing westward at 3:00 p.m. on August 23, 1883.[64]

At the meeting place, which lay in the Clark Fork Valley 55 miles west of Helena and 1,198 miles from Duluth, the tracklayers left a 1,200-ft.-long gap in the main line and made an interim connection on a siding. On Saturday, September 8, 1883, five trains bearing 3,000 invited guests converged on that point to witness the driving of the last spike.[65] Two of the special trains originated on the Atlantic

Looking out of the Meacham end of OR&N Tunnel No. 4. The point at which the locomotive is standing was the site of a terrible head-on collision between freight trains on August 23, 1889. *Oregon Historical Society.*

Henry Villard, founder and president of OR&N, and later president of Northern Pacific, and Oregon & Transcontinental. *Washington State University Archives*.

Captain J. C. Ainsworth, commander and part owner of the *Lot Whitcomb*. He was also a Northern Pacific director, and later a director on the first boards of both OR&N and O&T. *Oregon Historical Society*.

Simeon G. Reed, major owner of OSN and prominent businessman who served on the first OR&N board of directors. (Photo by C. E. Watkins) *Oregon Historical Society*.

Robert R. Thompson, major shareholder of OSN. *Oregon Historical Society.*

Dr. Dorsey Syng Baker, a banker who founded Walla Walla & Columbia River Railroad, the first line in the Interior. *Washington State University Archives.*

Henry H. Thielsen, chief engineer of OR&N and NPRR. *Oregon Historical Society.*

A classic Howe-truss bridge. Thompson River, Montana, August 1890. *Haynes Foundation Collection, Montana Historical Society.*

Grading the Northern Pacific Railroad at Big Bluff three miles above Heron's Rapids on the Clark Fork River, Montana, 1882, looking upstream. *Davidson Photograph, Oregon Historical Society.*

Northern Pacific Railroad rock cut just east of Cabinet Landing, Montana excavated by filling underground galleries with explosives and staging a huge blast, as described on page 94. *Davidson Photograph. Denver Public Library, Western History Department.*

Construction camp on the Northern Pacific Railroad at Cabinet Landing, Idaho. Looking south on an early summer morning in 1882. The steamboat, *Henry Villard*, is tied up at the wharf. *Davidson Photograph. Denver Public Library, Western History Department.*

Starbuck, Washington looking southeast shortly after the opening of the OR&N Pataha branch. Note the steeply graded line to the Alto Summit heading southwards across the Tucannon River. The locomotive is on the Riparia line. *John Foster Adams Photograph. State Historical Society Wisconsin, acquired from Oregon Historical Society.*

The OR&N line at Wallula, Washington. *John Foster Adams Photograph. State Historical Society, Wisconsin, acquired from Oregon Historical Society.*

Wallula depot and hotel, circa 1895. *Washington State University Archives.*

Ainsworth, Washington, looking southwest toward the Columbia River, about 1887. The railway in the foreground is the line to the transfer boat incline, further up the Snake River to the left. *Oregon Historical Society.*

The Northern Pacific bridge across the Snake River at Ainsworth, Washington. Photo taken from the Ainsworth end soon after completion in April 1884. Note the upstream-downstream false-work upon which the swing span was erected. *Eastern Washington State Historical Society.*

The Pack River trestle, crossing part of Lake Pend d'Oreille, Idaho. Looking north-east from Hawkins Point on the original NPRR alignment via Sunnyside, 1883. *Haynes Foundation Collection, Montana Historical Society.*

The cause of many collisions. A work train on the main line, just west of Sprague, Washington, February 1892. Note the small child on the running plate of the engine and the dog on the first flatcar. *Haynes Foundation Collection, Montana Historical Society.*

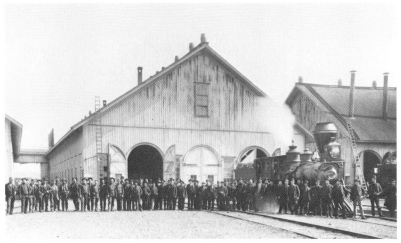

Northern Pacific Railroad shops and roundhouses at Sprague, Washington Territory, April 1887. *Haynes Foundation Collection, Montana Historical Society.*

The Northern Pacific depot at Spokane Falls, Washington, looking west, in the fall of 1881. The depot is on the opposite side of the tracks. The freight house is under construction in the foreground. *Eastern Washington State Historical Society.*

Windmill pump and water tank. Photograph at an unknown location on the OR&N system, later in the 1880s. New ties have been put in the track. The building with the tall chimney probably houses a steam pump which has phased out the windmill. *Oregon Historical Society.*

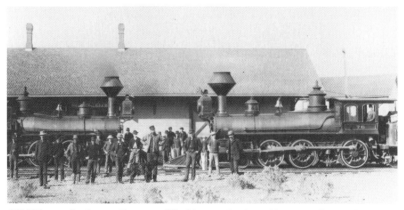

OR&N ten-wheelers at Prescott, Washington in the mid-1880s. *Oregon Historical Society.*

Eastbound OR&N passenger train at LaGrande, Oregon late in 1885 or early in 1886. *Oregon Historical Society.*

A view of LaGrande, Oregon late in 1885 or early in 1886 looking northwest. The roundhouse has already been enlarged to twelve stalls but the townsite is still mostly undeveloped. *Oregon Historical Society.*

Believed to be a photograph of the earliest eating house on the OR&N Baker City branch at Meacham, Oregon. *John Foster Adams Photo. State Historical Society Wisconsin, acquired from Oregon Historical Society.*

Wives and sweethearts. OR&N locomotive no. 9 at Huntington, Oregon. The extra headlight pointing to the rear suggests that by the time the photo was taken the engine was already in switching service. *Oregon Historical Society.*

Said to be the OR&N depot at Hood River, Oregon about 1887, this picture offers a good view of a caboose car of the kind widely used at that time. The telegraph pole in front of the building still has no more than four (or perhaps five) lines connected. *Oregon Historical Society.*

Clearing the track of the OR&N from Rooster Rock to Oneonta Falls in the Columbia River Gorge, Oregon. *Oregon Historical Society.*

J. C. Ainsworth, Engine No. 1, Middle Cascades Railroad. *Washington State University Archives.*

A posed shot of the completion of the Albina to Bonneville section of the OR&N Columbia Valley line, looking east on the Sandy River Bridge, October 1882. Note the rip-rapping at the base of the middle pier. *Oregon Historical Society.*

The great shops at Albina, Oregon. The photograph appears to have been taken shortly after the old roundhouse burned down in January 1888. The chimney coping was 156 ft. above ground and incorporated a bottle containing the workmens' names. *Oregon Historical Society.*

Portland, Oregon from the south, 1883. *Haynes Foundation Collection, Montana Historical Society.*

First train from Portland to New York at The Dalles. The Villard excursion and the opening of the Northern Pacific Railroad, September 1883. *Oregon Historical Society.*

seaboard, the third began its journey at Chicago, the fourth joined the cavalcade at St. Paul, and the fifth came from Portland.

Villard's guests must surely have been the most unlikely group of people ever to assemble in the wilds of the American West. The list included, from Great Britain: Lord Justice Bowen, former Lord Chief Justice Charles Russell, Mr. James Bryce, Mr. Justice (later Lord) Hannen, Mr. Horace (later Lord) Davey, Lord (later Earl) Carrington, Mr. Albert H. (later Earl) Gray, The Earl and Countess of Onslow, and the Hon. St. John Broderick: and from Germany: the great chemist Dr. A. W. Hofmann, the famous geologist Professor Zittel, Herr Georg von Bunsen, the novelist Dr. Paul Lindau, Dr. Georg Siemens of the Deutsche Bank, Herr Otto Braunfels of the Jacob Stern Co., and official representatives of the cities of Berlin, Hamburg, Bremen, Stettin, and Frankfurt am Main. Americans included former President Grant, several members of President Arthur's administration, some former secretaries, United States senators and representatives, governors of seven states, and many others.

The ceremonies[66] began with an address by Henry Villard, who spoke, in part, as follows:

> We deemed it fit and proper to bid both the Old and the New World to this celebration, or in other words, to arrange a sort of international festival. Thanks to the foresight of President Thomas Jefferson, well nigh four score years ago, Lewis and Clark toiled through these mountains as the first explorers of Anglo-American origin, and lifted the veil which hid from civilised mankind the region watered by the Upper Missouri, the Yellowstone, the Columbia, and their tributaries.
>
> We are permitted today to behold a mighty task as all but finished. It was my proud privilege to exercise the chief direction over its latter stages. No light duty it was, but wearisome, and brain and nerve exhausting. Still, its very grandeur inspired the will and power to perform it, and there was comfort and elevation in the thought that we have built what cannot perish, but will last to the end of all earthly things.

The principal oration of the day was then made by William M. Evarts, the former secretary of state, who spoke ". . . eloquently and at length." He was followed by Henry M. Teller, the incumbent secretary of the interior, and by former Northern Pacific president Frederick Billings. Short remarks were then made by the British and German ambassadors to the United States, by Dr. Gneist, by the governors of Wisconsin, Minnesota, Oregon, Washington, Dakota, and Montana, and by United States Senator Nesmith of Oregon. And finally there was a short address by the most popular figure present that day, United States General and former President Ulysses S. Grant.

The speaking at last being over, rival steel gangs from the east and west ends engaged in a prearranged race to lay the remaining 1,200 ft. of main line track. This they accomplished in 13 minutes, with the east end gang winning by a short head. Henry Villard then " . . . proceeded with much ceremony to drive the last spike and the Northern Pacific road was formally pronounced complete."

The ceremony at Gold Creek was to have commenced at 10:00 in the morning and been concluded by noon. However, due to an accident on the switchbacks above the still unfinished Mullan tunnel the trains were late arriving and the exercises had to be postponed until 4:00 in the afternoon. The cavalcade[67] consequently did not resume its westward course until after 10:00 that night. Designated alphabetically A, B, C, D, and E, the five sections of Villard's excursion left on 30 minutes' headway and took telegraphic precautions to remain at safe distances apart. Villard and his foreign guests traveled in Section A, the Portland group made up Section B, and the easterners followed in sequence. On reaching Sand Point the next day, Villard took his guests for a 4-hour steamer trip around Lake Pend d'Oreille. To the utter confusion of the inhabitants of Spokane Falls, Cheney, and Sprague, Section B then took the lead. At Spokane elaborate preparations had been made for a civic reception, and 2,000 people had assembled to cheer Villard's arrival. There was great disappointment when the trains arrived in the wrong sequence, paused but briefly, and left with what was seen locally as indecent haste.

Residents of Cheney were also disconcerted not to find Villard in the first train. Their preparations, however, were not entirely in vain, for many of the passengers, including the *Oregonian* correspondent traveling in Section B, commented favorably upon their well-illuminated lineside display of locally grown produce. The correspondent also noted, somewhat poetically, that the bright tapers placed in the windows of the town's most impressive buildings " . . . threw a flood of light far and wide through the surrounding darkness."

Sprague was also a blaze of light. Several buildings had been " . . . appropriately decorated . . . " and one even bore " . . . an attractive transparency of a complete locomotive . . . ." Notwithstanding the lateness of the hour, every man, woman, and child in this railroad division town turned out, determined to make the most of the event. In the absence of other celebrities aboard Section B, they enthusiastically welcomed Governor Newall of Washington who, rising magnificently to the occasion, gave a lengthy midnight speech!

At Ainsworth, the five sections of the excursion, sixty cars in all, had to be ferried across the Snake River, four cars at a time, aboard the transfer boat *Frederick Billings*. Each round trip took almost an hour, so that the entire process was not completed until noon on Monday, September 10, 1883. Nor was the passage achieved without incident, for at least one car ran away on the incline and " . . . several Lords and mahogany hued porters came close to being transferred to silvery realms."[68] The parade, however, was reassembled in correct alphabetical order at Wallula, and by midday both Villard and his guests had regained enough composure to arrange themselves in front of their locomotive for a group photograph. At 12:30 p.m. a pilot train, consisting of an engine and two coaches, in charge of OR&N Superintendent H. S. Rowe, and Assistant Engineer H. B. Thielsen (eldest son of H. Thielsen) set out ahead of the main cavalcade to ascertain that the line was clear. The other trains then followed in sequence, running from Wallula " . . . over the hot and sweltering sand plains . . . " to The Dalles at speeds of up to 60 mph.

Arriving at The Dalles at about 6:45 p.m., Henry Villard and his guests received a welcome surpassing all others.[69] As soon as the locomotive headlight cast its great glare along the shining rails there was a spontaneous outburst of firing, salutes, shouts, and cheers. Passing under a triumphal arch specially erected for the occasion, the highly decorated locomotive and cars drew slowly toward the depot while the Fifth Infantry Band, which had accompanied the excursionists all the way from Fort Keogh, struck up an appropriate air. Illuminated by calcium lights and the glow of numerous bonfires, the train of trains drew to a halt, and as it did so twenty-four beautifully attired young ladies stepped nimbly onto the end platforms of the cars and presented each emerging passenger with a buttonhole bouquet. In response to vociferous calls for a speaker Henry Villard alighted and proceeded to the porch of the Umatilla House. Punctuated by intermittent flashes of red and blue light he delivered a short oration that was received with cheers, followed by music from The Dalles Ladies Silver Cornet Band. The crowd, however, was hardly satisfied by a speech from Villard. The man they really wanted to see and hear was General Grant, who was eventually found in Section C. "Grant! Grant! Grant!" they cried, and at last, reluctantly, the victor of Appomattox stepped out onto the end platform of the car. He could not, however, be induced to speak.

Villard's train arrived in East Portland during the early hours of Tuesday, September 11, 1883, and was immediately sidetracked to allow the occupants to rest. Their slumber, however, was soon disturbed, for the vessel *State of California* lying in the Willamette River immediately delivered a cannon salute lasting for nearly half an hour. Fortunately for those passengers then requiring a soporific, a "tempting repast . . . " was conveniently available aboard the stern-wheeler *Wide West*, which had been moored directly alongside. The guests remained in Portland for two days and were treated to a gigantic civic parade and display, ably organized by General Morrow of the United States Army.[70]

On Thursday morning the party sailed from Ash Street dock aboard the steamers *S. G. Reed* and *R. R. Thompson* bound for Kalama.[71] Thence, they traveled by train to Tacoma where Mr. Villard:

. . . put himself at the head of his guests, and, preceded by a military band, marched them from the station to Commencement Bay where they first saw the waters of the Pacific Ocean. . . . The magnificent giant of the Cascades, Mount Tacoma, rose right before them, covered with an alpine glow wonderful to behold, for the sun was just setting . . . .[72]

Villard might perhaps have regarded that sunset as ominous, for although the Northern Pacific Railroad had been more or less completed, his several companies were nearly bankrupt, and his days of empire were numbered.

11

HENRY VILLARD'S DOWNFALL

Construction of the Northern Pacific main line was attended by continuous financial difficulty. Although the $40 million first mortgage bond issue, announced in November 1880, was expected to provide enough money to complete the line, the stipulations governing the issue of the bonds caused acute hardship. The mortgage applied not only to the railroad but also to the land grant. Neither bonds nor lands could therefore be sold until the United States government had inspected and approved completed sections of the railway. Unfortunately, at the instigation of Collis P. Huntington and the California railroad lobby, the land grant was attached in Congress and Northern Pacific was threatened with forfeiture. Pending the outcome of lengthy investigations, the government refused to convey land to the company, and for a whole year construction had to be carried on without access to funds derived either from bond issues or land sales.[1] The possibility of losing the land grant compelled Villard to make every effort to complete the line at the earliest possible date, and thus led to unnecessary and costly haste. Interim financing had to be provided by the Oregon & Transcontinental Co., and when matters became more desperate no less than $3,450,000 was advanced by Henry Villard himself. Fortunately, in August 1882 the government relented and the proceeds of bond sales once more became available. Given the rate at which these funds were spent, however, it must have been clear that any respite thus afforded would be but brief.

By the summer of 1882 money was becoming harder to get and stock market prices had already begun to decline. Immediate steps therefore had to be taken to bolster the value of shares providing the collateral needed to obtain further loans. In Villard's experience the best way to do this was to pay dividends. Despite the fact that Northern Pacific had absolutely no money to spare, he nevertheless decided to implement his previous proposal to pay for all construction with capital funds and distribute surplus earnings to stockholders. Accordingly, the company's *Annual Report*, issued in September 1882, declared that surplus earnings amounting to $4,667,490, used since 1875 for construction purposes, rightly belonged to holders of preferred stock, who would therefore receive an 11.1 percent dividend.[2] Payment was to be made in the form of certificates bearing 6 percent interest after five years, but redeemable after one year at the pleasure of the company, in amounts of not less than 20 percent to each holder. The desired result was at once attained. Northern Pacific preferred stock rose to par, and Oregon & Transcontinental Co. nearly to par. Thus encouraged, Villard abandoned restraint. On May 25, 1883, the Oregon & Transcontinental Co. undertook to finance completion of the Oregon & California Railroad line through the Siskiyou Mountains to the California boundary, and agreed to lease that property commencing January 1, 1884.[3] Grandiose plans were simultaneously made for a huge union depot and hotel in Portland, and the Northern Pacific Terminal Co., financed jointly by the three railroads involved, was formed to bring these and related projects to fruition.[4] The building of the Northern Pacific main line was pushed ahead with all dispatch and scant concern for cost.

Late in June 1883, Villard (as he afterward claimed) received first indications that Northern Pacific construction costs would greatly exceed the estimates prepared by the engineering department.[5] The proceeds of first mortgage bond sales would not be enough to complete the line. A great deal more money, unfortunately, would be required. Villard was thunderstruck. He had already encountered difficulty renewing loans, even at 8 percent interest.[6] Now he had to cover a deficit which might eventually reach $10 million. Worse still, to obtain loans and to eliminate the risk of having them prematurely called, he felt compelled to spend more and more money to maintain the value of stocks pledged as collateral.

As a first step toward correcting the situation he again resorted to paying dividends. The Oregon & Transcontinental Co. *Annual Report*, issued on July 17, 1883, declared that the approaching completion of the Northern Pacific main line would soon allow the reimbursement of advances, and as O&T had no directly owned property to preserve, there was " . . . no good reason why this Company should not give to the stockholders the benefit of all its income and profits." Despite the fact that both companies were in serious trouble, the O&T dividend was increased.[7] In an attempt to bolster the prices of the Villard railroad stocks, arrangements were made for O&T to acquire as many of the outstanding shares as possible.[8] To enable the company to do this, and to simultaneously meet its other commitments, the reluctant Endicott and other close colleagues were persuaded to buy more O&T stock. Villard, meanwhile, advanced the proceeds of a huge personal loan, secured by his holdings in the Oregon Improvement Company. These frantic maneuvers were best described by Endicott's comment made in a letter addressed to Villard earlier in the year. "I cannot quite make up my mind," he wrote, "whether it is you or Barnum that has the greatest show on earth."[9]

The investing public, all the while, innocently assumed that the Northern Pacific land grant would yield more money than the principal of the first mortgage bonds, and believed that when the main line was finished the preferred stock would quickly be retired by the sale of lands set aside for its redemption. They naively imagined that within the forseeable future the common stock would pay a satisfactory dividend. This optimistic view, however, resulted from a complete disregard of the facts. The Northern Pacific Railroad could not immediately generate enough surplus income to pay both bond interest and stock dividends. An *Oregonian* editorial of January 2, 1884, written at the climax of these events, lucidly explained Villard's dilemma, saying:

> It is a vice of the American system of building railways that the stocks are issued without benefit to the property while the roads are built on the proceeds of bond sales. The 90 millions of Northern Pacific stocks, for example, do not represent the money that built the road, but only a bonus which the original owners of the franchise divided among themselves. The roads ought to be built on the proceeds of their stock but instead of this the stock is distributed among the parties on the inside and then the road and all its properties are mortgaged to secure the sums borrowed to build. Thus the Northern Pacific, having incurred a debt for construction equal to the entire cost of the property, a debt which was a first lien on the road and land grant, was loaded besides with a vast amount of stock, and as the road cannot at once earn a greater sum than will pay the expenses of operation and meet the charges on the bonds, the stock is in a condition to be raided by its enemies . . . .[10]

It was predictable that as soon as the construction deficit became common knowledge and there was any suggestion that another issue of bonds would take precedence over the preferred stock, the shareholders would sell. The price of the stocks might then collapse. Villard evidently realized that if he was to avert disaster he would have to prevent the imposition of a second mortgage. He therefore sought another means of funding the debt incurred by the construction cost overrun. During the week before the Northern Pacific annual meeting held on Thursday, September 20, 1883, a desperate attempt was made to perform what can only be described as a feat of financial acrobatics. According to the New York special correspondent of the Philadelphia *Press*, Villard's plan was to sell Oregon & Transcontinental Co. holdings of Northern Pacific stock to raise the money to buy Northern Pacific income bonds, or debentures, at par.[11] In this way the railroad would be provided with the funds it so urgently needed, and the holding company would be promised repayment as soon as earnings permitted, all without placing another lien on the property.

Unfortunately, Villard was still away on the grand railway opening junket in the west and could not orchestrate the maneuver personally. Not enough time was left to bring the matter to a successful conclusion before the annual meeting and the attendant announcement of the deficit. Moreover, the old holders of Northern Pacific stock, betrayed by Billings in 1881, now sensed that their chance to regain control of the company had at last arrived. They badly wanted Northern Pacific stock but had no intention of paying Villard's artificially high price for it. The annual meeting was held, and Northern Pacific announced a shortfall of $7,986,508.[12] Then, on the very next morning, whoever had bought the shares sold by the Oregon & Transcontinental Co., resold them, thus initiating a great rush to sell.[13] Before the day was over 96,100 shares of Northern Pacific preferred stock, and 25,900 common had been turned in. In June 1882 these shares had been quoted at prices of 90 and 52 respectively. By Saturday, September 22, they had fallen to 64-3/4 and 34-3/4 and were still going down. OR&N suffered similar losses and O&T fell from over 80 to 54-1/4.[14] Villard and his associates were now in deep trouble, for there was a grave risk that unless the slide could be halted the loans incurred by and for the Oregon & Transcontinental Co. might well be called. All available resources were therefore diverted to buying up stocks, and the idea of purchasing Northern Pacific income bonds was abandoned.

By early October 1883 the Northern Pacific floating debt had increased to $9,459,921 and Villard estimated that another $5,500,000 would still be needed to complete the main line.[15] On October 6 the directors authorized a $20 million second mortgage bond issue, subject to the consent of three-quarters of the preferred stock.[16] The circular distributed at the time stated that arrangements had already been made with Drexel Morgan & Co., Winslow Lanier & Co., and August Belmont & Co. to take $15 million of the issue at 87-1/2 less 5 percent commission in bonds, with a six-month option to take another $3 million on the same terms. Northern Pacific, meanwhile, ordered severe economy measures put into effect on the railroad.[17] These were taken to such lengths that the lamps were even removed from the switch stands, thus jeopardizing the safety of operations. Less than a month later, general manager Herman Haupt resigned in disgust, stating that because so much of the money set aside for operations had to be used to make up for construction deficiencies, not enough funds remained to pay for the safe and efficient running of trains.[18] His resignation further undermined confidence in Villard's handling of Northern Pacific affairs.

News of the second mortgage brought about another onslaught upon the Villard stocks.[19] On October 16, O&T was reported to have fallen to 41. With characteristic optimism Villard continued to hope that the completion of the main line would bring about a marked increase in earnings. Unfortunately, he failed completely to take into account the cessation of construction traffic, and the railway receipts, instead of increasing, actually fell.[20] On November 22, the removal of the last legal barriers to the Northern Pacific second mortgage resulted in another rush to sell.[21] Then, on December 7 the introduction into Congress of another bill to rescind the land grant[22] finally forced stock prices down to levels at which, it seemed, Oregon & Transcontinental Co. could no longer remain solvent.[23]

Villard, in his own words,

> . . . was now in such desperate straits that he called a council of his most faithful and influential friends and disclosed to them his condition, with an appeal for advice and help, pledging himself in advance to accept any decision they might reach as to himself, no matter what consequences it might have for him personally.[24]

William Endicott, Jr., E. P. Fabbri of Drexel Morgan & Co., and Rosewell G. Rolston of Farmers Loan & Trust Co. immediately undertook an investigation of his affairs. During the night of December 16-17 Villard was aroused at his hotel and told that both he and the Oregon & Transcontinental Co. were close to bankruptcy. A syndicate of bankers, however, was willing to take $9 to $10 million worth of securities held by O&T and help him out personally, provided that he agreed to give up the presidencies of both the O&T and OR&N companies. There was nothing else Villard could do. The price of Northern Pacific preferred stock had now fallen to 50 and OR&N was down to 100-1/2. O&T stock, meanwhile, had fallen to 32-1/4 and more and more of the shares were being sold. On December 17, 1883, he complied with the bankers' wishes and resigned from the presidencies of both companies. Endicott thereupon took

charge of the Oregon & Transcontinental Co. and T. Jefferson
Coolidge, also of Boston, assumed control of the Oregon Railway
& Navigation Co. The disastrous decline in stock market prices was
checked, and a more serious panic was narrowly averted.[25]

An investigation committee consisting of Endicott, Fabbri, and
Rolston was then set up to determine the true extent of the Oregon
& Transcontinental Co. assets and liabilities. With only a short break
to allow Endicott to return to Boston for the holidays, this difficult
work went on night and day, while brokers anxiously awaited the
results. On December 29, 1883, the Philadelphia *Press* reported that:

> . . . the labours of the committee have not been very satisfactory. The Hugo
> accounts are found to be in a somewhat mixed (up) condition, and to follow
> all their complications will likely be a labor of many days. Many of the com-
> pany's affairs are found to be inextricably involved.[26]

Despairing of ever being able to understand the accounts, the committee eventually resorted to physically counting the bonds and share
certificates on hand, and finally concluded that Oregon & Transcontinental Co. possessed assets with a par value of about $52 million.
At current prices these were worth about $31 million. Despite the
fact that advances to Northern Pacific had already been repaid, the
outstanding Oregon & Transcontinental Co. liabilities still amounted
to just over $11 million.[27] How much of this debt had been con-
tracted in abortive attempts to hold up the market, and in paying
high interest rates and commissions on loans taken out to meet
emergencies, was never determined.

Henry Villard himself was found to be in even more dire straits.
To secure a personal loan from Drexel Morgan & Co., he had pledged
11,468 Oregon Improvement Co. shares. The market price of this
stock had then fallen from 91-1/2 to 10-1/4 and the loan had been
called.[28] He had also lost a great deal of money in the collapse of
the New York, West Shore, & Buffalo Railroad, a line that he had
planned to use as part of a combined Great Lakes steamer and railway
transportation scheme to move grain to the east.[29] By year's end his
fortunes were at a low ebb and he lay psychologically exhausted. At
a board meeting held on Thursday, January 4, 1884, his resignation
from the presidency of the Northern Pacific Railroad Co. was at last
laid upon the table.[30] It read as follows:

> I hereby offer my resignation as President of your board. I feel constrained to
> take the step for two reasons. One is, I am suffering from nervous prostration
> which renders me no longer capable of properly discharging my official duties,

and my physicians advise absolute abstention from active employment as a condition of the recovery of my health. The other reason is that in my own opinion, no less than in that of my personal and business friends, the interests of the Company call for the severance of my connection with it. It is a sad reflection that such should be the unjust result of years of severe labor and consuming anxiety which I have spent in my endeavors to relieve the Company, and to the best of my ability. I am consoled by an abiding confidence that the future will completely vindicate my actions. I may, as soon as my health will permit, ask for the privilege of submitting to you a summary of my administration of the Company's affairs. Allow me to express to you my sincere thanks for the cordial support and appreciative sympathy that you have at all times extended to me.

(signed) H. Villard.[31]

The resignation was accepted. The directors then adopted a resolution complimenting Mr. Villard, and voted him $10,000 for each year he had served the company as president. A committee was then set up to select his successor. The following day Villard assigned title to his recently completed mansion on Madison Avenue to William Endicott Jr. and Horace White, as trustees, for the benefit of his creditors.[32] The property was to be disposed of at public or private sale, and the proceeds applied: to the payment of interest on the $200,000 mortgage; to fulfillment of existing contracts for completion of the edifice; and to payment of his indebtedness to the Oregon Railway & Navigation Co., from which he had also, apparently, borrowed money. After convalescing for several months at his country house at Bogg's Ferry on the Hudson River, he left the United States on June 4, 1884, to take up permanent residence in Germany.[33]

On January 9, 1884, it was announced that the officers of the Oregon & Transcontinental Co. had made arrangements with a syndicate of Boston capitalists for a one-year loan of $8 million, secured by large blocks of Northern Pacific and Oregon Railway & Navigation Co. shares.[34] A month later another syndicate, said to include Cyrus J. Field, Russell Sage, Jay Gould, and most significantly, Anthony J. Drexel of Philadelphia, " . . . with whom are associated Charles B. Wright and one or two other friends there," were reported to have bought a block of 90,000 shares of Oregon & Transcontinental Co. treasury stock.[35] The block was made up of 30,000 shares each of OR&N, Northern Pacific preferred, and Northern Pacific common at prices of 75, 35, and 15, and was purchased for something less than $4 million. The stocks, it was said, were not to be sold but held for investment. Oregon & Transcontinental Co. thus obtained the funds needed to pay off the remaining part of the debt contracted during the decline in stock market prices and, for a very modest outlay, the old proprietors were able to regain control over the Northern Pacific Railroad.

The deliberations of the committee appointed to select the new Northern Pacific president went on for almost two weeks. Charles B. Wright, who had been associated with the company since 1864, and was said to be the largest individual stockholder, was the most eligible candidate. His health, however, was poor and for that reason he declined the committee's offer.[36] On January 17, 1884, Robert Harris, vice president of the New York, Lake Erie, & Western Railroad, and longtime official of the Chicago Burlington & Quincy Railroad, was named president.[37] Harris was an able, experienced, and careful railway manager, enjoying the full confidence of Charles B. Wright, with whom he was already associated in the Tacoma Land Co. His appointment quite clearly marked the beginning of a new chapter in Northern Pacific affairs. Six weeks after he took office the directors were called together to consider construction of the Cascade branch, and by early July 1884 Nelson Bennett and his Mormon crews were hard at work in the Yakima Valley. Northern Pacific was to bypass Portland and have its own direct line to Puget Sound.

12

THE BRIDGE
AT AINSWORTH

Consummation of the October 1880 traffic agreement between the Northern Pacific Railroad and Oregon Railway & Navigation companies required a means of crossing the mouth of the Snake River at Ainsworth. As there was still considerable reluctance to abandon the idea of an independent Northern Pacific line to Puget Sound either along the Columbia River Valley or over the Cascade Mountains, no immediate commitment was made to the construction of a bridge. Instead the Northern Pacific directors decided, as an interim measure, to use a train ferry. Early in 1881, therefore, a stern-wheel steamer designed to serve that purpose was laid down at Celilo.[1] Named *Frederick Billings*, the vessel was 220 ft. long, 37 ft. beam, 6 ft. deep, and had 20 X 96 engines.[2] With a load capacity of 550 tons she was able to take on eleven loaded freight cars and one locomotive at each trip. Commanded by Captain W. P. Gray, the *Billings* steamed up-river to Ainsworth in June 1881. Despite the fact that permanent slips were not yet ready and railway vehicles could not be taken on board, she was nevertheless placed in service on Monday, July 4, 1881.[3] Five months or more elapsed before the inclines were completed and during that period all freight had to be transshipped.[4]

By May 1882, the vessel was reported to be carrying the through sleeping cars for Ritzville and accomplishing the task so quietly that the repose of the passengers was not disturbed.[5] Fluctuations in river level nevertheless posed recurring problems. In September 1882 the water was so low that landings could only be made with great difficulty.[6] Twenty-five men were put to work blasting and dredging out a channel, and another incline was built. The troubles, however, were not entirely eliminated, for when Henry Villard and his excursionists were on their way to Portland in September 1883, low water and the steep approaches to the slips very nearly resulted in disaster.[7] New inclines, consequently, were built farther downstream and located nearly opposite each other. Much of the risk and delay was thus eliminated, but by then the days of the train ferry were numbered.

When Henry Villard took control of the Northern Pacific Railroad his intention was to channel all the northern transcontinental railway traffic onto the OR&N line to Portland. A bridge across the Snake River was an essential part of this scheme, and first steps were soon taken to build one. In November 1881 soundings were made and test piles were driven.[8] Then, early in March 1882, D. D. McBean was awarded a $350,000 contract to build piers and abutments, which were to be finished by April 1, 1883.[9]

The bridge was to be 1,540 ft. long,[10] designed to utilize the drawspan already on order at the Phoenix Iron Works, Phoenixville, Pennsylvania, for the aborted OR&N project at Grange City. Arrangements were therefore made to space the piers accordingly.[11] By March 20, 1882, McBean had fifty men working at the Granite Point quarry near Wawawai.[12] As the year went on, more and more of the stone required for pier construction was brought down the Snake River aboard the steamer *Spokane* and accumulated at Ainsworth.[13] Including the drawspan pivot there were to be seven piers, all built on bedrock and averaging 62 ft. in total height.[14] The work of building them proceeded within caissons, two of which were pneumatically pressurized. Progress, however, was slow. The first caisson was not sunk until July 1882, and by January 1883 only the north abutment and the first pier at the north end had been completed. Erection of the round drawspan pivot pier had commenced but the stonework had only been laid from bedrock to the elevation of the river bottom and was still 27 ft. below the surface of the water.[15] McBean evidently lacked the resources to complete the work in the time available. In February 1883, therefore, Northern Pacific took over the project and appointed the noted diver Captain Ed Spencer to be superintendent.[16] During this period the Wawawai quarry was largely abandoned in favor of a source of better material located near Granite, Idaho.[17] By mid-November 1883 Piers no. 2, 4, 5, 6, and 7 (numbered from the south end) had been finished, the caisson for Pier no. 1 was in place, and that for Pier no. 3 was being lowered into position.[18] Pier no. 1 was completed at the end of the year[19] and Pier no. 3 was finished early in February 1884.[20]

Beginning at the north end of the bridge the iron superstructure consisted of a 146-ft. Pratt through-truss span, the 346-ft. swinging drawspan, four 248-ft. Pratt through-truss spans, and a 65-ft. deck girder span.[21] The first step toward erecting the upperwork was taken in November 1883 when a gang of carpenters, using 12 X 15 section material, constructed two 70-ft.-high triangular timber supports for the drawspan. In January 1884 these were floated out into the river, filled with cobbles, and sunk in positions immediately upstream and downstream of the pivot pier. Resting on the riverbottom they then served as supports upon which the drawspan was erected.[22] False-work, meanwhile, was put up for the fixed spans, and as soon as it was in place the iron-workers began to assemble the final structure.[23] Work commenced at Pier no. 1 at the south end of the bridge and progressed northward. By the end of December 1883 the false-work was completed out to Pier no. 3 and the erection of the first 248-ft. span was well under way.

Work on the superstructure proceeded night and day, and progress was rapid. Haste, however, led to at least one accident, for on the night of Thursday, January 3, 1884, a workman named William Hughes was struck on the head by a heavy timber and badly injured.[24] Despite this mishap, and the fact that a lot of ice was running in the river, work proceeded apace, and by the end of January 1884 two of the four long spans had been completed. The drawspan and the short fixed span at the north end of the bridge were finished early in April, and the two remaining long spans were ready by mid-month. As the plate girders for the short span at the south end had not yet been delivered, a temporary timber trestle structure was built to fill the gap, thus allowing the railway track to be laid.[25] The biggest bridge west of the Missouri then stood ready for test.

At 9:25 a.m. on Sunday, April 20, 1884, a train consisting of transfer Engine No. 298 and three cars loaded with rails passed slowly over the bridge in a northerly direction. Yardmaster William Hollingsworth was in charge of the movement and was assisted by William Clark. Aboard the train were civil engineer George Lederle, Idaho Division general roadmaster Paul Munn, and general timber inspector James S. Rogers. The engine was driven by C. S. Larison and fired by Herman Ahrons. At Ainsworth, Engine No. 297 and another car of railroad iron were added to the consist and " . . . a large number of ladies and gentlemen . . . " were taken aboard as passengers. The train then returned to the bridge, stopping on each span while deflections were measured. The tests took two hours to complete but demonstrated satisfactorily that maximum deflection did not exceed half an inch. After a whistling contest between the railway locomotives and the steamer *Frederick Billings* the bridge was declared safe and opened to traffic.[26] Its cost, according to the 1884 *Annual Report* of the Northern Pacific Railroad Co., was $1,135,743.[27] The first regular train to cross was No. 14 eastbound, which consisted of thirty-five cars hauled by Engines No. 190 (engineer Lohr) and 298 (engineer Larison), all in charge of conductor J. Mahoney.

The completion of the Snake River bridge removed a significant gap in the Northern Pacific Railroad-OR&N route via Portland to Puget Sound. Other bottlenecks, however, remained. The Northern Pacific line from Portland down the left bank of the Columbia River to Goble, Oregon, had been substantially completed in September 1883,[28] but the prefabricated components for the Goble-Kalama train ferry did not reach Portland from the East Coast until mid-January 1884.[29] The assembled ferry was not therefore launched until the third week in May 1884,[30] and not handed over to the operating department until July 24, 1884.[31] Even then the Villard route to Puget Sound remained incomplete, for the construction of a bridge across the Willamette River at Portland was indefinitely delayed by a protracted legal dispute concerning rights of fluvial navigation.[32]

In the meantime the Northern Pacific Railroad was divorced from the OR&N and returned to its original owners. Pursuing an independent course, the new president, Robert Harris, began to place all emphasis on building a direct route from the confluence of the Snake and Columbia rivers over the Cascade Range to Puget Sound. Less than three weeks after the Snake River bridge was completed a survey party left Tacoma to make a final assessment of the several mountain passes. Work on the Yakima Valley line was also resumed with vigor. In June 1884 the *Frederick Billings* was sent downriver for an overhaul and modifications,[33] and by September of that year she had been pressed into service ferrying trains of construction materials and supplies across the Columbia from Pasco to Kennewick. The push through the mountains was on, and the future role of the Snake River bridge already seemed uncertain.

13

COLUMBIA & PALOUSE

Within the framework of Henry Villard's railway empire in the Columbia Interior the Northern Pacific Railroad and OR&N companies were given separate zones of influence on opposite sides of the Snake River.[1] The October 1881 decision to abandon plans for the OR&N crossing above Grange City and build but one bridge at Ainsworth placed the territory north of the Snake River firmly under Northern Pacific control. The roadbed between Texas Ferry and Union Flat was left to the teamsters and plans were made to link the remainder of the OR&N Colfax line with the Lake Pend d'Oreille Division of the Northern Pacific.[2] Some time elapsed before the main line connection was located, for at least two different routes were considered. Early in March 1882, a survey party was reported to be laying out a line from Sprague to Endicott.[3] Two months later, however, it became clear that a railway was to be built eastward along the Washtucna Coulee from a point named Palouse Junction, 39 miles north of Ainsworth and 51 miles from Wallula.[4] The revised link with Colfax, chartered separately as the Columbia & Palouse Railroad, was financed by the Oregon & Transcontinental Co. and built for the Northern Pacific.[5] From the very beginning, however, associations with OR&N were quite strong. Engineer E. H. Mix supervised grading operations[6] carried out by the Oregon Construction Co.,[7] and when track was eventually laid OR&N operated the construction and supply trains.[8]

Grading began at Palouse Junction on May 22, 1882, and within seven weeks about 300 Chinese laborers and forty teams of horses were hard at work. The lower Washtucna Coulee was ". . . a waterless, sandy region, fit only for the abode of rattlesnakes and coyotes," and thus attracted few whites. The Chinese, therefore, were able to secure employment normally reserved for Europeans and found themselves in a relatively strong bargaining position. A short strike was enough to increase the Chinese drivers' wages to $1.50 per day, while the few disgruntled whites had to be satisfied with only 50 cents more.

Individuals with their own teams, meanwhile, were hired for $4.00 per day but had to pay 2 cents per lb. for feed grain provided by the company. Water was brought up in tanks from Bluff Wells and sometimes, it was said, took an uncomfortably long time to arrive. These difficulties notwithstanding, the forces working at the junction succeeded in excavating a cut 2,300 ft. long and up to 9 ft. deep, and quickly threw up embankments forming a "Y."[9] The roadbed was then extended eastward into the basalt palisaded confines of the Washtucna Coulee.

In the open country of the Columbia Interior the railway builders were frequently able to use routes formed by one of the most spectacular natural events ever to occur.[10] During the last great ice age ten thousand years ago, glaciers extended tentacle-like from the ice cap covering the mountains to the north. As moisture became locked up in ice formations great dust storms were created by fierce winds. The fallout from these storms gradually covered the beds of lava laid down during recent periods of intense volcanic activity. Over the whole area windborne dust was eventually deposited to a depth of several hundred feet. When the climate again became warmer, vast lakes accumulated in east-west mountain valleys still blocked by the slowly receding fingers of the ice cap. The most ominous of these great impounded masses of water built up behind a barrier of ice damming the valley of the Clark Fork River. Wave-formed terraces, which can still be seen on the mountainsides above Missoula, Montana, give us an idea of the extent and depth of the water. Inevitably, as the glacier blocking the valley melted and the level of the lake behind it became higher and higher, a day came when water began to spill over westward and cut down into the ice as it did so. The resulting breach in the dam became enlarged at a rapidly increasing rate and what was quite possibly the greatest torrent of water in the earth's history poured out toward the Interior basin. Once it reached the lower lying country the vast flow of water divided, each part quickly cutting its own channel through the accumulations of windborne dust and ripping lumps of rock from the lava beds below. Following the lay of the land, the water went roaring west and south toward the Wallula Gap in great rivers of unimaginable size and speed. In a matter of days, or at most weeks, it was all gone. But the channels or "coulees" the water had cut remained to provide routes that the railways later followed, and the intervening islands of wind-blown deposits became the rich "palouse" soils upon which grain is grown today.

The Columbia & Palouse line followed the Washtucna Coulee eastward and northeastward into virtually unsettled country. Passing by way of Kahlotus and Washtucna it met and crossed the Palouse River just below the confluence with Cow Creek, near Hooper. After proceeding about 6 miles on the south bank of the Palouse River the line diverged eastward. Climbing steeply along Willow Creek it reached a junction with the existing Texas Ferry to Colfax roadbed just beyond Pampa. From that point it followed the original OR&N route northward across Union Flat to the confluence of Rebel Flat Creek and the Palouse River. Turning to the east the road ascended with the Rebel Flat Creek through Endicott to a point about 4 miles southwest of Colfax. The engineers thus avoided the incised meanders of the Palouse River and saved a lot of rock work but placed the railway at a considerably higher elevation than the town. The only way the line could reach its destination was to climb over the top of the intervening hill and descend on a steep gradient all the way down to the canyon bottom. The Colfax depot and yard then had to be located on a very limited area of flood-prone ground just at the fork of the Palouse River.

Distances[11] measured in miles eastward from Palouse Junction (later Connell) were originally given as:

> Sulphur, 9; Kahlotus, 18; Washtucna, 29; Hooper, 39; Pampa, 48; Endicott, 69; Crest, 86; and Colfax, 88.

Elevations[12] in feet above sea level have recently been given as:

> Connell (formerly Palouse Junction), 832; Washtucna, 991; Hooper, 1,057; Pampa, 1,339; La Crosse (5 miles east of Pampa), 1,473; Winona (at the confluence of the Palouse River and Rebel Flat Creek, 6 miles west of Endicott), 1,482; Endicott, 1,594; summit (formerly Crest), 2,264; and Colfax, 1,945.

Starting out cold from Colfax, westbound trains had to climb for more than 2 miles on a 3 percent grade to reach Crest. Eastbound trains, by comparison, faced nothing worse than the 1.28 percent climb up the Willow Creek Valley to Pampa.

For a short while during the early summer of 1882 there was some doubt about whether the railway would actually descend into Colfax or proceed directly over higher ground to Moscow. Engineer Mix was quoted on June 20, 1882, as saying that it would pass through Endicott and not go into Colfax.[13] Less than two weeks later, however, H. Thielsen announced that the line would definitely pass through the town.[14] Unfortunately, by mid-July there was no town left to go through, for Colfax had been burned to the ground for a second time.[15] This crime, for it was said to have been the work of an incendiary, may have given the Oregon & Transcontinental Co. an excuse for not pressing the Columbia & Palouse line to completion in 1882 as originally planned. Failure to finish the road in one year may also have been deliberate, for in March 1882 Villard's branch line construction policy was stated to be ". . . to let about a year intervene between grading and tracklaying." The rationale given for this approach was that "during the year's delay the settlers come into the country on the assurance of early completion of the branch, and thus by the time it is opened for business there is traffic to sustain it."[16] The exact reasons for the delay are now obscure. Tracklaying, however, does not seem to have commenced until the spring of 1883.

By the end of the Northern Pacific fiscal year, in June 1883, track had been extended eastward to a point 32 miles from Palouse Junction.[17] On July 11, 1883, the railway was reported complete to the 35th mile,[18] and a force was being organized to lay a mile of track a day. Such a rapid rate of advance apparently was not achieved. In mid-October the track was reported laid to Endicott and work was said to be "continuing steadily."[19] Not until November 20, 1883, was the *Oregonian* able to state that daily trains were running between Palouse Junction and Colfax and connecting with the transcontinental expresses on the Northern Pacific main line. At that time the road was still being operated on an interim basis by the OR&N.[20]

The responsibility for operating the Columbia & Palouse line was transferred to the Northern Pacific Railroad Co. on January 1, 1884,[21] just three days before Villard relinquished control. The Palouse road, however, remained the property of the Oregon & Transcontinental Co., and in mid-January 1884 that concern decided to sell it to OR&N for a sum of $3 million.[22] The Oregon company encountered legal difficulties with the bond issue that was to have provided the necessary funds, and completion of the transaction was delayed for several months.[23] Later in the year, however, the line became a detached segment of the OR&N system.

Meanwhile, in March 1884 natural calamity forced the cessation of operations.[24] When the winter snows melted, the level of Washtucna Lake (now Lake Kahlotus) suddenly rose to a level not previously foreseen and permanently inundated about 2 miles of track. Two months later the rails were still 3 ft. under water and the line remained closed.[25] A new alignment was clearly required, but until the question of ownership was resolved apparently nothing was done. Eventually in June 1884 a contract was let to P. O'Neill for the construction of a 2-1/4 mile long detour to be located at 25 ft. higher elevation.[26] This work was completed late in July 1884. The railway was then reopened in true "after the flood" style by running the closest possible approximation to Noah's Ark. To the delight of local inhabitants the first train to re-enter Colfax was a special, carrying, of all things, a traveling circus![27]

Thereafter, the western part of the Columbia & Palouse line had a checkered history.[28] The through mail service from Palouse Junction to Colfax survived only until 1888, when a bridge was built across the Snake River at Riparia and track was at last laid on the long-abandoned roadbed up the Alkali Flat Creek. Service on the section west of La Crosse was then reduced to a weekly round trip to Washtucna,[29] and the remainder of the railway to Palouse Junction was closed and eventually torn up. That, however, was not the end of the story, for in 1901 track was relaid to Kahlotus and in 1904 the entire line was reopened right through to Connell. This surprising resurrection was part of the power play between the railroad giants. By reopening the railway, Harriman blocked plans to turn the lower Washtucna Coulee into a reservoir for the Palouse irrigation scheme and thus prevented Hill's Northern Pacific Railway from selling large tracts of otherwise worthless land. Unfortunately, having reopened the line, Union Pacific was then obliged by the government to keep it open, and for the next three-quarters of a century empty trains continued to trundle backward and forward along it. Surviving well into the diesel locomotive era, the Hooper Junction to Connell section of the erstwhile Columbia & Palouse line was eventually closed for the third and perhaps the last time in 1980.[30]

14

BLUE MOUNTAIN STATION AND CENTERVILLE

The uplands between Walla Walla and Pendleton were soon exploited as prime grain-growing country and produced greater crops each year. Within a very short time the narrow gauge branch line from Whitman to Blue Mountain Station was overwhelmed with traffic. In October 1881 Henry Villard and a party of guests including Mr. Pillsbury, the Minneapolis flour-milling magnate, visited Walla Walla and traveled the length of the narrow gauge branch. Arriving at Blue Mountain Station they climbed to the top of an immense pile of wheat and wondered at the productivity of the surrounding area. Mr. Pillsbury, it was said, even ". . . doffed his beaver . . . " in salute to the local agricultural potential.[1] Villard, however, may have felt uneasy, for such large piles of grain must have underlined the need for better rural transportation.

Action to alleviate the situation was not long delayed. In March 1882 OR&N was reported to be conducting surveys for a standard gauge railway from Walla Walla to Pendleton.[2] The surveys took three months and terminated at Pendleton early in June 1882.[3] Further action was held in abeyance until after the OR&N annual general meeting on June 19, 1882, when the stockholders were asked to approve charter amendments sanctioning the construction of various additional branch lines.[4] After this legal formality, the Walla Walla to Pendleton line was located, and steps were taken to procure land. Working in conjunction with a right-of-way committee appointed by the local board of trade, the OR&N land agent, Mr. A. S. Watt, spent the month of August 1882 negotiating property purchases along the line.[5] His special skills were amply demonstrated, for no individual property owner was paid more than $700 and the entire right-of-way was secured for $7,000.[6] By mid-September 1882 the graders were able to start work. Proceeding southward from Walla Walla they crossed the Oregon state line, and by the end of the month they were reported to be approaching Milton.

The railway, as planned and eventually built, swung westward from Milton to meet the existing narrow gauge line at Barrett. Above that point the steeply graded WW&CR roadway up the Dry Creek Valley to Blue Mountain Station was widened to accommodate standard gauge track.[7] Beyond Blue Mountain the surveyed line described a 10-degree horseshoe curve in the valley bottom and climbed out northwestward. Reversing direction again it struggled up to the height of land above the Pine Creek Valley and descended southeastward toward Weston. Completing yet another about-face, it topped another rise to reach Centerville (later Athena). Thence, the route followed the Wild Horse Creek down through Adams to the confluence with the Umatilla River. Crossing the latter stream it joined the Baker City line at a point about a mile east of the Pendleton depot.

Distances in miles northward from Pendleton and elevations in feet above sea level were: junction with Baker City branch, 0 (1,069); Adams, 13 (1,527); Centerville, 17 (1,714); summit at mile 20 (1,823); Weston, 21 (1,797); summit at mile 22 (1,854); Blue Mountain Station, 27 (1,398); Barrett, 33 (884); low at mile 33.6 (845); Milton, 36 (1,003); lows near miles 43 and 44 (886); Walla Walla, 47 (906).[8]

Between Barrett and mile 22, southbound trains climbed almost 1,000 ft. in 11 miles, on a 2 percent ruling grade. The northbound climb from Pendleton was much less severe.

The most significant structure on the line was the Umatilla River bridge, which consisted of two 150-ft. timber Howe-truss spans.

Completion of the entire line took much longer than originally anticipated, for despite Villard's good intentions agricultural branches were always accorded a lower construction priority than strategic main lines. Indeed, the railway from Walla Walla to Pendleton was not completed until it was needed as part of a through route to Spokane Falls and the Coeur d'Alene mines. Almost immediately the work between Walla Walla and Milton suffered from competition with main line requirements for materials. Bridge construction was held up for lack of timber and did not commence until early in November.[9] Then a shortage of rails delayed tracklaying. Eventually enough steel was found to link Walla Walla with Milton, and on November 30, 1882, Henry Bateman, his brother "Clayt," and the steel gang arrived in Walla Walla from Albina and made camp near the old depot.[10] By December 7, 1882, they had laid 2-1/2 miles of track, and five days later they were reported to be halfway to Milton.[11] More 56-lb. rails became available, and by January 18, 1883, track had been extended to a point just beyond Milton.[12] The heavy iron, meanwhile, was also distributed along the narrow gauge right-of-way to Blue Mountain Station, so that whenever the gauge was changed, the original 36-lb. rails could be replaced. On January 22, 1883, forty men were reported to be putting full-length standard gauge ties into the narrow gauge track south of Barrett. Ominously, however, a force of carpenters working at Blue Mountain Station was said to be installing a turntable for standard gauge locomotives.[13] As no grading had been done beyond that point, it became clear that, for the time being at least, the line was to terminate there.[14] By February 7, 1883, standard gauge trains were able to run through to Blue Mountain Station, but there they came to a premature halt.

Farmers working the high land were no nearer to a railway line than they had been before. Those residing near Centerville and Adams had to haul their grain considerable distances to the nearest railhead and, as a result, suffered great hardship. When Villard again visited the Interior, in mid-April 1883 they sent a deputation to meet him and plead for completion of the railway from Blue Mountain Station to Pendleton.[15] To induce OR&N to bring the line into operation before the next season's harvest their committee was even authorized to offer a $30,000 subsidy. Despite the fact that the railway company had previously accepted such subsidies, and sometimes even demanded them, Henry Villard adopted a puritanical stance and declared that such was not his policy. He magnanimously undertook to look the country over and see that the road was promptly built. Despite many other difficulties, he kept his promise.

By mid-September 1883 grading was well under way between Pendleton and Centerville, and the roadbed had already been completed to Adams.[16] Above Blue Mountain Station, meanwhile, six gangs of men were busy cutting the horseshoe grade by which the railway was to climb out of the Dry Creek bottom.[17]

Secondary construction work followed without delay. The first piles for the truss bridge across the Umatilla River were driven on Sunday morning, November 4, 1883,[18] and within a month the superstructure was in position.[19] As soon as the bridge was finished the pile driver was moved ahead to prepare foundations for several trestle bridges over the Wild Horse Creek.[20] Conveniently, just as the roadbed became ready for track, men also became available to lay it.

As winter descended on the Blue Mountains, work on the Baker City road came to a halt, and the main line steel gang, which had been camped at the mouth of Meacham Creek, moved down the valley to Pendleton to await delivery of rails for the branch. Tracklaying[21] began on or about January 5, 1884, and just over a month later trains were running between Pendleton and Centerville.

The first 25-car train, carrying 250 tons of wheat shipped from both Centerville and Adams, was brought down to Pendleton on February 7, 1884.[22] The railway, however, could hardly have been fully ballasted and surfaced, for on February 11 there was a derailment 2 miles below Adams.[23] The wrecking train had to be summoned to recover a locomotive and one car. Nevertheless, business continued to be brisk, for there were still another 300 carloads of grain awaiting shipment.

With railheads at both Centerville[24] and Blue Mountain Station, the plateau farmers' transportation problems were greatly eased. Completion of the 10 miles of line between the two interim termini was not regarded as an urgent matter. Following the collapse of Villard's empire, OR&N's first imperative was to link up with Union Pacific's Oregon Short Line. Every priority was given to completion of the main line to Huntington, and the Walla Walla to Pendleton road was left in limbo. Weston had to wait another three years for a train.

15

OVER THE BLUE MOUNTAINS

When the Oregon Railway & Navigation Co. was first formed, Henry Villard reached a general understanding with Jay Gould and Sidney Dillon concerning an eventual connection with the Union Pacific railroad. It was agreed that when the time was ripe a westward branch of the narrow gauge Utah & Northern Railway would be built to link up with an OR&N line at Baker City in eastern Oregon.[1] Beset by the trials and tribulations of the Kansas Pacific merger[2] yet secure in the knowledge that Northern Pacific remained impecunious, Dillon postponed the work for more than a year. In November 1880, however, the unexpected announcement of the financial agreement to complete the Northern Pacific Railroad changed the situation completely. Union Pacific was already threatened by diversion of traffic from the Central Pacific to the Southern Pacific and could ill afford the added risk of being shut out of the Northwest. Suddenly a connection with OR&N became a matter of the utmost urgency, and Dillon reacted accordingly.

Union Pacific at once revised its plans for an Oregon branch and made overtures to OR&N for a joint venture.[3] In January 1881, Dillon offered Villard two seats on the Union Pacific board and expressed willingness to contribute $10 million toward construction. Bent on pursuing his own dreams of empire and already on the way to gaining control of Northern Pacific, Villard, however, declined. The two companies nevertheless agreed to extend their respective lines to an end-on junction at Baker City. During the second week of February 1881, Union Pacific announced that a standard gauge railway would be built northwestward from a junction with the main line at Granger, Wyoming, by a route coinciding closely with the Hudnutt survey of 1868-69.[4] The line was to proceed by way of the Ham's Fork, Bear, and Portneuf rivers to the upper reaches of the Snake River and follow that stream to Old Fort Boise and the Oregon boundary. Baker City would then be reached by ascending the Burnt River Canyon and crossing the height of land to the Powder River basin. The total distance was to be almost 590 miles. Since the new route would meet the Utah & Northern line at Portneuf,[5] 204 miles from Granger, and share a common roadbed for the next ten miles to Pocatello, work could be undertaken on three fronts simultaneously. Progress was expected to be rapid.

Legal and financial arrangements were quickly completed and during the second week of April 1881 a Union Pacific subsidiary named the Oregon Short Line Railway was duly incorporated under the laws of Wyoming Territory.[6] The Union Pacific Railway Co. retained half of the Oregon Short Line stock and offered the remainder to its own shareholders as a bonus for subscribing to a $25,000 per mile first mortgage bond issue.[7] Significantly, the wording of the mortgage bore evidence of lingering distrust between the Union Pacific and OR&N companies. To meet every eventuality the document provided for construction ". . . from a point near Granger, Wyoming . . . to Baker City" and "thence to such point or points on the Columbia River or the Pacific Ocean as the Company may select."[8] Gould and Dillon, it appeared, were taking no chances!

Anticipating Dillon's moves, and anxious to check the Union Pacific advance at Baker City, Villard immediately ordered Oakes to secure the southeastern approach to the Columbia River.[9] On November 26, 1880 Thielsen invited tenders for clearing a right-of-way from the mouth of Meacham Creek all the way over the Blue Mountains to La Grande in Union County.[10] Engineer E. H. Mix hastened to verify the previously surveyed line[11] and during the second week of December 1880 clearing contracts were let to G. W. Redding of Pendleton and Daniel Chaplin of La Grande.[12] Engineer P. Zahner and party, meanwhile set out to make preliminary surveys for a railway from Umatilla to Pendleton. First steps were then taken to procure land.

Below Pendleton the Umatilla Valley had already been extensively settled. The right-of-way had to be purchased from individual property owners, all of whom expected to receive substantial compensation. OR&N was determined to acquire the land at little or no cost to themselves, and did so by exploiting fears that the railroad might bypass Pendleton altogether. Speaking in the dining hall of the Villard House hotel on December 24, 1880, Thielsen told Pendleton citizens that although a railway along the Umatilla valley was feasible, it would be expensive to build. OR&N was willing to follow that route and establish a depot within half a mile of Pendleton only if local residents would raise enough money to pay for the right-of-way from the Columbia River to the boundary of the Indian Reservation.[13] Despite the fact that the deep-cleft valleys of the Umatilla River and Meacham Creek offered the only good railway route into the mountains, the leaders of the community hastened to cooperate. A right-of-way committee was appointed forthwith and undertook to raise subscriptions for a $10,000 bond. The twice-weekly *East Oregonian*, meanwhile, urged the people ". . . not to let the golden opportunity pass, for it may not come again soon."

Threatened with relegation to limbo, Pendleton merchants responded so liberally that by January 15, 1881, Thielsen was graciously pleased to confirm that the railway would in fact follow the Umatilla River and pass within the city limits.[14] The actual negotiations for purchase of the right-of-way were conducted in May 1881 by OR&N land agent, Mr. A. S. Watt,[15] who not only obtained all the property at very low cost but accomplished the task with such skill that the Pendleton Committee was blamed for the poor prices paid. On July 1, 1881 the *East Oregonian* at last reported that all but two parcels of the land had been acquired.[16] Then, to rationalize the unsatisfactory compensation and put an end to recriminations, the paper concluded that "the road has increased the worth of every place through which it passes."

Above Pendleton the OR&N Baker City branch, as the line was called, passed through the Umatilla Indian Reservation. To obtain a right-of-way through these aboriginal lands the company first had to negotiate an agreement with the Indians and then obtain ratification by the United States Secretary of the Interior. This procedure should not have presented any great difficulty, but certain parties in Walla Walla decided to make a last ditch attempt to have the railway diverted to their own town. They therefore persuaded the Indians to object to the OR&N proposal to follow the Warm Springs road through Thorn Hollow.[17] The *Weekly Statesman* reported on May 21, 1881, that "it is thought in Walla Walla that it is too bad that the railroad follows the Umatilla Valley so closely, and there are hopes that the redskins may change this." Quite a lot of mischief was done and the trouble was not put to rest until H. Thielsen and the Hon. J. N. Dolph personally met Homly and Young Chief in council at the Umatilla Agency on June 8, 1881.[18] In return for per acre payments of $2.50 for wild land and $2.75 for all cultivated property, amounting in all to $43,000, the Indians agreed to grant the company right-of-way and depot grounds within the reservation.[19] This agreement, described in the OR&N *Annual Report* as being "mutually fair and reasonable," allowed the location plan of the line from Umatilla to Baker to be submitted to the Interior Department and approved. At last the company's land problems seemed to be settled, and construction was expected to continue apace.

The Baker City branch left the Columbia Valley railway just east of the Umatilla bridge, 186 miles from Portland, and proceeded southeastward towards the foothills of the Blue Mountains. The route diverged briefly from the Umatilla River at the old Four Mile House, passed over higher ground near the present-day town of Hermiston, and descended into the valley again near Twelve Mile House. Passing through what was then known as Foster's and is now called Stanfield,[20] the line turned almost due south across the lush bottomlands to Echo City, where the military road from The Dalles to Walla Walla crossed the Umatilla River. Above Echo the Umatilla Valley becomes a narrow cleft in the hills, and, in the days before the river was restrained, the bottomlands were often flooded. At a point 24 miles from Umatilla the line crossed the river and swinging eastward through Nolin took up an elevated position on the south side of the valley. Just above Yoakum, however, it again descended to water level and hugged the base of high lava bluffs containing a southerly bend in the river. Then, to negotiate higher ground within the stream's next northerly excursion it was forced into a tight 10-degree full horseshoe curve.[21] At a point 33 miles from Umatilla the railway recrossed the river and, following the base of cliffs forming the north side of the valley, passed by Barnhardt's and Rieth's to a third crossing just a mile below Pendleton. In 43 miles the first section of the Baker City branch climbed a net 773 ft. from an elevation of 296 ft. at Umatilla to 1,069 ft. at Pendleton. The maximum adverse grades were said to have been 47 ft. per mile eastbound and 26 ft. per mile westbound.[22]

The key to passage of the Blue Mountains was Meacham Creek, which rises high on the dissected plateau just over 20 miles southeast of Pendleton. The creek follows a generally northeastward course, but in the first 10 miles below Meacham it makes two complete reversals in direction. Its valley thus forms a great incised S curve in the hills and provides a feasibly graded railway route onto the high ground. Leaving Pendleton the OR&N line proceeded eastward up the Umatilla Valley through Cayuse and Thorn Hollow, 22 miles to Mikecha[23] (now Gibbon), at the mouth of Meacham Creek. The road then turned abruptly southward to follow the course of the creek 28 miles to Meacham, whence there were only 7 more uphill miles to the Blue Mountain summit 4,205 ft. above sea level at Kamela.[24]

In 57 miles from Pendleton the line climbed 3,136 ft. Much of the altitude, however, was gained in the final ascent from Laka (now Huron) to Kamela, where eastbound trains were forced to climb 1,292 ft. in 13 miles on grades as steep as 116 ft. to the mile. Fortunately, the curvature was limited to 8 degrees, and many of the curves were no sharper than 6 degrees, so that the ascent was not as difficult as it might have been otherwise.

From the summit at Kamela the line descended steeply southeastward by way of Railroad Canyon[25] and Pelican Creek[26] to Hilgard, which lies in the valley of the Five Point Creek just above that stream's confluence with the Grande Ronde River. Beyond Hilgard and the meeting of waters known as The Five Points, the railway proceeded eastward down the Grande Ronde Canyon to Oro Dell and at last emerged onto the broad intermontane plain at La Grande. On the descent from Kamela to Hilgard the line fell 1,202 ft. in just over 11 miles, thus presenting westbound trains with a climb just as steep but not quite as long as the final ascent eastbound.

At La Grande the railroad turned southeastward onto an almost level tangent alignment and traversed the southern part of the Grand Ronde plain at elevations of just over 2,700 ft. above sea level. For more than 10 miles ideal conditions prevailed but, as there was no natural outlet to the south, the engineers were obliged to carry the line over the height of land between the Grande Ronde and Powder river basins. To do this they had the choice of two existing routes, one on each side of Craig Mountain.

The old Oregon Trail pursued a westerly course through Ladd Canyon, while the more recently used stage road wended its way through a narrow gap known as Pyle's Canyon, south of the established town of Union. The Ladd Canyon route (now used by interstate highway 84) was shorter, but its summit lay at an elevation of over 3,600 ft. Any railway grade built on its north side would therefore have been very steep. The Pyle's Canyon road was longer but it crossed the divide at a lower elevation several miles farther to the south. It therefore offered a much easier grade for eastbound trains.[27] From an elevation of 2,718 ft. near Union, the line climbed 730 ft. in just over 10 miles. Ascending southward on the flank of Craig Mountain, it swung to the east around Hutchinson's Point and turned south again to pass through the narrow Pyle's Canyon defile. Emerging at Crook's it continued to climb along the west side of a broader valley to reach a bleak and windswept summit 3,448 ft. above sea level at Telocaset.[28] Beyond the summit the line swung away to the southwest, descending 258 ft. in 6 miles to reach an elevation of 3,190 ft. at the confluence of Antelope Creek and the Powder River. After following the Powder River upstream for several miles it turned southeastward onto 15 miles of tangent track and climbed gently through Haines to Baker City.

Between Umatilla and Baker City the original aligment required two tunnels.[29] Tunnel No. 4, 356 ft. long, was excavated in weathered volcanic rock a mile west of Meacham. Tunnel No. 5 was driven in sheared and fractured granite near the meeting of Antelope Creek and Powder River, just over 4-1/2 miles east of Telocaset. Primitive rock-drilling methods were used in both cases.

Distances in miles from Umatilla and elevations in feet above sea level were: Foster (now Stanfield), 15 (592); Echo, 18 (639); Barnhardt, 36 (907); Pendleton, 43 (1,069); Mikecha (now Gibbon), 65 1,740); Laka (now Huron), 87 (2,913); Meacham, 93 (3,680); Kamela, 100 (4,205); Hilgard, 111 (3,003); La Grande, 119 (2,788); Telocaset, 142 (3,448); North Powder, 152 (3,251); Haines, 162 (3,335); and Baker, 171 (3,457).

Construction of the Umatilla to Pendleton section of the Baker City branch began near Umatilla during the third week of March 1881.[30] On the grassy plains near the Columbia River and in the sandy hills of the hinterland grading was easy. Rapid advances were made and by April 19, 1881, more than 20 miles of roadbed were nearly complete.[31] Just beyond Echo City, however, the graders encountered rock and the work slowed down.[32] To avoid delaying the scraper teams, which were urgently required on the Columbia Valley line, loose earthwork between Echo and Pendleton was undertaken on a priority basis and the hard rock excavations were left until later. By August 6, 1881, all the scraper work had been wound up, and the men and teams transferred to points west of The Dalles.[33] Meanwhile, at Barnhardt's Ranch and several other places within 12 miles of Pendleton, the heavy rock work continued.[34]

Late in June 1881, the Northern Pacific Railroad and Oregon Railway & Navigation companies were brought under common control, and within a short time new policies were adopted. In mid-October it was made abundantly clear that first priority would henceforth be given to construction of the Northern Pacific main line. Despite the fact that completion of the Umatilla grade required only three weeks' work by 300 men, the entire force was suddenly transferred to Lake Pend d'Oreille to join in Hallett's "winter seige." The remaining rock work between Yoakum and Pendleton had to

await the release of men from The Dalles-Cascades section of the
Columbia River line.

The steel gang started work at Umatilla early in February 1882[35]
and proceeded eastward at a leisurely pace, reaching the river crossing at Nolin on April 22, 1882.[36] By that time, work on the bridge
was already well under way.[37] Piling had been driven for an approach
trestle on the west side and piers had been built to carry a main Howe-
truss span 155 ft. long.[38] As soon as the railway track reached the
crossing, the main timbers were brought up, and before the end of
May the truss bridge and 550 ft. of trestle work had been erected.
Construction of the railroad then suffered several setbacks. Early in
May, 400 Chinese working on final preparation of the grade went
on strike demanding that their pay be increased from $25 to $30 per
month.[39] After a stoppage of ten or more days the work was resumed,
but by June 13, 1882, the men were again idled by a shortage of
materials.[40] Then, a week later, they were all sent farther west to
repair flood damage along the Columbia River.[41] Consequently the
track did not reach the second crossing of the Umatilla, west of Barnhardt's, until about July 10, 1882.[42]

As the railway approached Pendleton, progress quickened. The
bridge at the second crossing was finished about the end of July
1882,[43] and by August 20 the track had been laid to the third crossing, just below Pendleton. At this point there was another Howe-
truss span with long approach trestles, totaling, in all, 900 ft. in
length.[44] Again, the piling had already been driven and, once the
track reached the site, less than ten days were required to bring up
the main timbers and erect the bridge. Using iron rails the steel gang
laid the last mile.[45] At 3:30 p.m. on August 31, 1882, the construction train rumbled into Pendleton. Track work was finished on the
following day and a regular train service was established within three
weeks.[46] As the Walla Walla *Weekly Statesman* remarked on September 9, 1882, "The railroad is at Pendleton and the Siwashes better be careful how they try to lassoo the iron horse!"[47]

While the Umatilla to Pendleton section of the railway was under
construction, preliminary work began on the Mountain Division.
Clearing and grubbing contracts were let in mid-December 1880 and
a complementary agreement for the supply of 220,000 ties was signed
in January 1881.[48] As all the higher land was heavily forested, clearing the right-of-way was a big job requiring many months to complete. No other operations were initiated until mid-August 1881 when
it was announced that J. R. McLean of Chicago had been awarded

a construction contract for all the piling, trestle work, and bridges required between Pendleton and Meacham's Station.[49] At that point, when $200,000 had already been spent[50] on the line, real estate problems suddenly recurred.

The trouble[51] arose over a toll road through the Blue Mountains, built by Harvey Meacham in 1865. Meacham was deceased but his widow had married F. A. Foster, who now demanded an extortionate fee for right-of-way. For a while rumors abounded. It was even said that the Oregon Short Line had acquired the toll road and Villard would be forced to use another route. After two months of haggling, however, the matter was settled. During the third week of December 1881 the Blue Mountain Consolidated Wagon Road Company formally agreed that for a consideration of $20,000 they would grant an easement allowing OR&N to cross their toll road.[52] A deed was filed in the county clerk's office at Union and the air was cleared at last, but by that time the mountains were locked in the grip of winter.

The contract for rock work and grading on the Mountain Division was let to the Oregon Construction Company, previously known as R. M. Steel & Company, who had recently completed the roadbed between Texas Ferry and Colfax. The officers of this company were D. P. Thompson, president; R. M. Steel, vice president; J. B. David, secretary; and C. D. Bates, superintendent.[53] Having made an exploratory trip to Baker with Thielsen in December 1881,[54] these gentlemen promptly made all the necessary arrangements for labor, tools, and supplies, and began work in the spring of 1882. By April of that year 800 men were heavily engaged east of Pendleton and 12 miles of roadbed had already been completed. As soon as the mountain snows melted the company built comfortable offices and dwelling houses near Meacham and moved their headquarters staff onto the high ground.[55] A start was then made on Tunnel No. 4 and the numerous rock cuts on the upper reaches of Meacham Creek. In mid-July 1882 hundreds of men were hard at work. At Encampment blasting took place twice daily and before long the roofs of several nearby houses had been perforated by flying missiles![56] Meanwhile, down in the valley, the graders had already advanced to a point beyond Mikecha.[57] Messrs. Steel, David, and associates were under no illusions about the magnitude of the task ahead of them. The road was nearly all rock cut and fill. Meacham Creek, moreover, was a treacherous stream, able to transform itself from a mere trickle, ". . . not large enough to float a Racine canoe . . ." into a raging mountain river within a few hours. Wherever the embankments were likely to be scoured by rushing waters "log cabin crib" retaining walls had to be built. The cost of grading was expected to reach $40,000 per mile.[58] Bridge building, too, was clearly going to be expensive and time consuming. The line crossed Meacham Creek in nine places, and there were numerous tributary streams, so that between Pendleton and Meacham alone no less than twenty-five Howe-truss bridges had to be erected.[59] Even without delays due to unforseen events the track was not expected to reach the summit until well into 1883. Early in September 1882, however, Villard suddenly countered the Union Pacific threat to his empire, and work on the Baker City branch was abruptly thrown into a state of upheaval.

The OR&N and Oregon Short Line tracks were originally to have met at Baker City. The relationship between the two companies, however, remained uneasy, and when Villard gained control of Northern Pacific other disputes caused further alienation. Trouble arose over access to mining areas in Montana. In 1878 Union Pacific had acquired the bankrupt, Mormon-built, Utah Northern Railroad, linking Ogden, Utah with Franklin, Idaho.[60] Reorganized as the Utah & Northern Railway, this narrow gauge line was extended slowly northward over the Monida Pass into Montana Territory. Villard was bitterly opposed to the invasion of an area he regarded as the rightful preserve of Northern Pacific. As early as June 1881 he asked United States Senator J. H. Mitchell of Oregon to initiate moves designed to revoke the Utah & Northern right-of-way through public lands. Mitchell complied, but after prolonged hearings the Secretary of the Interior ruled in favor of Union Pacific and the narrow gauge advance was allowed to continue.[61] Aiming for Helena, the Utah & Northern Railway reached Silver Bow, just west of Butte, in October 1881. Two months later a branch was extended from Silver Bow to Butte.[62] Negotiations between Northern Pacific and Union Pacific held in January 1882 resulted in an agreement whereby that section of the Utah & Northern extension to Helena lying between Silver Bow and a junction with the projected Northern Pacific main line at Little Blackfoot (later Garrison) would be built with a full width standard gauge roadbed and laid with three identical rails. Northern Pacific was to make up the difference in cost and pay for similar modifications to the branch between Silver Bow and Butte. Utah & Northern narrow gauge trains would then be used to bring up all the supplies needed for construction of the Little Blackfoot and Hell's Canyon sections of the Northern Pacific main line, and Northern Pacific standard gauge trains, by grace of running powers, would eventually have access to Butte.[63] Villard, however, failed to persuade Dillon to abandon plans for an independent Utah & Northern line paralleling the Northern Pacific Railroad east of Little Blackfoot. If the narrow gauge reached Helena on its own track there was no guarantee that it would stop there and no telling where it would finally end. Union Pacific, however, refused to be contained. As the year 1882 progressed and the relationship between the two groups deteriorated, hostilities were extended to eastern Oregon. For several months OR&N and Union Pacific exchanged threats to extend their respective lines to points beyond Baker City. There were persistent rumors that OR&N would advance southward to link up with an impending Central Pacific thrust to the east, or that the Oregon Short Line would be extended, not only to Portland but all the way to Puget Sound. As Dillon's emissaries roamed the Northwest,[64] Villard's anxiety grew, until at length he felt compelled to make a preemptive strike.

On September 12, 1882 the Pendleton *East Oregonian* reported that OR&N engineers and draftsmen had been hastily sent forward to examine new routes. Leading officials had been holding secret consultations and Pendleton teamsters had been asked to move a large amount of supplies to the Powder River basin.[65] Oregon & Transcontinental Co., it was said, would locate an extension from Baker to Boise with all dispatch! Three days later the same paper confirmed that engineer Mix of OR&N had taken possession of the narrowest part of the Burnt River Canyon, about 35 miles southeast of Baker.[66] Within a week 500 men set out on a forced march from Meacham,[67] and by mid-October they had reached and secured their objective. The Oregon Short Line right-of-way agent was forced to look on helplessly as Oregon Construction Company forces consolidated Villard's hold on the Burnt River defile. There was no room for a second railway.[68] Union Pacific, quite clearly, had been headed off at the Snake River.

Presented with a *fait accompli* there was little the Oregon Short Line people could do but bluster. Matters had to be resolved at a higher level, and for that purpose a conference was held at New York in February 1883. The terms of the resulting agreement were as follows:[69]

1. Upon completion of the Northern Pacific Railroad to Little Blackfoot, Montana Territory, a point about 48 miles west of Helena, the Northern Pacific Railroad would lay a third rail between Helena and Little Blackfoot. The Utah & Northern would

also lay a third rail between Little Blackfoot and Butte City, thus giving to each company a through rail connection to the most important cities in Montana.

2. The Oregon Short Line would be extended to the Snake River where it would be met by the Oregon Railway & Navigation Co. and where the business of the Pacific Coast would be exchanged.

3. Upon the junction of the Oregon Short Line and the Oregon Railway & Navigation Co. at the Snake River, freight between the Pacific Coast and Salt Lake would be interchanged by the new route.

4. Freight between Colorado and the Pacific Coast would also be exchanged by the new route.

5. The rates between all eastern points and Portland would be the same as between the same points and San Francisco.

6. Rates of freight between the Pacific Coast and points in Montana would be the same as rates from St. Paul.

It soon became clear that by "Snake River" the parties meant a crossing of the Snake River on the Oregon-Idaho boundary at or near the confluence with the Burnt River. In fact, since Villard had no desire to pay for the Snake River bridge and there was not enough flat land for interchange facilities in the immediate vicinity of the crossing, a junction was eventually established 2 miles away at Huntington, Oregon.

Villard emerged victorious from his disputes with Union Pacific, but railway construction in the Blue Mountains was seriously set back. Departure of the expedition to the Burnt River cut the work force on Meacham Creek by almost a third.[70] Moreover, there were simultaneous disasters of other kinds. During the second week of September 7,000 ties were burned in a fire at Meacham.[71] Later that month part of Tunnel No. 4 caved in,[72] and during October heavy rain caused serious rock slides in the cuts.[73] Nevertheless, by December 27, 1882, 40 miles of roadbed lay ready for track.[74] Rock work went on throughout the winter and the tunnel was finished in mid-March 1883.[75] Early in the spring the steel gang got off to a good start and before the end of April track had been laid to a point 25 miles east of Pendleton.[76] By June 1, 1883, therefore, regular trains were running through to Mikecha. The rest of the summer, however, was needed to finish the Meacham Creek grade, and the train service was not extended to Meacham's Station until mid-October.[77]

The winter of 1883-84 was bitter indeed. Heavy snow was reported at the front on November 27 and by December 6 grading had been suspended.[78] On Wall St. the financial climate deteriorated. For almost three months the value of the Villard railroad stocks declined and by the end of the year the debacle was complete. As these events unfolded confidence was lost and uncertainty prevailed. Early in January 1884 the Oregon Construction Company therefore stopped all work on the Baker City branch and discharged the majority of their men.[79]

In Pendleton the social effects were felt almost immediately. Large numbers of men descended from the mountains and congregated in town. Many of them said they had no money, for the layoff came just after the New Year celebrations. Others complained that they had signed on in Portland for three months' work and could not cash their time checks without returning there. All claimed to be destitute and clamored for food. To avert unrest, Umatilla County Sheriff Martin arranged for them to be fed, and on the evening of Tuesday, January 8, 1884, no less than 135 men were given a free meal at the Golden Rule Hotel. On the following day nearly as many had breakfast and fifty-three took dinner. On Thursday the men again became restless and at 2:30 p.m. about 140 of them descended on the Pendleton depot, boarded the afternoon mixed train, and demanded a free ride to Portland. The conductor refused to break the rules and insisted that they either pay the fare or get off. The laborers sat tight, vowing that they would never let the train leave without them. The result was an impasse.

In reply to a telegraphed request for instructions, the head office in Portland suggested that county officers should try to resolve the problem. The OR&N authorities, however, overlooked the fact that the Pendleton depot lay within the Umatilla Indian Reservation and was thus outside Sheriff Martin's jurisdiction. Unsuccessful attempts were made to secure help from local federal officials. During the evening the OR&N agent, E. F. Hilgard, made a formal complaint charging some individuals with obstructing the mails. United States Commissioner Tustin, however, held that no sufficient offense had been committed and refused to issue warrants for the men's arrest. A message was again sent to Portland and at that point somebody decided to call upon the military. General Miles was given an exaggerated account of the affair and within a matter of hours a detachment of the United States Army was on its way (by train) from Walla Walla. The expeditionary force, consisting of thirty-five cavalrymen and their horses, commanded by Captain Wagner, arrived in Pendleton at 3:00 on Friday afternoon. Wagner asked the laborers to get off the train, and when they refused he gave the order to have

them forcibly evicted. Unfortunately, the soldiers were greatly out-
numbered and made but mild attempts to comply with the captain's
command. Failure to dislodge the men was then greeted with a deafen-
ing howl of derision from a large crowd of local spectators, and the
soldiers, not knowing quite what to do next, withdrew. Encouraged
by irresponsible elements in the local populace, the laborers held out
for a while longer, but after 24 hours on the train most of them were
beginning to tire of the whole affair. Common sense was therefore
allowed to prevail. The men finally acceded to United States Marshall Morse's request that fare-paying passengers and mail be permitted to leave, and at 6:00 that evening the baggage car and passenger
coaches went their lawful way. Having received another meal and
rations for the road, the men were then advised to leave, and by Saturday noon, January 12, 1884, most of them had quietly drifted away
down the valley.[80] For the time being the problem was solved, but
it was to recur in place after place throughout that bitter winter. Early
in February the *Umatilla Examiner* stated that at least 1,700 men
had been discharged from railroad work in eastern Oregon and
Washington in the previous two months, many of them without homes
or money. The larger towns, it was said, were full of vagrants and
tramps depending on charity for subsistence.[81]

On December 17, 1883, T. Jefferson Coolidge of Boston replaced
Henry Villard as president of the Oregon Railway & Navigation Co.[82]
Coolidge's first task was to unravel the financial tangle left by his
predecessor. Funds then had to be found to complete the line to Huntington. OR&N was an exception among American railroads of the
time, for it was built largely with share capital.[83] The only loan capital
was that derived from the initial $6 million bond issue of 1879. The
remainder of the $24 million needed to construct the railway was
in fact raised by selling stock at par. This enviable state of affairs,
however, had only existed because Villard's dubious policy of paying large dividends had kept the shares consistently overpriced. Unfortunately, during the latter half of 1883 loss of confidence drove
the price of OR&N stock down dramatically from over 140 to less
than 100, and by January 20, 1884, it stood at no more than 90.[84]

To raise the funds needed to complete the line to Huntington,
therefore, the company was forced to revert to the money market.
Coolidge planned to float a 5 percent mortgage bond issue for $14.28
million, of which $6 million would be allocated to retiring the ex-
isting first mortgage bonds, $1.2 million to paying off outstanding
8 percent scrip, $2.7 million to buying the Columbia & Palouse

branch, and the remainder to meeting ongoing construction costs. Some $3 million worth of the bonds were to be taken by Boston bankers and the remainder by Baring Brothers of London.[85] Unfortunately, these arrangements had no sooner been announced than they were found to contravene a newly enacted Oregon state mortgage law that could not be amended until the next session of the legislature.[86] To pay off the floating debt and provide the funds so urgently required for construction OR&N was therefore obliged to take out $4 million in 7 percent, three-year debentures. These were placed with Lee, Higginson & Company of Boston during the third week of March 1884,[87] and within a month railway construction was once again well under way.

At Meacham, the first sign that work was about to resume came on February 17, 1884, when R. M. Steel and J. W. Bates passed through en route to Hilgard.[88] Any prospects of an early start were immediately smothered by a blizzard that buried the line and blockaded the Meacham passenger train.[89] On February 23 the bridge gang, sent out from Pendleton four days previously to make repairs along the line, arrived on the scene and dug the train out, thus restoring communications with the outside world.[90] Any serious work on the east side of the summit was set back until the weather improved and all the snow had been shoveled off the grade. No real progress was made until mid-April, but with large numbers of Chinese again at work matters then improved rapidly. Just beyond the front, final preparations were made for tracklaying, while farther down the line at Stumptown and in the Grande Ronde Canyon major earthworks were rushed to completion. To keep well ahead of the tracklayers the carpenters hurriedly completed the truss bridges near Pelican and Hilgard and then moved on quickly to the Grande Ronde River crossing just above Oro Dell.[91] Daniel Chaplin, meanwhile, was awarded another contract for two million board feet of lumber and arrangements were made to put in sidings at his Meacham and Five Point sawmills.[92] During the month of April rails were brought up to the summit at a rate of ten carloads per day.[93] The steel gang resumed their advance early in May and by June 28 track had been laid right through to a point several miles beyond the Grande Ronde River.[94] Some time was then required to ballast and surface the new railway, and a regular train service to the new town of La Grande was not inaugurated until Monday, July 21, 1884.[95]

On the Grande Ronde plain most of the grading had been completed in 1883, and little work remained to be done.[96] Rock excavation at Pyle's Canyon and the driving of Antelope Creek tunnel, however, threatened to delay the opening of the line. Work at Pyle's Canyon was briefly suspended following Villard's downfall but resumed at the end of January 1884[97] and was finished within the next five months. The Antelope Creek tunnel drive apparently proceeded without interruption through December 1883 and January 1884.[98] When the workings had advanced about 100 ft. from the north end the company announced that due to financial stringency the wages of the Chinese would be reduced from $1.00 to 80 cents per day. As a result there was an angry protest and the men went on strike until the middle of March.[99] Work then had to be pushed night and day, and in the prevailing atmosphere of haste at least one fatal accident occurred.[100] The tunnel was finished on Friday, July 4, 1884.[101] The steel gang, meanwhile, advanced steadily. The construction train passed through Pyle's Canyon during the second week of June, reached the summit at Telocaset in the third week of July, paused at North Powder early in August, and rolled into Baker on or about August 20.[102] The first passengers for Baker City left Portland on Saturday, September 6, 1884, and reached their destination the following day.[103]

Beyond Baker City the 47-mile OR&N extension to Huntington crossed the height of land and descended nearly 2,000 ft. through a series of rugged mountain valleys leading to the Snake River. Starting out from Baker in a southeasterly direction, the line first followed the Sutton Creek gently uphill for almost 6 miles. It then climbed more steeply for another 4-1/2 miles to a summit 3,968 ft. above sea level on desolate moorland at Encina.[104] Thence there was a rapid descent for 9-1/2 miles down the Alder Creek Valley to Unity (now Oxman). At that point the railway reached the edge of a 500-ft. escarpment overlooking the western end of the broad Durkee Valley and was forced to follow a circuitous route downhill. To obtain a feasible grade the line swung around to the north, dropped sharply into the valley of Pritchard Creek, described a full hairpin bend, and headed southward again.[105] In a distance of 12 miles between Encina and the horseshoe curve on Pritchard Creek the railway descended fully 1,058 ft. on grades as steep as 2.2 percent. The gradient then eased, and for the next 9 miles the road was able to traverse open country on predominantly tangent alignments. Unfortunately the only route from the enclosed Durkee basin to the Snake River Valley lay through the forbidding Burnt River Canyon. The railway was therefore obliged to head directly southeastward into the towering limestone gateway at Nelson and follow the river's rushing waters through the narrow defile. For 14 miles the line wended its way through a gorge more than 2,000 ft. deep and in places so constricted that it was believed no second railway could ever be built.[106] Several times over, sharp bends forced the road to cross from one side of the river to the other. Four truss bridges were required,[107] and to make matters more difficult a tunnel over 500 ft. long had to be driven through a high spur of rock 1-1/2 miles below Weatherby.[108] At last, within 4 miles of the meeting with the Snake River, the Burnt Valley widened to form a crescent shaped area of flat land suitable for railway yards. And there, 2,111 ft. above sea level and 404 miles from Portland, the junction with the Oregon Short Line was effected and the town of Huntington grew up.

Distances from Baker City and elevations in feet above sea level were:[109] Encina, 10 (3968); Pleasant Valley, 13 (3766); Unity (now Oxman), 19 (3,166); Durkee, 27 (2657); Weatherby, 36 (2,405); and Huntington, 48 (2,111).

The details of construction progress on the OR&N extension to Huntington are largely obscure. Indeed, when work in the Burnt River Canyon first got under way nobody in the outside world knew exactly what was happening there. On November 13, 1882, Oakes wired Thielsen for enlightenment, saying:[110]

> We have indirect information that in Burnt River Pass Short Line forces are working alongside our own. Advise me in cipher the exact situation, giving such material facts as will enable us to treat understandingly with the Short Line people here. We are now in the dark.

Although the Oregon Short Line Railway had surveyed and located a line to Baker City, and there was speculation in the press about what would happen when their Italian laborers caught up with the Oregon Construction Company's Chinese,[111] it seems unlikely that they ever moved much earth in the Burnt River Canyon. A correspondent of the *Oregonian*, writing from Baker on November 30, 1882, noted that although the Oregon Short Line contractors were vigorously pursuing work on the Idaho side of the Snake River, and materials had already been brought up for a bridge, OR&N nevertheless appeared ". . . to have the best of the game so far as the Burnt River Canyon is concerned. . . ."[112] Union Pacific, it seemed, was determined to prevent Villard from making any farther advance to the east but was already resigned to accepting the OR&N coup on the Burnt River. The initial Oregon Construction Company force, consisting of 500 men, appears to have been concentrated at the most constricted parts of the canyon, such as the rock barrier below Weatherby. As time went on, more and more men were brought in until in the summer of 1884 there were 1,600 Chinese and 600 whites.[113] In June 1884, 17 miles of heavy work (presumably the section between Encina and Durkee) remained to be done.[114] Two months later the steel gang was able to push on directly from Baker and lay track to Pleasant Valley without pause.[115] Some time, however, seems to have elapsed before they could proceed down Alder Creek and finish the railway through the Burnt River Canyon. Track did not reach Huntington until early in November 1884.[116] The delay, however, was unimportant, for the Oregon Short Line could not complete the Snake River bridge and effect a union with OR&N any earlier.

On Monday, November 24, 1884, private cars nos. 99 and 100, belonging respectively to Messrs. C. H. Prescott and Wm. H. Starbuck, were coupled onto an eastbound passenger train to convey OR&N representatives from Portland to a "last spike" railway opening ceremony at Huntington, Oregon.[117] The distinguished passengers left Albina at 6:00 in the evening and reached their destination at 3:00 the following afternoon. The OR&N party consisted of: H. S. Rowe, superintendent; H. B. Thielsen, chief engineer; E. R. Willis, clerk to the chief engineer; W. Shaw, roadmaster; P. T. Keen, private secretary to C. H. Prescott; R. M. Steel of the Oregon Construction Company; J. M. Brandt, superintendent of the Oregon & California Railroad; and three Portland journalists. United States Senator James H. Slater and his daughter, who joined the train in Baker and traveled on directly over the Short Line to the east, were guests of honor. Union Pacific assistant chief engineer E. C. Smeed accompanied the Portland group on their journey, and Oregon Short Line manager Hickensdorfer welcomed them to Huntington. A crowd of about 300 construction workers and others had assembled at the depot grounds, and as the sun was sinking below the hills the ceremony commenced. A gap of two rails' length had been left in the track and at a given signal a crew of a dozen burly Irishmen, ". . . each one of them tall enough and stout enough to have claimed descent from Brian Boru or Finn McCool himself . . . ," took up appropriate positions. In teams of three the Irish giants simultaneously lifted all four rails from the deck of a flatcar and laid them in place upon the ties. The men stood waiting with uplifted mauls as the fishplate bolts were tightened and then gave a resounding demonstration of professional spike driving. As the echos died away in the hills, young Henry Thielsen set the ultimate spike and called upon Mr. Smeed to strike the first blow. Senator Slater, Mr. Rowe, Mr. James W. Virtue, Dr. Keen, and Mr. Steel all ". . . had a whack at it . . . " and the rest of party drove it home.

The locomotives then eased ahead pilot to pilot on the newly laid rails, three cheers were given for the Oregon Short Line and three more for the Oregon Railway & Navigation Co., and the job, at last, was done. Six days later the two companies inaugurated a through Pullman and emigrant sleeping car train service between Portland and both Omaha and Kansas City.[118] The Omaha service was billed as being " . . . 462 miles the shortest and 29 hours the quickest." The journey time was 84 hours, and the trains were the wonder of the country through which they passed.

The last spike ceremony at Huntington, Oregon, was the least pretentious such event to have taken place in America until that time. It was a low-key, businesslike affair, done properly and quickly. Occurring not long after Villard's ostentatious opening of the Northern Pacific Railroad and overshadowed immediately by the Cleveland-Blaine presidential election, it was given little space in the press. The lack of fanfare, however, belied the importance of the event, for as a milestone in regional history it marked the debut of a second transcontinental railroad. At 3:30 p.m. on Tuesday, November 25, 1884, the Union Pacific became established as a growing, counterbalancing force in the development of the Pacific Northwest.

16

"ON THE ROAD, AND OFF"

For two years after the collapse of Villard's empire, construction of new railways was severely curtailed. While New York and Boston financiers licked their wounds and the Philadelphia group struggled to retain advantage, railway men took up the challenge of running regular trains over barely completed lines.

Before the railroads could function efficiently a variety of fixed facilities had to be provided. First priority was given to installing side tracks, water tanks, and telegraph lines. Depots, roundhouses, and shops were erected at the earliest opportunity. Unforeseen problems, meanwhile, were confronted as they arose. Embankments washed away by flood waters were rebuilt and protected with riprap, and trestle bridges, which presented a continuous fire hazard, were filled with earth. Many lines nevertheless remained a liability. In areas vulnerable to rock falls and slides little could be done but clear away the fallen debris and wait for slopes to stabilize. Winter, moreover, brought its own problems. Before the invention of the steam rotary snowplow, hundreds of men with shovels could hardly keep certain sections of railway open.

When OR&N was first formed Villard recruited a team of experienced managers from the Kansas Pacific.[1] These gentlemen introduced architectural features bearing a marked similarity to those of the aborted transcontinental far to the south. Some of the depots in the Interior, indeed, were said to have been built to drawings sent directly from Kansas City to the OR&N construction office at Walla Walla.[2] Northern Pacific, meanwhile, had its own standards, and the depots at Cheney, Spokane Falls, Rathdrum, and elsewhere were built accordingly. The first Spokane Falls depot was said locally to be ". . . the handsomest on the line so far . . . " being ". . . more thoroughly finished with mouldings, cornice, and brackets, and such things as are generally added by superior mechanics."[3] The passenger depot was 22 ft. X 28 ft., two storeys high, with ticket, telegraph, and paymaster's offices on the ground floor and rooms for the agent and his family upstairs. The nearby freight shed was 24 ft. X 75 ft. with a 10-ft.-wide platform all around.

Wherever possible water needed for locomotives was obtained by gravity from nearby flowing springs. At Sprague the Northern Pacific water tank was thus filled from a hillside spring " . . . large enough to supply the wants of a city of considerable size."[4] At Spokane Falls the 15,000-gallon tank was filled with water brought from an 84-ft. higher elevation through a buried 2-inch pipeline 2,900 ft. long,[5] and at Rathdrum similar conditions prevailed. In the arid areas farther to the south, however, wells were a necessity. At Palouse Junction the well had to be sunk 185 ft. before an adequate flow of water was encountered. At that depth the ground was uncomfortably cold and the men digging the well had " . . . to wear heavy clothing and wrap their feet and legs in dunny bags to keep from freezing. . . ." A steam pump was required to bring the water to surface.[6]

The railway companies entrusted their communications to the Western Union Telegraph Company, which installed the pole lines and telegraph equipment. On Northern Pacific's Lake Pend d'Oreille Division only two lines were put up at first,[7] a third being strung late in 1882 when overland communication was established with company headquarters at St. Paul.[8] Similarly a single wire carried all telegraph traffic on the OR&N route between Umatilla and Pendleton. In that case, however, the cross arms were bored to carry four insulators, thus making allowance for future expansion. It may be of interest that by 1882 telephone service was already well established in many areas, and often preceded the construction of railways. During the first four months of train service to Pendleton OR&N was able to rely completely on voice communications provided by the local telephone system.[9]

The earliest railway workshop facilities in the Interior were the OSN shops at The Dalles, greatly enlarged by OR&N in 1880. These enhanced facilities included a car shop, a machine shop, a locomotive erecting shop, a blacksmith's shop, a paint shop, a storehouse, a master mechanic's office, and two roundhouses. The machinery was driven by a 150 HP Corliss engine supplied with steam by a boiler plant boasting a new chimney 81 ft. high.[10] The Dalles shops not only coped with routine repair work but also produced new rolling stock. In December 1880 a first order was accepted for 240 new cars, which were then turned out at a rate of seven per week. Northern Pacific, meanwhile, carried out repairs at Ainsworth. Early in 1882, however, all the shop equipment was moved northeastward to Sprague, where the company opened new facilities including a car shop 75 ft. X 225 ft., a machine shop 75 ft. X 150 ft., a twelve-stall roundhouse, and ". . . a splendid office building."[11] To commemorate the opening of these premises a grand ball was held in the car shop, which was elaborately decorated for the occasion. According to the Walla Walla *Weekly Statesman* correspondent, there were:

> Flags o'er head and evergreens and mottos artistically arranged in graceful profusion. The music stand in the center of the hall was a model of beauty. Two large headlights threw their radiance from end to end of the building. . . . A string band of six pieces, under the leadership of Prof. J. Ziminski played music by Offenbach, Strauss, and other composers. Ninety couples sat down to supper, besides others who had no partners, two hundred and seventy-five in all. Ainsworth, Cheney, and Spokane Falls, and all the towns up towards the front, represented by manly grace and female beauty. Vedder and Burton of the Villard House furnished the supper, which was the best ever gotten up in the Spokane Country, the table fairly groaning under the weight of good things.[12]

In 1883 the shops at The Dalles and Sprague were threatened with eclipse by the Northern Pacific Terminal Company's grandiose plans for huge works at Albina. The new installations, to be used jointly by Northern Pacific, OR&N, and Oregon & California, were to include a forty-four stall roundhouse 316 ft. in diameter, with a central 56-ft. turntable, a locomotive erecting and machine shop 120 ft. X 464 ft., a car manufacturing and painting shop 130 ft. X 464 ft., a foundry 90 ft. X 290 ft. with two melting cupolas, a blacksmith shop 80 ft. X 340 ft., a boiler shop 80 ft. X 200 ft., a two-story office and stores building 50 ft. X 302 ft., a two-story wood-working shop 84 ft. X 262 ft., and several smaller edifices. The erecting shop was designed to allow twenty-one locomotives to be repaired simultaneously and, in common with the car shop, was to be served by a 60-ft. transfer table running on four pairs of rails laid on a depressed runway 625 ft. long. To serve the shop machinery the intention was to install two 150 HP Corliss engines and four Babcock & Wilcox water tube boilers, the latter being fired with sawdust and shavings extracted from the wood-working shop by means of a large exhaust fan. Roots blowers were to provide forced draft for the foundry cupolas. The shops were expected to employ 1,500 men.[13]

Construction got under way at Albina during the summer of 1883, and by the end of that year the foundry was complete and footings had been laid for several other buildings. The dissolution of Villard's empire, however, brought the work to a halt. The site lay derelict until late in 1886 when OR&N and Northern Pacific reached a new agreement to resume construction.[14] The machinery was at last started up in December 1887 but after several months of intermittent operation the plant was again shut down. It did not finally reopen until after OR&N was ceded to Union Pacific in October 1889.[15]

Smaller roundhouses and workshops were built at division points established about 150 miles apart on main lines. Thus, in the spring of 1883, Northern Pacific built another twelve-stall roundhouse and machine shop at Heron, Montana.[16] Engines and crews then began to work through from Sprague to Heron on a regular basis. On the OR&N lines, meanwhile, Blalock's and Prescott were set up as division points between Portland and Riparia, and late in 1882 six-stall roundhouses were built at both places.[17] The Baker City branch was initially worked from Umatilla, but as the line became longer a second division was headquartered at LaGrande. Early in 1885 the small existing roundhouse there was given six more stalls and supplemented by a shop building 60 ft. X 100 ft. with a wing 20 ft. X 50 ft.[18]

On the newly completed railroads the trains were allowed plenty of time to complete their journeys. In August 1881, for example, the 149-mile trip over the Northern Pacific from Ainsworth to Spokane Falls took no less than 12 hours 25 minutes.[19] A year later, however, the trains were running faster. Passengers were then able to reach Spokane in 8 hours 30 minutes and travel onward to Sand Point, Idaho, another 70 miles, in 4 hours 40 minutes.[20] Fortunately, those coming from Portland were able to complete the overnight journey from The Dalles in comfort. On May 2, 1882, the *Oregonian* carried the following announcement:

> Sleeping cars to Ritzville. Commencing this evening a Pullman sleeper will run eastwards every other night to Ritzville on the Northern Pacific. This is done to accommodate the large and steadily increasing traffic and will be permanent. Another sleeping coach has been ordered by telegraph and will probably arrive within a month, when sleepers will run to Ritzville every night. For the present they will run Tuesdays, Thursdays, and Saturdays.[21]

When OR&N opened the Portland to Bonneville section of the Columbia Valley line, in November 1882, train no. 1 eastbound was scheduled to cover the 213 miles from Albina to Wallula in 14 hours 20 minutes.[22] In January 1883 the Northern Pacific time between Ainsworth and Spokane Falls was cut to 6 hours 57 minutes,[23] and Spokane was brought within 24 hours of Portland.

As soon as the last spike was driven, the designation of Northern Pacific trains was changed to give the eastbounds the even numbers. The through passenger trains then became known as Pacific Express

No. 1 (westbound) and Atlantic Express No. 2 (eastbound). In November 1883 the Northern Pacific main line between Sprague and Heron carried three regularly scheduled trains each way each day, the two expresses being supplemented by two "freights" and two "emigrants," all of which carried some accommodation for passengers.[24] By June 1886 the latter trains were designated "express freight" (nos. 13 and 14) and "local freight" (nos. 15 and 16).[25] Other revenue trains ran as extras when required.

Traffic on the new railways grew slowly. In the fiscal year 1882-83 Northern Pacific points west of Marshall all received more passengers and freight than they shipped, probably reflecting the arrival of settlers and their effects. At Ritzville, for example, 644 passengers arrived and only 229 departed. At the same time, 1,245 tons of freight were received and only 92 tons were shipped.[26] In the timberlands farther east outgoing lumber shipments inverted the ratio for freight, but in 1883 the discovery of gold on the North Fork Coeur d'Alene River caused Rathdrum to be overwhelmed by incoming passengers. Due to the mining excitement, and to the economic distress accompanying Villard's downfall, there was something of a hiatus in agricultural settlement. Each fall and winter OR&N continued to carry about a thousand tons of flour, wheat, and flax daily to Portland for export,[27] but no great increase in grain traffic was experienced until after the bumper harvest of 1885. On the wide expanses of still unbroken land, cattle-raising continued to flourish, and for several years the livestock traffic was brisk. In May 1885 alone, no less than 626 carloads of stock, 37 trains in all, were sent eastward over the Northern Pacific from the newly completed Yakima branch and from Wallula, Lind, Sprague, and Spokane Falls.[28] Three hundred and thirty cattle shipped from Walla Walla on March 30, 1885, were reported to have reached Chicago on April 10 after being unloaded and rested five times en route. Only one animal was lost.[29] In eastern Oregon, meanwhile, the wool trade also expanded. In May 1885 new rates were announced for the rapid shipment of wool over the Oregon Short Line to Omaha, New York, Boston, and Philadelphia, thus enabling producers to earn prompt returns on the year's clip.[30]

The railroads relied upon agricultural products for their bread and butter but promoted other traffic whenever the opportunity arose. In the days before electric power and domestic refrigerators, ice was an important commodity. During the winter of 1884-85 the Portland Ice Company cut 6,000 tons of ice on Cocolalla Lake in northern Idaho, 3,000 tons of which was used by the Northern Pacific and

OR&N companies. Two thousand tons was sold in Portland, 500 tons went to Puget Sound Transfer Company at Tacoma, and the remainder satisfied the needs of towns along the line.[31] The ice not only provided local traffic but also enabled the railroads to move perishable goods over great distances. In March 1885 rates were published for moving green fruit and vegetables from the Pacific Coast to Omaha, Kansas City, and St. Paul, $1.40 per hundred by express freight and $2.40 per hundred by passenger train. In the latter case the produce was shipped in cars ". . . specially constructed for that purpose and nearly perfect in ventilation."[32]

Innovations in the movement of livestock and perishables stimulated the development of valuable long haul traffic to the east. The glamor, however, was stolen by the tea trains. In July 1885 Northern Pacific undertook to carry New York-bound Oriental tea from Tacoma to St. Paul and agreed to do so in the most expeditious manner possible.[33] Early in August of that year 23,000 cases of tea, discharged from the ship *Isabel*, were put aboard ten special trains and rushed eastwards on express time. All other traffic was sidetracked, and the trains crossed the continent in eight days and four hours.[34] Future consignments, however, were not as lucky, for the relentless pace at which the tea specials were operated resulted in at least two serious accidents on the Pacific slope alone.

Freight rates soon became a contentious issue in the Interior communities, for the railroads charged less to ship eastern goods all the way through to the West Coast. In March 1884 businessmen in Pendleton and Walla Walla universally denounced newly established tariffs ". . . making greater discrimination in favor of Portland as against the Interior towns than ever before," and accused the railroads of compelling them ". . . to feed the Portland merchants."[35] The companies, for their part, argued that the coastal points had to have lower rates to compete with ocean shipping, and steadfastly refused to grant concessions. The Inland Rates controversy lasted as long as the railroads enjoyed a monopoly of overland transportation and was the subject of recurring litigation.

Farmers, meanwhile, complained about the rates charged for shipping grain. In September 1884 OR&N charged $7 per ton, or 21 cents per bushel, to move wheat from Pendleton to Portland. Out of a total price of 32 cents per bushel farmers were thus left with 11 cents.[36] Early in the following month the rate was reduced to $6 per ton, provided that shipments were made by October 15. The intention, apparently, was to extend the shipping season to achieve better utilization of the available cars. The farmers, however, complained of being forced to sell their grain before the price reached its peak.[37] In 1885, the Northern Pacific Railroad, seeking a way of balancing predominantly westbound loaded traffic, offered to haul grain from Ainsworth to Duluth for $8 per ton. With lower ocean shipping charges farmers could have gained 10 cents per bushel, but those living in the Pendleton and Walla Walla areas had no independent means of getting their wheat to Ainsworth.[38] Another four years were to pass before OR&N was confronted with meaningful competition in the grain-growing areas of the southern Interior.

Compared with prevailing wage rates, railway passenger fares were quite high. In 1881 a regular one-way ticket from Walla Walla to Portland[39] cost $14 and round-trip excursions were advertized at $16.50.[40] In May 1885, the Oregon legislature, in regulatory mood, decreed that passenger fares charged by railroads operating in the state be set at 4 cents per mile for adults and 3 cents for children, and obliged ministers of the church to pay full fare. The one-way tariff between Walla Walla and Portland was thus reduced to $10.45.[41] Meals taken at eating houses en route generally cost $1.00 each and added to the expense of a trip.

Before the introduction of dining cars meal stops were the order of the day. OR&N trains on the Portland to Walla Walla run stopped twenty minutes at both Bonneville and Wallula, while those crossing the Blue Mountains paused at Meacham. On the Northern Pacific, meanwhile, dinner was served at Ritzville. The eating houses and the railroad company hotels appear to have catered not only to passengers but also to railway men. The prime purpose of certain hotels, indeed, seems to have been to accommodate train crews laying over away from home. At Heron, for example, the Northern Pacific's ". . . large, artistically finished . . ." hotel, opened on May 7, 1884, was said to make life ". . . much pleasanter for the U.S. Mail agents and train men on the Pend d'Oreille and Rocky Mountain divisions who lay over here."[42] When the company finally got around to promoting tourist traffic in the area in 1886, a new hotel with a fine view of Lake Pend d'Oreille was opened at Hope, Idaho, especially for the purpose.[43]

Among the various railroad employees there was a large spread in rates of pay. In 1881 OR&N paid three grades of locomotive engineers $90, $100, and $125 per month, while firemen and brakemen received only $66 per month. Laborers, meanwhile, earned $1.85 per day and the Chinese had to be content with $1.00.[44] Labor unrest, however, remained muted, for during the 1880s the railroad brotherhoods functioned primarily as mutual benefit societies. By 1885 the Brotherhood of Locomotive Engineers had nearly 300 locals with 17,000 members and had already paid out $1,650,000 to widows and orphans.[45] In that year BLE Willamette Division No. 277 was organized at East Portland and elected J. W. Miller, J. Kehoe, and J. McFadden as principal officers. The *Oregonian* of April 20, 1885, recorded that during the inaugural meeting:

> . . . a recess for refreshments was taken at Campi Restaurant. The tables were spread lavishly and attacked unsparingly, the general good humour characteristic of railroad men conspiring with the palatable viands in aiding digestion. Toasts were severally drunk to Division No. 236 (at The Dalles), Division No. 277, the OR&N Co., the O&C Co., and the Press, and when the toasts were disposed of the incense of Havanas, symbol of peace, brought the festivities to a fitting conclusion.[46]

Locomotive engineers, clearly, were gentlemen and not agitators. Militancy did not emerge until the rise of Eugene V. Debs's American Railway Union during the depression years of the 1890s. In the meantime the brotherhoods looked after their own and the railroad companies, to their credit, promoted and encouraged self-help schemes. In October 1885, for example, OR&N urged its employees ". . . to avail themselves of the opportunity to buy Portland General Hospital annual certificates," $5 per year for ward treatment and $10 per year for a private room. The arrangement with the hospital was made, it was said, ". . . with the intention of enabling every employee of this company, for a small sum within his reasonable command, to make provision for himself in case of sickness or accident."[47]

Railroaders were all too frequently injured, for the air brake was still in its infancy and the automatic coupler had not yet been invented. The lack of continuous train brakes demanded that men ride on the car roofs to screw down the hand brakes. Brakemen often fell between cars and were run over, and when derailments occurred they were thrown headlong to the ground and crushed beneath overturning vehicles. The old link and pin coupler, meanwhile, was a dangerous abomination costing many men their fingers and hands. Tramps stealing rides on the trains also suffered injuries, some accidental, some self-inflicted, and more at the hands of irate railroaders. In September 1883, a young man named Tom Dallam, riding on the brake beams of a westbound Northern Pacific freight, drank too much of his elderly companion's whiskey. Falling into a stupor, he allowed his legs to dangle on the track, and when the railroaders at

Cocolalla found him, his feet had been completely worn away.[48] Hardly more fortunate was Adolph Lendburg, who was thrown off Northern Pacific freight No. 13 by an overzealous brakeman, and suffered a broken leg. He lay beside the track 8 miles east of Ritzville for twelve hours until the station agent was forced by the sheriff to send out a handcar to pick him up.[49] Railroaders' brutality, however, occasionally backfired, as happened near Sprague in January 1886, when passenger brakeman Harry Kilduff, who was trying to eject a tramp, got thrown off the train himself![50]

Between 1881 and 1886 trains running in the Columbia Interior were hauled by quite small locomotives using wood for fuel. "American Standard" 4-4-0 engines drew the passenger trains, while "Mogul" 2-6-0 engines pulled the freights. The American Standard locomotive had a uniquely flexible three-point suspension system enabling it to run at quite high speeds on relatively poor track. Lack of adhesion, however, restricted the starting tractive effort, and the small firegrate placed a severe limit upon power output at speed. While the engines occasionally ran at phenomenally high speeds with featherweight special trains, they were unable to achieve more than about 30 mph with day-to-day loads. The Moguls used in freight service had more adhesion and could develop a higher tractive effort but produced about the same power output at lower speed. Freight cars were still small and carried only about 15-ton loads. Nevertheless, thirty cars was considered to be a longish train and forty cars drew comment in the press. On the steeper gradients two, and sometimes three, locomotives were used. In the Blue Mountains two locomotives were needed to haul twenty-two loaded cars, and on the 3-1/2 percent grade between Starbuck and the Alto summit a pair of engines, struggling hard, could only manage fourteen cars.[51] In wet weather wood was poor fuel and locomotive performance suffered. Cordwood, moreover, was bulky and took a lot of handling. In January 1882 a hundred cords a day had to be shipped up-river from points west of The Dalles for use on the OR&N lines in the Interior.[52] It was no surprise therefore, that when coal became available it was quickly adopted as the universal locomotive fuel. In 1883 OR&N began to use Newcastle coal shipped from Seattle to Portland by sea. The supply, however, was limited and delivery was sometimes interrupted by bad weather. Northern Pacific continued to use wood on their lines east of the Cascade Mountains until late in 1886, when a plentiful supply of good, low cost, steam coal was secured from mines at Roslyn, on the upper Yakima. Thereafter, the company's locomotives never regularly burned wood again.

During the first six years of railway operations in the Columbia Interior accidents were surprisingly few. In no case was a fare-paying passenger killed or injured. This fortunate state of affairs was probably due to the new condition of the track and rolling stock, the low traffic density, and very modest train speeds. Accidents occurring after the various lines had been handed over to railway company operating departments, and reported in the press, fell into the following categories.

Collisions between trains: head-on 1; rear-end 0; with work trains 3; during switching operations 2.

Collisions with obstructions: due to rockslides 2; due to cattle 1.

Derailments: due to track defect 0; due to vehicle defect 3; due to misplaced switch 1; due to shifting cargo 1; unexplained 2.

Train falling through open swing bridge: 1.

Snowplowing accidents: 2.

Unspecified "wreck": 1.

Total: 20.

The first accident of any consequence was a collision between a westbound special and a work train, occurring near Cheney on December 23, 1881. Northern Pacific Rule No. 7 required any extra or special train on the territory of a work train to flag around all curves and obscure places. In other words, a flagman was to proceed on foot half a mile ahead of the extra to given warning of its approach. When locomotive engineer Ellis was given his orders to run from Hangtown to Ainsworth as a special, he was told the work train was between Spokane Falls and Cheney, and he acknowledged receipt of the information. However, he failed completely to send out a flagman, and despite pleas from his conductor to slow down was still running at speed when the collision occurred. At least one person was killed and both Ellis and the conductor, whose name was also Ellis, were arrested on charges of negligence and manslaughter.[53] Another very similar accident occurred 8 miles east of Ritzville on August 17, 1882.[54]

In the case of derailments nobody was usually blamed. Such was the case on February 24, 1882, when the rear truck of a passenger coach attached to the tail end of a service train came off the track between Cheney and Marshall. The train hands sprang for the brakes and signaled for the enginemen to stop, but smoke from the two locomotives obscured the view. The passenger coach and a boxcar caboose slid down the embankment and threatened to drag the whole train with them, but a coupling broke and the remaining vehicles, including the locomotives, remained on the track. No one was injured.[55]

Rock slides presented a continuous hazard, especially in precipitous areas such as the Columbia Gorge. In July 1882 a freight train was swept off the track at the sliding mountain near the Cascades, and a valuable stationary engine, bound for Spokane Falls, was deposited in the river.[56] From time to time, areas of more gentle relief could also offer unpleasant surprises. At 6:15 a.m. on October 31, 1886, an OR&N grain extra, hurrying westward through a cut 2 miles east of Arlington, struck a large boulder that had rolled down onto the track. The engine and fifteen cars ended up in a huge heap of wreckage, and fireman Sanctus Silva and head-end brakeman T. F. Burke both lost their lives.[57]

Railroaders were frequently killed or injured when snowplow trains were bucking drifts. Wedge type snowplows, propelled by multiple locomotives, were driven pell-mell into the accumulated snow, with the result, all too frequently, that locomotives and tenders jack-knifed vertically, crushing the enginemen in their cabs. Thus, on December 27, 1884, a locomotive engineer named Hudson was fatally injured on board one of seven engines propelling the Blue Mountain snowplow westward from Hood River to the relief of a passenger train blockaded near Wyeth.[58] Two years later Charles Elks died of internal injuries sustained under similar circumstances at Wallula. In the latter case, Dr. Y. C. Blalock of Walla Walla made a heroic attempt to reach the scene of the accident, walking six miles through deep snow, but arrived too late to save the man's life.[59]

On any given line of railway the presence of a swing bridge was always an invitation for trains to plunge into the waters below. Ainsworth bridge was no exception, for on November 20, 1885, a train attempted to cross the Snake River when the drawspan was open, and the engine, along with its tender and at least one car, fell headlong into the shipping channel. Recovery was attempted in January 1886 but the divers were unable to endure the icy water. The operation was therefore called off until the following August. The tender was recovered fairly easily. Three times the locomotive was brought to the surface, however, and three times the lifting tackle broke. Tragedy then struck, for the Northern Pacific superintendent of construction, Alexander Shearer, who was directing operations, fell into the river and was drowned. Three frustrating weeks of difficult work were eventually required before the errant engine was brought to shore.[60]

A fascinating glimpse of railroad operations in the mid-1880s may be obtained from contemporary accounts[61] of the worst accident to occur in the Columbia Interior at that time. Those, remember, were the days before track circuits and automatic block signals, when safety depended entirely on the train order and the rule book and the manner in which they were interpreted.

At 5:00 in the morning of Friday, November 27, 1885, a fast tea special, 39 hours out of Portland, drew briskly into Missoula, Montana. The crew had gained valuable time on the run from Heron but the train's early arrival disrupted plans for its onward journey. Missoula train dispatcher J. G. Bristol had already sent orders to Bearmouth for regular express freight No. 13 westbound to meet the tea special at Turah, and to run 25 mph from Bearmouth to Turah to avoid delay. An advance in the tea train's schedule meant that it would reach Turah before the freight and be forced to stop there. As the company had stressed that the tea specials were to be kept moving, Bristol felt obliged to make revised arrangements for a meet at Wallace, 6 miles east of Turah. With some misgivings he therefore disregarded a rule requiring train crews to be given their orders at least one station ahead of meeting points, and instructed night operator W. D. McGee at Wallace to hold the freight there for a meet. Upon receipt of the message McGee duly hung out a green light as a signal for No. 13 to stop.

According to the company's rules all trains had to halt at night telegraph stations to obtain written clearance orders, which were to be picked up by the conductor and passed to the engineer. Most crews, however, abbreviated the procedure. When a train approached such a station the engineer would reduce speed and take the orders from the operator without actually stopping. A whistle signal would then be given to tell the conductor that the orders had been picked up, and normal speed would be resumed. Company officials were well aware of this practice, but because it saved time they turned a blind eye to it. Unfortunately, on that particular night, circumstances combined to transform such rule-bending into an infallible formula for disaster.

Engineer Michael Rech of the westbound freight was Belgian, aged about thirty-five, with no relatives in the United States. He was described as being ". . . an excellent workman, generally sober, and very popular among his acquaintances." Accompanying him on board the engine were relief fireman Alvin S. Moffat, head-end brakeman Frank Bohnert, and twenty-two-year-old William Andrews, the latter "working his way" from Butte to Portland to visit an elder sister. At the far end of the train, meanwhile, conductor W. D. Doremus and rear-end brakeman S. M. Burrus shared the caboose with an unofficial passenger named Fitzgerald.

To Michael Rech, his orders were clear. He was to meet the tea special at Turah and make every effort to get into the hole there before it arrived. The company had emphasized the importance of the tea trains and he had no desire to be blamed for any delay. He therefore planned to run at reduced speed through Wallace and then push on quickly westward to Turah. As the train approached the Wallace depot he shut off steam and slowed down. Despite a warning whistle blast, however, no one emerged from the station building. Certainly there was a green light indicating, theoretically, that he should stop. The rules, however, said that he should stop anyway, and, in practice, unless he received a clear hand signal to halt, he always ran by. If the engine passed the depot before the operator came out the orders could always be handed to the conductor. Impatiently Rech gave two short blasts on the whistle to tell the trainmen to release the car brakes. Then, as the train began to roll easily onwards, he dropped the Johnson bar to the far end of its quadrant and opened the throttle wide. Hearing the whistle blasts and the quickening beat of the engine, conductor Doremus naturally assumed that clearance had been received. Without looking back, he therefore settled into his seat for the remaining 6 miles to Turah.

In the Wallace telegraph office McGee and several prospective passengers heard No. 13 approaching. As the train slowed down the engine whistled but McGee made no move to go outside. The engine passed the building and whistled again, two shorts to throw off the brakes, and still McGee sat there. Somebody said, "He's not going to stop," but McGee merely pointed to the green light outside the window. "He'll stop," he said. At that moment the engine was given steam again and the train began to gather speed. As the occupants of the telegraph office stared at each other in disbelief the caboose rolled smoothly by, and before any of them could collect their wits No. 13 had disappeared down the line.

At Missoula a fresh engine was put on the tea train, and within a few minutes the cars and their precious Oriental cargo were rolling eastward again. Engineer J. B. Waite and his fireman, Norman Rice, were determined not to waste any time. When the train passed through Turah, it was already running at 25 mph. The collision occurred suddenly. On a sharp curve 2 miles beyond Turah, Waite caught a glimpse of light from No. 13's headlamp, reflected momentarily on the rocks. He yelled to Rice, who was on the other side of the engine, and then jumped. In the following instant both locomotives and a dozen cars were completely wrecked, and five men were killed or mortally injured. Confronted on his own side by a sheer rock face, Rice attempted to cross the cab, but he was too late. His leg was badly crushed above the knee and he received serious internal injuries. Following an amputation he died in the hospital two days later. Head-end brakeman Thomas Devine of the tea train (who was riding on the roof of the first car), fireman Alvin Moffat of No. 13, and young William Andrews, were all killed instantly. The unfortunate Michael Rech was trapped in the wreckage of his engine and terribly scalded by escaping steam. He died a painful death at Missoula later the same morning, saying at last that ". . . he forgave the man whose fault caused the accident."

A Coroners Jury ruled the following week that the collision had been caused by ". . . the disregard of orders of the NPRR Co. and the nonattention to signals at Wallace Station MT on the part of M. L. Rech, engineer of train No. 13," and that ". . . W. Doremus, the conductor of 13 is censurable in not seeing that the said orders and signals were obeyed." The jury further found that ". . . J. G. Bristol, dispatcher at Missoula, did not use sufficient discretion in arranging a meeting place for the trains." Of telegraph operator W. D. McGee's omissions nothing was said at all.

EPILOGUE

When Henry Villard's railroad empire disintegrated, the Oregon & Transcontinental Co. retained control of Oregon Railway & Navigation Co. and resolved to use it to best advantage. In an attempt to recoup their recent losses, the O&T directors sought to lease the OR&N property to Northern Pacific at an exorbitant rental. The Philadelphia group controlling that company, however, rejected the proposition, preferring instead to build their own line from Pasco over the Cascade Mountains to Puget Sound. In April 1887 O&T leased OR&N to Union Pacific, but the opening of the Northern Pacific Cascade branch immediately took away much of the traffic. With revenue reduced, the rental threatened to be an impossible burden for Union Pacific alone to bear. In a desperate bid to secure redress, O&T tried to buy control of Northern Pacific but due to a minor panic on the stock market became financially overextended. They then had to appeal to German banks for help. Prostrated by the cost of building the Cascade branch, Northern Pacific was forced to do likewise, and the door was opened to outside arbitration of differences. Henry Villard, who had recently returned to America as financial agent of the Deutsche Bank of Berlin, was thus drawn back into the Northwest railroad arena.

In order to provide O&T with a 6 percent return on OR&N stock, without excessively encumbering one railroad company, Villard proposed that Northern Pacific should join Union Pacific in a joint lease of the OR&N property. Moreover, to prevent duplication of lines and eliminate unnecessary competition, he insisted that Northern Pacific and OR&N again be given separate zones of influence north and south of the Snake River. In the financial centers of the east Villard's proposal was well enough received, but in Oregon its territorial provisions were considered outrageously unfair. In March 1888 Portland capitalists, who wanted the OR&N lines extended northeastward to serve their interests in the Coeur d'Alene mines, secured an injunction preventing the company's Oregon directors from ratifying the joint lease agreement. The scheme fell through, and within two months OR&N set out to build railways to both Wallace and Spokane Falls. Later that year Villard introduced an alternative proposal for joint-trust ownership of the lines in the Interior, but it, too, was rejected, and for the same reasons. In April 1889 Union Pacific backed out, precipitating a struggle for control of O&T. In a hard-fought stock market battle Villard prevented Union Pacific and their newfound St. Paul, Minneapolis, & Manitoba allies from gaining a foothold on the way to outright control of Northern Pacific. His opponents, however, threatened to bring in Oregon legislation denying O&T control of OR&N, and to that extent his victory was pyrrhic. On June 17, 1889, a compromise was reached and the over-lapping ownership of the Northern Pacific Railroad and Oregon Railway & Navigation companies was at last brought to an end. Paying dearly, Union Pacific assumed sole control of OR&N, and O&T became little more than a fund-raising auxiliary to Northern Pacific.

Throughout the 1880s the financial condition of the Northwest's railroads worsened. Between 1880 and 1885 the Villard companies built 900 miles of main line guiding two transcontinental routes to a single extremity at Portland.[1] During the next six years the Northern Pacific and OR&N companies more than doubled the railway mileage in the Columbia Interior. The benefits of expansion, however, remained elusive. Of all the additional lines, only the Northern Pacific Cascade branch could be termed a "trunk route," and it drew traffic away from the existing Columbia Valley road. The remainder, amounting to more than a thousand route miles, consisted of secondary lines of limited earning capacity, often paralleling each other to common destinations. As time went on, payment of interest on the money borrowed to build these competing railways and the cost of operating them became onerous burdens for the old companies to bear. Dilution of income, moreover, bode ill for hard times ahead. In November 1887 Southern Pacific gained access to Portland, and in January 1893 Great Northern completed a new main line to Puget Sound. Northern Pacific spent large sums of money upgrading their road to compete with Hill's Great Northern, while Union Pacific struggled with the cost of purchasing OR&N. After the near failure of the London financial house of Baring Brothers in November 1890, money became tighter throughout the world. The Northern and Union Pacific companies tried desperately to survive on short-term loans, but in the end both of them were overtaken by the great financial collapse of 1893.

The revitalization of the bankrupt railroads took several years to complete. Under the auspices of J. P. Morgan & Company, investment bankers, a new Northern Pacific Railway Co. took over the assets of the old Northern Pacific Railroad on August 31, 1896. Because of the need to satisfy financial obligations to the United States government, the resurrection of the Union Pacific took longer. The reorganization process, spearheaded by Kuhn, Loeb, & Company, was not finally completed and the property handed over to the new Union Pacific Railroad until January 1, 1898. Meanwhile, OR&N, which had fallen by the wayside in 1893, emerged from separate metamorphosis as the independent Oregon Railroad & Navigation Co. Among the northwestern lines only James J. Hill's Great Northern Railway survived the debacle. Allied with Morgan, Hill became a power in the land. Great Northern and Northern Pacific formed a defensive alliance and agreed to share traffic at points, such as Butte, where their lines overlapped. Hill, moreover, encouraged the directors of the Oregon Short Line and Oregon Railroad & Navigation companies to remain independent from the new Union Pacific Railroad and exchange traffic with all comers. The Union Pacific president, Edward H. Harriman, however, outwitted Hill, and in 1899 the old subsidiaries were brought back into the fold.

As economic conditions improved the railroads prospered as never before. Earnings were ploughed back into the new companies, and unprecedented improvements were made. Reinvestment of the profits strengthened the ability to produce ever greater returns, and the wealth and power of the railroad companies grew apace. Inevitably, conflict occurred between the rival groups. By 1901 Hill had gained control, not only of Northern Pacific, but also of the Chicago Burlington & Quincy. Harriman, meanwhile, married Union Pacific and Southern Pacific. Allying himself with James Stillman of National City Bank and William Rockefeller of the Standard Oil Company, he attempted to wrench Northern Pacific from Hill's grasp. The resulting stock market battle, which very nearly caused another financial collapse, ended in a standoff. Sobered by the side effects of the struggle, the participants agreed to establish a holding company in which their respective interests in Northern Pacific, Great Northern, and Chicago Burlington & Quincy would be vested. The Northern Securities Company, as it was called, was incorporated in the state of New Jersey on November 12, 1901, and was thought to be large enough to deter any other group from attempting to purchase control.

The founders of the huge company, however, failed to reckon with Theodore Roosevelt, who made its dissolution an election issue. In February 1902 the United States Government brought suit against the Northern Securities Company, claiming that it violated the Sherman Anti-Trust Act of 1890. The case was hard-fought but the courts upheld the government's position, and in 1904 the company was ordered dissolved. The Harriman-Rockefeller group then tried to recover their investment in terms of Northern Pacific shares alone and another court case ensued. A decision of 1905, however, allowed Hill to retain separate controlling interests in all three companies. Having failed to gain control of Northern Pacific, the Rockefeller faction then set out to extend their Chicago, Milwaukee, & St. Paul Railroad westward to Butte and eventually all the way to Puget Sound, paralleling the Northern Pacific for over 400 miles.

By 1900 the advantages of the Columbia Gateway had again become clear. The shipping channel between Portland and the open sea, moreover, had been greatly improved. When Harriman regained control of OR&N, Hill had to decide whether to pay high charges for using it or build his own railway on the other side of the valley. For several years he hesitated, but the need to secure the right banks of the Snake and Columbia rivers to prevent their use by the Milwaukee Road eventually forced his hand. At great expense, the Spokane, Portland & Seattle Railway, jointly owned by Great Northern and Northern Pacific, was completed between Vancouver, Washington, and Kennewick in March 1908 and extended from Ainsworth Junction to Fort Wright Junction (Spokane) in May 1909. Harriman then sought to restore the balance of power.

During the early years of the century, the greatest unresolved problem arising from the legacy of the old companies was that of Union Pacific access to Puget Sound. The compromise agreement between the Oregon & Transcontinental Co. and the old Union Pacific Railway, made in June 1889, originally included at least a verbal understanding that Union Pacific would be allowed to use Northern Pacific trackage between Portland and Tacoma. The Northern Pacific Railroad Co., however, quickly welched on any such commitment. In April 1890 Union Pacific consequently organized a subsidiary named Portland & Puget Sound Railroad, and set out to build their own line to Seattle. Unfortunately, within a year financial difficulty intervened. Construction was then suspended and never resumed. When Hill began to build the Spokane, Portland & Seattle Railway, Harriman decided that the time had at last come for Union Pacific to gain access to Puget Sound. To avoid the expense of building a Union Pacific line, pressure was brought to bear on Northern Pacific to concede trackage and traffic rights on the Kalama route. The Northern Pacific Railway put up a strong resistance and did not offer reasonable terms until Union Pacific made threatening moves to build yet another railroad through the Cascade Mountains. In May 1909 the long-sought concessions were granted. Implementation of the agreement between the two companies, however, was delayed by further hostilities in central Oregon, provoked by the aging Hill himself. Union Pacific trains began to run between Portland and Seattle on January 1, 1910, and with the settlement of the Deschutes Canyon dispute two months later, peace eventually descended on the Northwest railway scene. Unfortunately, by that time the railroads were already beginning to feel the first effects of competition from road motor transport.

In 1914 the outbreak of war in Europe brought further investment in new railways to an abrupt end. Three years later American entry into the conflict resulted in the railroads being brought under government control, which was not relinquished until 1920. The western roads then felt the combined impact of the post-war slump and the opening of the Panama Canal. Only brief recovery preceded the Depression of the 1930s, and before the railroads could recover from those lean years they were called upon to perform the prodigious feats of transportation associated with the Second World War. Afterwards, economic emphasis was unfortunately placed on other forms of transport, and the railways, burdened by the mass of regulation imposed on them over the years, deteriorated into a condition from which it seemed they might not recover. Eventually, profound changes, not the least of which was the long-delayed union of the Hill lines in Burlington Northern, turned the situation around. During the 1970s operations were rationalized and a fresh commitment was made to improving and maintaining track. In 1980 the Staggers Act removed many of the handicaps imposed by government regulation and set the railroads free to compete with other modes of transportation.

In the Columbia Interior region, extending northward to the Canadian border; eastward to Columbia Falls and Missoula, Montana; southeastward to Huntington, Oregon; westward to the Stevens, Snoqualmie, and Stampede passes; and southwestward down the Columbia Valley to Portland, the record of railroad construction and abandonment, expressed in route miles, may be summarized as follows:

Period	Opened	Closed	Net Mileage at End of Period
Before 1880	70	0	70
1880-84	1,149	18	1,201
1885-93	1,877	4	3,074
1894-1914	2,989	151	5,912
1914-83	185	1,462	4,635
Totals	6,270	1,635	

These figures are only approximate and do not include or otherwise take into account subsequent line relocations.

Over the years the railways built between 1880 and 1884, being predominantly main lines, have fared relatively well. Indeed only 84 miles out of 1,149 have been abandoned and not replaced either by line relocation or track-sharing agreement. Between Ainsworth and Missoula the old Northern Pacific main line, albeit realigned and improved in many areas, remains virtually intact, various sections now forming parts of Burlington Northern's Portland, Spokane, and Rocky Mountain divisions. For some years the Pasco to Spokane section has been paired with the former Spokane, Portland & Seattle main line, the trains running in one direction only (currently eastbound through Ritzville and westbound through Washtucna). Between Spokane and Sandpoint, Idaho, all of Burlington Northern's traffic is concentrated on the former Northern Pacific line, thus making it the busiest stretch of railway in the whole Interior. Further east, however, two-thirds of all trains now use the Great Northern line to Whitefish, Montana. The abiding peace of the Clark Fork Valley, therefore is little disturbed. At Ainsworth the Snake River bridge has been rebuilt with an enormous lift span and heavier steelwork to carry Lewiston traffic no longer able to use the inundated Snake River Junction to Texas Ferry connection between the Northern Pacific lines and the Camas Prairie Railroad. Six of the original granite piers of the bridge are nevertheless still in use. Beyond the Wallula Gap the former OR&N lines, westward along the Columbia Valley to Portland and eastward over the Blue Mountains to La Grande and Huntington, now form the Oregon Division main line of the Union Pacific Railroad. Since 1915, trains from Pendleton to Portland have used the Munley cutoff between Echo and Coyote, leaving Umatilla to one side. With the exception of a remnant between Umatilla and

Irrigon, now used only for car storage, the Columbia Valley line between Coyote and Juniper has disappeared altogether. Union Pacific trains proceeding northeastward are now routed over a new connection between Hinkle and Juniper, and the first 10 miles of the old Baker City branch are only used for local traffic. Dr. Baker's road continues to link Wallula with Walla Walla, but OR&N's Pendleton-Walla Walla-Riparia line used in the 1890s as the southern part of a secondary main line from Pendleton to Spokane is now dismembered. Grain is no longer brought down Wild Horse Creek from Athena and Adams to Pendleton, and though the railway is still open between Walla Walla and Athena it carries little traffic. Further north, a daily way-freight is still worked from Walla Walla to Dayton, but it uses Burlington Northern (Northern Pacific-Hunt system) trackage beyond Waitsburg Junction.

The old OR&N line from Bolles Junction to Starbuck, once graced by through reclining chair cars and Pullman sleepers bound for Omaha, has been reduced to a 7-mile spur to the grain elevators at McKay. Beyond the end of track only a disjointed chain of washed-out embankments and weathered cuts mark Thielsen's route to Grange City. The line nevertheless evokes the spirit of railroad days gone by. High on the uplands, the Alto summit is a desolate and lonely place, overlooking a vast expanse of open country. At the north end of the cutting there, the wind blows strong and free, and if you listen to it and gaze intently at the scarred flank of the Kellogg Creek Valley, you can almost hear the engines and their helpers working hard on the long steep grade. After all, it was only a hundred years ago!

NOTES

CHAPTER 1 NORTHERN PACIFIC

[1]Eugene V. Smalley, *History of the Northern Pacific Railroad* (New York: G. P. Putnam's, 1883), pp. 57-67. Another proposal for a transcontinental railroad that gained some attention was forwarded in 1847 by George Wilkes in his *Proposal for a National Rail-Road to the Pacific Ocean for the Purpose of Obtaining a Short Route to Oregon and the Indies,* reprinted in New York in 1928.

[2]Isaac Ingalls Stevens, first governor of Washington Territory, commanded the U.S. Army railroad survey from Minnesota to Puget Sound in 1853-1854. His official report is contained in *Reports of Explorations and Surveys to Ascertain the Most Practicable and Economical Route for a Railroad from the Mississippi River to the Pacific Ocean, 1853-1854,* chap. 1, vol. 1, 1855, and vol. 12, bks. 1 and 2, 1860. Maps and survey profiles are found in vol. 11, 1861, of the same report. One of Stevens's surveyors, Lieutenant John Mullan, later supervised construction of a military wagon road along what he believed would be the best route for a railroad from Fort Benton to Fort Walla Walla. The route of the so-called "Mullan Road" differed considerably from what became the Northern Pacific Railroad route. The wagon road crossed the high, rugged Bitterroot Mountains over Lolo Pass in north central Idaho, while the railroad followed the more gentle gradient of the Clark Fork River to the north. For Mullan's survey and construction activities, see *Report on the Construction of a Military Road from Walla Walla to Fort Benton.* Senate Executive Document 43. 47th Congress, 3rd Session, 1863. See also, Smalley, *History of the Northern Pacific Railroad,* pp. 77-84.

[3]Ibid., pp. 106-110; Robert C. Athearn, *Union Pacific Country* (Chicago: Rand McNally, 1971), pp. 27-30; Stuart Daggett, *Railroad Reorganization* (Boston: Houghton Mifflin & Company, 1908), pp. 220-221.

[4]Ibid.

[5]Athearn, *Union Pacific Country,* pp. 98-101; *The Union Pacific Story* [A Centennial Brochure, 1969], p. 11. Promontory Point has long been the misnomer applied to the meeting place of the Central Pacific and Union Pacific railroads. The driving of the golden spike actually occurred on high ground in the Promontory Mountains many miles north of Promontory Point, which is situated on a peninsula jutting into the Great Salt Lake. At present, the Southern Pacific line crosses Promontory Point via the Lucien Cutoff, but the original meeting place was known as Promontory Summit, or simply Promontory.

[6]Smalley, *History of the Northern Pacific Railroad,* pp. 113-116; Daggett, *Railroad Reorganization,* pp. 263-264. A more recent history of the Northern Pacific can be found in Louis Tuck Renz, *The History of the Northern Pacific Railroad* (Fairfield, Washington: Ye Galleon Press, 1980).

[7]Smalley, *History of the Northern Pacific Railroad,* pp. 128-132.

[8]Ibid., pp. 141-146.

[8]Daggett, *Railroad Reorganization,* pp. 263-264; Smalley, *History of the Northern Pacific Railroad,* pp. 146 and 159-162.

[10]Smalley, *History of the Northern Pacific Railroad,* pp. 148-158. For additional details on Jay Cooke and the early development of the Northern Pacific, see John C. Harnsberger, *Jay Cooke and Minnesota: The Formative Years of the Northern Pacific Railroad, 1868-1873* (New York: Arno Press, 1981).

[11]Henrietta M. Larsen, *Jay Cooke—Private Banker* (New York: Greenwood Press, 1968—reprint of 1932 edition), pp. 261-262. See also, W. Milnor Roberts, *Special Report of a Reconnoissance [sic] of the Route of the Northern Pacific Railroad Between Lake Superior and Puget Sound via the Columbia River Made in 1863 by*

W. Milnor Roberts, U.S. Civil Engineer Under the Direction of Jay Cooke & Co., Bankers (Philadelphia: n.p., 1869); and Edward William Nolan, "Exploring the Northern Pacific Railroad Route: W. Milnor Roberts' Letters from the Expedition of 1869," unpublished M.A. thesis, University of Oregon, 1967.

[12]Smalley, *History of the Northern Pacific Railroad*, pp. 161-162.

[13]James Blaine Hedges, *Henry Villard and the Railways of the Northwest* (New Haven: Yale University Press, 1930), pp. 21-22.

[14]Smalley, *History of the Northern Pacific Railroad*, p. 164.

[15]Ibid., pp. 168-169.

[16]Daggett, *Railroad Reorganization*, p. 264; Smalley, *History of the Northern Pacific Railroad*, pp. 164-166.

[17]Larsen, *Jay Cooke*, pp. 277-278.

[18]Smalley, *History of the Northern Pacific Railroad*, p. 166.

[19]Ibid., pp. 185-186.

[20]Ibid.

[21]Ibid., pp. 187 and 426.

[22]Ibid., p. 169; Daggett, *Railroad Reorganization*, pp. 264-265.

[23]Larsen, *Jay Cooke*, pp. 345-347.

[24]Ibid., pp. 332, 349-353, 373-375, and 387; Smalley, *History of the Northern Pacific Railroad*, p. 188.

[25]Larsen, *Jay Cooke*, pp. 345 and 362-364.

[26]Ibid., pp. 376-377 and 381-382.

[27]Ibid.

[28]Smalley, *History of the Northern Pacific Railroad*, p. 188; Larsen, *Jay Cooke*, pp. 386-387.

[29]Smalley, *History of the Northern Pacific Railroad*, pp. 157-158.

[30]Ibid., pp. 187-188.

[31]Ibid., pp. 193-194; Hedges, *Henry Villard*, pp. 25-26.

[32]Northern Pacific Railroad Company, *Annual Report, 1872*.

[33]Athearn, *Union Pacific Country*, pp. 123-127; Charles P. Kindleberger, *Manias, Panics, and Crashes: A History of Financial Crises* (New York: Basic Books, 1978), pp. 109-110.

[34]Larsen, *Jay Cooke*, pp. 401-403.

[35]Ibid., pp. 399-401.

[36]Ibid., pp. 390-391 and 401-405.

[37]Kindleberger, *Manias, Panics and Crashes*, p. 106.

[38]Larsen, *Jay Cooke*, pp. 406-411; Daggett, *Railroad Reorganization*, p. 265.

[39]Smalley, *History of the Northern Pacific Railroad*, pp. 198-200.

[40]Ibid., pp. 426-427. For an added perspective on the early development of Tacoma and the role of the railroad in that city, see Herbert Hunt, *Tacoma, Its History and Its Builders: A Half Century of Activity* (Chicago: S. J. Clarke, 1916).

[41]NPRR Co. *Annual Report, 1876*.

[42]Ibid.

[43]NPRR Co. *Annual Report, 1872, 1874, 1876*.

[44]Smalley, *History of the Northern Pacific Railroad*, p. 214; Hedges, *Henry Villard*, pp. 63-64.

[45]Smalley, *History of the Northern Pacific Railroad*, pp. 206-210; Daggett, *Railroad Reorganization*, pp. 265-270.

[46]Smalley, *History of the Northern Pacific Railroad*, pp. 214-215; NPRR Co. *Annual Report, 1876, 1877, 1878*; Hedges, *Henry Villard*, p. 27.

[47]NPRR Co. *Annual Report, 1877*. By 1877 the Seattle and Walla Walla Railroad had been built fifteen miles, linking Puget Sound with the New Castle coal mines. Eventually the line became part of the Pacific Coast Railroad, providing connections

to the Milwaukee Road that crossed Snoqualmie Pass, the original goal of the Seattle and Walla Walla Railroad promoters. For information on that and other Washington railroads, major and minor, see Bruce Bissell Cheever, "The Development of Railroads in the State of Washington, 1860-1848," unpublished M.A. thesis, Western Washington College of Education, Bellingham, 1949.

[48]Smalley, *History of the Northern Pacific Railroad*, pp. 428-429.

[49]Ibid., p. 230; NPRR Co. *Annual Report, 1879.*

CHAPTER 2   OREGON STEAM NAVIGATION

[1]E. W. Wright, *Lewis and Dryden's Marine History of the Pacific Northwest* (New York: Antiquarian Press, 1961), reprint of 1895 edition, pp. 15-18.

[2]Ibid., pp. 28-29.

[3]Ibid., pp. 29-31.

[4]Donald W. Meinig, *The Great Columbia Plain: A Historical Geography, 1805-1910* (Seattle: University of Washington Press, 1968), p. 155.

[5]Wright, *Lewis and Dryden's Marine History*, pp. 51-52; Frank B. Gill, "Oregon's First Railway," *Oregon Historical Quarterly* 25:3 (Sept. 1924): 175.

[6]Wright, *Lewis and Dryden's Marine History*, pp. 35, 45, and 51.

[7]Meinig, *Great Columbia Plain*, chap. 7. For Governor Stevens's role in treaty-making, see Kent D. Richards, *Isaac I. Stevens: Young Man in a Hurry* (Provo, Utah: Brigham Young University Press, 1979).

[8]Wright, *Lewis and Dryden's Marine History*, pp. 51-52; Gill, *Oregon Historical Quarterly* 25:3 (Sept. 1924): 175.

[9]Wright, *Lewis and Dryden's Marine History*, p. 56; Randall V. Mills, *Sternwheelers Up Columbia* (Palo Alto: Pacific Books, 1947), p. 68; Gill, *Oregon Historical Quarterly* 25:3 (Sept. 1924): 177-178.

[10]Union Pacific Railroad Company (untitled) historical outline for the OSL and OWR&N, p. 7. This outline is an untitled, undated work, distributed to the public by the company upon request to their head office at Omaha, Nebraska. Meinig, *Great Columbia Plain*, p. 177; James L. Ehernberger, and Francis G. Gschwind, *Union Pacific Steam-Northwestern District* (Callaway, Nebraska: E. G. Publications, 1968), p. 71.

[11]Gill, *Oregon Historical Quarterly* 25:3 (Sept. 1924): 177.

[12]Ibid., p. 179.

[13]Ibid., pp. 182-189.

[14]Wright, *Lewis and Dryden's Marine History*, p. 50.

[15]Ibid., p. 65; Gill, *Oregon Historical Quarterly* 25:3 (Sept. 1924): 180-181.

[16]Wright, *Lewis and Dryden's Marine History*, pp. 72-73, n.

[17]Ibid., pp. 75 and 80-81.

[18]Ibid., p. 86; Gill, *Oregon Historical Quarterly* 25:3 (Sept. 1924): 190.

[19]Wright, *Lewis and Dryden's Marine History*, pp. 90-91; Meinig, *Great Columbia Plain*, pp. 212-213 and 213, n.; Gill, *Oregon Historical Quarterly* 25:3 (Sept. 1924): 190; Dorothy O. Johansen, "The Oregon Steam Navigation Company," *Pacific Historical Review* 10 (1941): 180-181. See also Dorothy O. Johansen, "Capitalism on the Far-Western Frontier: The Oregon Steam Navigation Company," unpublished Ph.D. diss., University of Washington, Seattle, 1941.

[20]Gill, *Oregon Historical Quarterly* 25:3 (Sept. 1924): 191.

[21]Ibid., pp. 189-190.

[22]Ibid., pp. 188-189.

[23]Ibid., pp. 197-212; Ehernberger and Gschwind, *Union Pacific Steam-Northwestern District*, pp. 70-72; Mills, *Sternwheelers Up Columbia*, pp. 69-70; UPRR Co.

(untitled) historical outline for OSL and OWR&N, p. 7. Note that "Pony" had cylinders 6 X 12 ins., driving wheels 34 ins., wheelbase 7 ft., weight 9700 lbs., boiler 36 ins. dia., firebox 33 X 18 ins., 67 tubes 1.25 ins. dia. by 25 ins. long, reduction gear drive, tractive effort 810 lbs.

[24] Gill, *Oregon Historical Quarterly* 25:3 (Sept. 1924): 197.

[25] Ibid., p. 208.

[26] Ibid., pp. 211-212.

[27] Ibid., pp. 212-214.

[28] Wright, *Lewis and Dryden's Marine History*, p. 91.

[29] Dorothy O. Johansen, *Empire of the Columbia* (New York: Harper & Row, 1967), p. 280; and Johansen, *Pacific Historical Review* 10: 182.

[30] Wright, *Lewis and Dryden's Marine History*, pp. 100-101.

[31] Meinig, *Great Columbia Plain*, pp. 213-214; Johansen, *Empire of the Columbia*, p. 279; Johansen, *Pacific Historical Review* 10: 182; Wright, *Lewis and Dryden's Marine History*, p. 107.

[32] Wright, *Lewis and Dryden's Marine History*, p. 106.

[33] Mills, *Sternwheelers Up Columbia*, pp. 71-72; Meinig, *Great Columbia Plain*, p. 213; George W. Abdill, *This Was Railroading* (Seattle: Superior Books, 1958), pp. 11-12.

[34] Mills, *Sternwheelers Up Columbia*, p. 71; Abdill, *This Was Railroading*, pp. 11-12 and 90.

[35] Wright, *Lewis and Dryden's Marine History*, p. 51, n.

[36] Abdill, *This Was Railroading*, pp. 10-11 and 14-17.

[37] UPRR Co. (untitled) historical outline for OSL and OWR&N, p. 7; Ehernberger and Gschwind, *Union Pacific Steam-Northwestern District*, pp. 71-72; Mills, *Sternwheelers Up Columbia*, p. 71.

[38] Wright, *Lewis and Dryden's Marine History*, p. 125.

[39] Ibid., 115.

[40] Ibid., pp. 123-124.

[41] Ibid., p. 81.

[42] Ibid., p. 138; Mills, *Sternwheelers Up Columbia*, p. 86.

[43] Ibid., pp. 145 and 181-183.

[44] For firsthand accounts of the *Mary Moody* on Lake Pend Oreille, see Thomas Francis Meagher, "Rides Through Montana," *Harper's New Monthly Magazine* 35 (1867): 572-573 [entire article includes pp. 568-583] and "Around the Lake in the Year 1866," reprinted in the *Sandpoint Northern Idaho News*, 21 December 1920, p. 6. For more on the *Mary Moody*, as well as on the steamboats *Cabinet* and *Missoula*, and their roles in transportation development on the Clark Fork River before completion of the Northern Pacific, see Bette E. Meyer, "The Pend Oreille Routes to Montana, 1866-1870," *Pacific Northwest Quarterly* 72 (1981): 80-82 [entire article includes pp. 76-83] and Fritz Timmen, *Blow for the Landing: A Hundred Years of Steam Navigation on the Waters of the West* (Caxton Press: Caldwell, Id., 1973), pp. 125-126.

[45] Ibid., pp. 194-195.

[46] Ibid., p. 206.

[47] Ibid., p. 248; Mills, *Sternwheelers Up Columbia*, pp. 48-49.

[48] Wright, *Lewis and Dryden's Marine History*, p. 258.

[49] Ibid., p. 249.

[50] Ibid., p. 257.

[51] Ibid., p. 239.

[52] Ibid., pp. 249 and 410-411.

[53] Ibid., p. 250.

[54] Ibid., p. 258.

[55]Mills, *Sternwheelers Up Columbia*, p. 43.

[56]W. W. Baker, "The Building of the Walla Walla & Columbia River Railroad," *Washington Historical Quarterly* 14 (Jan. 1923): 3-13; *Railroad Gazette*, 13 February 1880, p. 96.

[57]Note that *Spokane* was built in 32 days, 6 hours, which suggests that during 1877 the boat builders were indeed under pressure to produce vessels rapidly; Wright, *Lewis and Dryden's Marine History*, p. 250.

[58]Meining, *Great Columbia Plain*, p. 214.

[59]*Railroad Gazette* 6 May 1881, p. 255.

[60]Meining, *Great Columbia Plain*, p. 256, n.

[61]Wright, *Lewis and Dryden's Marine History*, p. 268.

CHAPTER 3   HENRY VILLARD'S DEBUT

[1]Hedges, *Henry Villard*, p. 6.

[2]Ibid., p. 7.

[3]Ibid., pp. 7-8; Johansen, *Empire of the Columbia*, p. 309.

[4]Hedges, *Henry Villard*, p. 9; Johansen, *Empire of the Columbia*, pp. 309-310.

[5]Hedges, *Henry Villard*, pp. 10-11; Johansen, *Empire of the Columbia*, p. 310; Smalley, *History of the Northern Pacific Railroad*, p. 252.

[6]Smalley, *History of the Northern Pacific Railroad*, pp. 245-260; Benjamin Whitesmith, *Henry Villard and the Development of Oregon*, WPA Project, (Eugene: University of Oregon, 1940); Henry Villard, ed. by Oswald Garrison Villard, *The Early History of Transportation in Oregon* (Eugene: University of Oregon, 1944). At the authors request publication was delayed for many years. It first appeared in print in 1926 in serial form in the Portland fflIOregonian. It was then published as a monograph by the University of Oregon, Eugene, Oregon in March 1944.

[7]Smalley, *History of the Northern Pacific Railroad*, p. 254; Hedges, *Henry Villard*, pp. 12-14; Wright, *Lewis and Dryden's Marine History*, p. 196.

[8]Wright, *Lewis and Dryden's Marine History*, p. 238.

[9]Smalley, *History of the Northern Pacific Railroad*, pp. 255-256; Hedges, *Henry Villard*, pp. 15-17; Wright, *Lewis and Dryden's Marine History*, pp. 238, 242, 266-267 and 274.

[10]Note that the ruinous rate cutting was due not only to the Pacific Coast Steamship Co., formed in 1877, but also to Pierre B. Cornwall's side-wheeler *Great Republic*; Henry Villard, *Memoirs of Henry Villard: Vol. 2* (Boston: Houghton Mifflin & Co., 1904); Wright, *Lewis and Dryden's Marine History*, pp. 256-257 and 265-266.

[11]Smalley, *History of the Northern Pacific Railroad*, pp. 254-255; Hedges, *Henry Villard*, p. 56; Athearn, *Union Pacific Country*, p. 226.

[12]Athearn, *Union Pacific Country*, pp. 312-313, quotation; Villard, *Memoirs*, p. 284; UPRR Co. (untitled) historic outline for OSL and OWR&N, pp. 1-2.

[13]Villard, *Memoirs*, pp. 284-285; Smalley, *History of the Northern Pacific Railroad*, pp. 256-257.

[14]Villard, *Memoirs*, pp. 284-285; Smalley, *History of the Northern Pacific Railroad*, p. 256; Hedges, *Henry Villard*, p. 56.

[15]Villard, *Memoirs*, p. 287; Smalley, *History of the Northern Pacific Railroad*, pp. 257-258; Athearn, *Union Pacific Country*, pp. 314-315.

CHAPTER 4   WALLA WALLA & COLUMBIA RIVER

[1]The *Adeline Elwood* also took one hundred cases of salmon with a view to introducing it to the English market. Wright, *Lewis and Dryden's Marine History*, p. 178.

[2]Baker, *Building of the WW&CRR*, p. 4; *An Illustrated History of South Eastern Washington* (Spokane: Western Historical Publishing Co., 1906), p. 91.

[3]Baker, *Building of the WW&CRR*, pp. 4-5; Miles C. Moore, "A Pioneer Railroad Builder," *Oregon Historical Quarterly* 12 (June 1911): 171-189; *Weekly Statesman*, 4 June 1881. All of these sources give different lists of persons named as promoters or stockholders. The only individuals whose names are mentioned in more than one account were: D. S. Baker, J. F. Boyer, A. Kyger (or Kegger), Wm. H. Newell, B. F. Stone, B. L. Sharpstein and Wm. Stevens (or Stephens).

[4]*An Illustrated History of South Eastern Washington*, p. 97.

[5]Baker, *Building of the WW&CRR*, p. 5; Moore, *Oregon Historical Quarterly* 12 (June 1911): 197.

[6]Baker, *Building of the WW&CRR*, pp. 3-4; Moore, *Oregon Historical Quarterly* 12 (June 1911): 195-196; *Dr. Baker's Railroad* (Walla Walla: Walla Walla City – County Bicentennial Committee, 1976), pp. 3-4.

[7]Baker, *Building of the WW&CRR*, p. 6.

[8]*An Illustrated History of South Eastern Washington*, p. 97. *Dr. Baker's Railroad*, p. 23, gives the full text of Tilton's report.

[9]Baker, *Building of the WW&CRR*, p. 5.

[10]Ibid., pp. 8-9.

[11]*Beacon*, 6 October 1873; Baker, *Building of the WW&CRR*, p. 9.

[12]*Beacon*, 6 October 1873.

[13]Baker, *Building of the WW&CRR*, p. 7.

[14]Ibid.; Moore, *Oregon Historical Quarterly* 12 (June 1911): 198.

[15]*Dr. Baker's Railroad*, p. 22; UPRR (untitled) historical outline for OSL and OWR&N, p. 8, which gives the date of arrival of the first train as October 30, 1875.

[16]Baker, *Building of the WW&CRR*, p. 11; Moore, *Oregon Historical Quarterly* 12 (June 1911): 198; *Weekly Statesman*, 15 September 1877, advertisement.

[17]*Weekly Statesman*, 8 September 1877.

[18]Baker, *Building of the WW&CRR*, p. 11.

[19]Moore, *Oregon Historical Quarterly* 12 (June 1911): 199.

[20]*Weekly Statesman*, 9 March 1878.

[21]*Weekly Statesman*, 12 October 1878; George Abdill, *This Was Railroading* (Seattle: Superior Books, 1958), p. 60, ill.

[22]*Weekly Statesman*, 15 November 1879, quotation.

[23]Baker, *Building of the WW&CRR*, p. 10; *Railroad Gazette* 13 February 1880, p. 96.

[24]*Weekly Statesman*, 15 September 1877 and 3 November 1877.

[25]*Weekly Statesman*, 29 September 1877. There was great concern that the sacks would shrink and the grain would swell, thus leading to burst sacks. The sacks were carried on flat cars.

[26]Baker, *Building of the WW&CRR*, p. 12.

[27]Ibid., p. 8.

[28]*Weekly Statesman*, 29 December 1877.

[29]Baker, *Building of the WW&CRR*, p. 13; *Weekly Statesman*, 5 July 1879; *Railroad Gazette*, 16 January 1880, p. 31.

[30]*Weekly Statesman*, 20 September 1879.

[31]Meinig, *Great Columbia Plain*, p. 255.

[32]*Weekly Statesman*, 8 September 1877.

[33]Ibid., 23 August 1879.

[34]Ibid.

[35]Baker, *Building of the WW&CRR*, p. 8, quotation.

[36]Abdill, *This Was Railroading*, pp. 59 and 61-62; *Weekly Statesman* 23 August 1879; Cornelius W. Hauck, "Six Little Porters From Walla Walla," *Colorado Rail Annual* 5 (1967), published by the Colorado Railroad Museum, Golden, Colorado. *Mountain Queen* was sent to the Mill Creek railroad in 1881 (*Weekly Statesman*, 6 August 1881) and two other engines went to the Cascades railroad (*Railroad Gazette*, 6 April 1883, p. 224). A "new" engine was received by the Mill Creek line soon after the OR&N takeover (*Union*, 3 March 1888). *Mountain Queen* was then sent to The Dalles for repairs and returned soon afterwards (*Union*, 16 June 1888).

[37]Baker, *Building of the WW&CRR*, p. 12.

[38]*Railroad Gazette*, 21 May 1880, p. 279, 28 January 1881, pp. 50 and 59, and 11 March 1881, p. 150.

[39]*Union*, 27 November 1880.

[40]*Weekly Statesman*, 3 February 1883; *Railroad Gazette*, 23 February 1883 and 6 April 1883; Ehrenberger and Gschwind, *Union Pacific*, pp. 85-86; Meinig, *Great Columbia Plain*, p. 260, n.

[41]Baker *Building of the WW&CRR*, pp. 12-13; Moore, *A Pioneer Railroad Builder*, p. 200; Meinig, *Great Columbia Plain*, p. 299, n.; *Weekly Statesman*, 6 August 1881, 4 March 1882, 10 June 1882, and 19 August 1882.

[42]*Weekly Statesman*, 19 August 1882. Baker first offered the clay to the City of Walla Walla for making bricks to build schools.

[43]*Union*, 7 August 1886.

[44]*Oregonian*, 29 June 1888. The narrow gauge was extended about 300 yards into the Penitentiary grounds in August 1888 (*Oregonian*, 7 August 1888). The railway began hauling clay to the institution in March 1889 (*Union*, 9 March 1889).

[45]*Union*, 3 September 1887 and 8 October 1887.

CHAPTER 5   OREGON RAILWAY & NAVIGATION

[1]Smalley, *History of the Northern Pacific Railroad*, pp. 258-259; Villard, *Memoirs*, p. 288; Hedges, *Henry Villard*, pp. 57-58.

[2]Villard, *Memoirs*, p. 288, quotation; Hedges, *Henry Villard*, pp. 60-61.

[3]Smalley, *History of the Northern Pacific Railroad*, p. 259; Wright, *Lewis and Dryden's Marine History*, p. 268.

[4]Villard, *Memoirs*, p. 289.

[5]Hedges, *Henry Villard*, pp. 59-60; *Weekly Statesman*, 14 June 1879 and 2 August 1879.

[6]Villard, *Memoirs*, p. 288; Hedges, *Henry Villard*, p. 57; *Weekly Statesman*, 19 July 1879.

[7]Villard, *Memoirs*, p. 288.

[8]*Weekly Statesman*, 3 January 1880; *Railroad Gazette*, 2 January 1880, p. 11 and 6 February 1880, p. 84.

[9]Hedges, *Henry Villard*, p. 60.

[10]Ibid., p. 62.

[11]Ibid., pp. 62-63.

[12]*Weekly Statesman*, 23 August 1879, quotation.

[13]Ibid., 15 November 1879, 27 December 1879 and 17 January 1880.

[14]*Railroad Gazette*, 2 January 1880, p. 11; *Weekly Statesman*, 3 January 1880.

[15]*Railroad Gazette*, 6 February 1880, p. 84, quotation; Hedges, *Henry Villard*, p. 71; Smalley, *History of the Northern Pacific Railroad*, pp. 261-263; Villard, *Memoirs*, p. 291.

¹⁶Villard, *Memoirs*, pp. 291-292.

¹⁷The adoption of standard gauge and building of additional feeder lines required more money. This was acquired by selling another $6 million capital stock. Investors were pleased to buy the new issue at par because OR&N stock then stood at 180.

¹⁸*Railroad Gazette*, 20 August 1880; *Weekly Statesman*, 9 October 1880, quotation. In spite of repeated statements about the Palouse line, work did not apparently begin there until after contracts were let early in 1881 (*Weekly Statesman*, 26 February 1881 and *Railroad Gazette*, 6 May 1881, p. 255).

¹⁹*Railroad Gazette*, 16 July 1880 and 20 August 1880, p. 248.

²⁰*Weekly Statesman*, 9 October 1880.

²¹Hedges, *Henry Villard*, pp. 64-65.

²²Villard, *Memoirs*, pp. 292-293, quotation; Hedges, *Henry Villard*, pp. 65-66.

²³*Weekly Statesman*, 14 October 1880; Hedges, *Henry Villard*, p. 65; Sol H. Lewis, "A History of Railroads in Washington," *Washington Historical Quarterly* 3 (July 1912): 191; C. J. Smith, "Early Development of Railroads in the Pacific Northwest," *Washington Historical Quarterly* 13 (October 1922): 245.

²⁴Hedges, *Henry Villard*, p. 67.

²⁵Smith, *Washington Historical Quarterly* 13 (October 1922): 245.

²⁶Wright, *Lewis and Dryden's Marine History*, p. 274; *Weekly Statesman*, 14 May 1881.

²⁷Villard, *Memoirs*, p. 290. Edison invented electric lighting in 1879. Villard was one of his most enthusiastic patrons. The generator in question was installed at Spokane Falls in 1885 by George Fitch. See *History of the Washington Water Power Company*, p. 2. The ship mentioned was almost certainly the *Columbia*. Without doubt the electric power potential of the falls enabled Spokane to outpace rival settlements in the Interior.

²⁸Johansen, *Empire of the Columbia*, p. 438. Early in 1882 the Northern Pacific shops at Tacoma were using Carbondale coal and Oswego iron. Northern Pacific, it was said, intended to erect rolling mills at Tacoma (*Weekly Statesman*, 21 January 1882).

²⁹NPRR Co. *Annual Report, 1880*; Villard, *Memoirs*, p. 295.

³⁰Villard, *Memoirs*, pp. 295-296; Hedges, *Henry Villard*, pp. 72-73; Smalley, *History of the Northern Pacific Railroad*, p. 263.

³¹Hedges, *Henry Villard*, p. 73.

³²Ibid.; Villard, *Memoirs*, p. 296; Smalley, *History of the Northern Pacific Railroad*, pp. 263-264.

³³Villard, *Memoirs*, p. 296, quotation; Hedges, *Henry Villard*, pp. 73-74.

CHAPTER 6   THE LAKE PEND D'OREILLE DIVISION

¹*Times*, 26 June 1879 and 10 July 1879.

²Platted on February 13, 1878, the village of Spokane Falls became simply Spokane after its reincorporation in 1890. See Robert Hitchman, *Place Names of Washington* (Tacoma: Washington State Historical Society, 1985), p. 285; James W. Phillips, *Washington State Place Names* (Seattle: University of Washington Press, 1971), pp. 134-135; and Edmond S. Meany, *Origin of Washington Geographic Names* (Seattle: University of Washington Press, 1923); *Times*, 26 June 1879, 4 July 1879 and 25 September 1879; *Weekly Statesman*, 14 June 1879 and 19 July 1879.

³*Times*, 7 August 1879.

⁴Ibid., 2 October 1879.

[5]Ibid., 18 September 1879. Northern Pacific called for 350,000 ties 6 X 8 X 8 ft. long, in tamarack or red or yellow fir and 10 million board feet, more or less, of bridge timber, consisting of sills 12 X 12 X 18 to 20 ft. long, caps 14 X 14 in odd lengths, stringers 6 X 16 X 32 ft long, all in red or yellow fir or cedar, all to be delivered to the mouth of the Snake River.

[6]*Times,* 16 October 1879. General Sprague was said to have taken the shovel home with him as a "memento of the happiest day the company has seen for six years."

[7]*Chronicle,* 29 June 1881; *Railroad Gazette,* 30 September 1881, p. 545. Some confusion arises because distances were at first measured from Ainsworth. After the Villard takeover, however, they were computed from Wallula, an extra 12 miles being added.

[8]*Times,* 2 October 1879.

[9]Ibid., 19 October 1879.

[10]Ibid., 30 October 1879 and 5 June 1880; *Weekly Statesman,* 15 November 1879.

[11]*Times,* 18 December 1879.

[12]Ibid., 25 December 1879.

[13]NPRR Co. *Annual Report, 1879* and *1880*; *Times,* 2 October 1879; *Weekly Statesman,* 15 November 1879.

[14]*Times,* 25 December 1879.

[15]Ibid., 18 December 1879.

[16]Ibid., 4 December 1879.

[17]Ibid., 25 March 1880.

[18]Ibid.

[19]Ibid., 22 April, 1880.

[20]Ibid., 29 May 1880.

[21]Ibid., 12 June 1880.

[22]Ibid., 19 June 1880.

[23]Ibid., 22 May 1880.

[24]Ibid., 5 February 1880 and 20 May 1880; NPRR Co. *Annual Report, 1880.*

[25]Ibid., 18 December 1879.

[26]Ibid., 12 June 1880.

[27]Ibid., 15 May 1880 and 5 June 1880; *Weekly Statesman,* 19 February 1880, quotations.

[28]*Times,* 5 June 1880.

[29]*Oregonian,* 17 May 1881; *Weekly Statesman,* 9 April 1991.

[30]*Times,* 11 September 1880, quotation.

[31]NPRR Co. *Annual Report, 1880,* quotation.

[32]*Weekly Statesman,* 25 December 1880.

[33]*Times,* 27 November 1880.

[34]Ibid., 16 December 1880; *Oregonian,* 18 January 1881.

[35]*Weekly Statesman,* 19 February 1881.

[36]*Weekly Statesman,* 12 March 1881. For more on the boisterous nature of the infamous settlement, see Bette E. Meyer, *Ainsworth: A Railroad Town* (Fairfield, Wash.: Ye Galleon Press, 1983).

[37]NPRR Co. *Annual Report, 1880*; *Times,* 23 October 1880; *Oregonian,* 2 December 1880.

[38]*Times,* 4 December 1880.

[39]*Weekly Statesman,* 9 April 1881.

[40]Ibid.

[41]*Weekly Statesman,* 15 November 1879.

[42]NPRR Co. *Annual Report, 1880.* The Land Office was moved from Colfax to Cheney in June 1881 (*Weekly Statesman,* 28 March 1881).

[43]*Weekly Statesman,* 9 April 1881.

[44]Ibid.

[45]*Times*, 28 April 1881; *Oregonian*, 3 May 1881.

[46]*History of the Big Bend Country* (Spokane, Wash.: Western Historical Publishing Co., 1904), p. 772.

[47]*Weekly Statesman*, 22 April 1882.

[48]*History of the Big Bend Country*, p. 774.

[49]*Times*, 1 April 1880, 8 April 1880 and 2 October 1880. The *Times* added that Cheney had also been called "Section 13," which apparently it was at one time. Desiring an educational institution in their city, citizens appealed to Benjamin P. Cheney, a director of the Northern Pacific, for help. His gift of $10,000 allowed residents to see their way clear to rename the town for him, and to establish the Benjamin P. Cheney Academy, which became the State Normal School and later Eastern Washington University. Hitchman, *Place Names*, p. 45.

[50]*History of the Big Bend Country*, pp. 173-174.

[51]*Times*, 5 May 1881.

[52]*Weekly Statesman*, 28 May 1881.

[53]*Railroad Gazette*, 22 April 1881, p. 226, quotation.

[54]*Times* 12 May 1881; *History of the Big Bend Country*, p. 174. This probably indicates the date of inauguration of regular train service.

[55]*Times*, 12 May 1881.

[56]*Weekly Statesman*, 21 May 1881, quotation.

[57]*Oregonian*, 28 May 1881; *Times*, 26 May 1881.

[58]*Times*, 25 September 1879.

[59]NPRR Co. *Annual Report, 1880*; *Times*, 30 October 1880.

[60]*Times*, 29 April 1880.

[61]Ibid., 13 January, 1881; *Weekly Statesman*, 29 January 1881.

[62]*Times*, 20 January 1881 and 10 February 1881.

[63]Ibid., 16 December 1880.

[64]Ibid., 3 March 1881.

[65]Ibid., 14 April 1881.

[66]Ibid., 13 January 1881 and 12 May 1881.

[67]Ibid., 26 May 1881. During the construction period a lot of tents were used. Northern Pacific had a full-time tent maker in Spokane Falls, named J. N. O. Larken (*Times*, 12 May 1881).

[68]*Times*, 30 June 1881.

[69]*Weekly Statesman*, 21 May 1881, 26 May 1881, 16 June 1881 and 30 June 1881.

[70]Ibid., 21 May 1881 and 25 June 1881, quotations.

[71]*Chronicle*, 3 August 1881. Even at this early date Spokane promoters had formed a "Spokane Falls & Columbia River Railway & Navigation Company" to build a railroad from Spokane to Kettle Falls and operate steamers on the Upper Columbia.

[72]*Chronicle*, 29 June 1881. The accounts appearing in the *Chronicle* and *Times* are somewhat different. The *Chronicle* account seems to present a more balanced picture.

CHAPTER 7 THE BLIND POOL

[1]Smalley, *History of the Northern Pacific Railroad*, pp. 233-234 and 264; Villard, *Memoirs*, p. 296; Hedges, *Henry Villard*, pp. 73-74; *Oregonian*, 22 November 1880 and 30 November 1880.

[2]Smalley, *History of the Northern Pacific Railroad*, p. 233; Hedges, *Henry Villard*, pp. 108-109.

[3]Villard, *Memoirs*, p. 296, quotation, written in third person singular context; Hedges, *Henry Villard*, pp. 73-74; *Oregonian*, 22 November 1880.

[4]Hedges, *Henry Villard*, pp. 74-77.

[5]Smalley, *History of the Northern Pacific Railroad*, p. 265; Villard, *Memoirs*, p. 297.

[6]Hedges, *Henry Villard*, p. 77 and p. 77, n.

[7]Smalley, *History of the Northern Pacific Railroad*, pp. 265-268; Villard, *Memoirs*, pp. 297-200; Hedges, *Henry Villard*, p. 77.

[8]*Railroad Gazette*, 25 February 1881, p. 119.

[9]Hedges, *Henry Villard*, pp. 78-79.

[10]Ibid., pp. 82-85; *Oregonian*, 6 April 1881, quotations.

[11]*Railroad Gazette*, 18 March 1881, p. 163.

[12]Smalley, *History of the Northern Pacific Railroad*, pp. 206-207.

[13]Ibid., p. 270; Hedges, *Henry Villard*, pp. 78-79; *Railroad Gazette*, 25 March 1881; *Oregonian*, 22 March 1881.

[14]Smalley, *History of the Northern Pacific Railroad*, p. 270; Villard, *Memoirs*, p. 300; Hedges, *Henry Villard*, p. 79; *Railroad Gazette*, 8 April 1881, p. 190.

[15]*Railroad Gazette*, 29 April 1881, p. 243 and 20 May 1881, p. 285; *Oregonian*, 2 May 1881.

[16]*Oregonian*, 8 June 1881, quotations; *Weekly Statesman*, 11 June 1881.

[17]Smalley, *History of the Northern Pacific Railroad*, p. 270.

[18]*Chronicle*, 6 July 1881 (Special to St. Paul *Pioneer-Express*, 10 June 1881), quotations.

[19]Smalley, *History of the Northern Pacific Railroad*, p. 268; Villard, *Memoirs*, p. 299.

[20]Villard, *Memoirs*, p. 297; Hedges, *Henry Villard*, pp. 79-81.

[21]*Oregonian*, 29 June 1881, says the O&T articles were filed "yesterday." Hedges says that the documents were dated July 15.

[22]Smalley, *History of the Northern Pacific Railroad, p. 270;* Villard, *Memoirs*, p. 300.

[23]Villard, *Memoirs*, p. 300, quotation.

CHAPTER 8   THE UPPER RIVER AND THE SOUTHERN INTERIOR

[1]*Times*, 12 February 1880 reported that the work of modifying the locomotives and cars began on January 24, 1880. *Times*, 26 February 1880 reported the track gauge changed by four gangs of men in only five hours.

[2]*Times*, 15 May 1880.

[3]*Railroad Gazette*, 16 July 1880.

[4]*Times*, 21 August 1880. The ship lost was the *Orient*.

[5]*Railroad Gazette*, 20 August 1880, p. 446.

[6]Ibid., 21 May 1880, p. 279; *Times*, 21 August 1880 and 6 November 1880; *Oregonian*, 16 November 1880.

[7]*Oregonian*, 19 November 1880.

[8]Ibid., 30 November 1880, 2 December 1880, 15 December 1880 and 17 May 1881. Passengers for Pendleton travelled from Blalock's on the UI&O Stage Line, calling at Rockville, Olex, Heppner and Pilot Rock. Intermediate railway stations between Celilo and Blalock's were Des Chutes (now Miller), Grant's, John Day's, and Quinns (later Quinook and now Quinton).

[9]*Oregonian*, 19 November 1880 and 23 November 1880.

[10]*Weekly Statesman*, 25 December 1880.

[11]*Oregonian*, 17 January 1881.

[12]Ibid., 7 February 1881.

[13]Ibid., 15 December 1880.

[14]*Weekly Statesman*, 12 March 1881.

[15]*Oregonian*, 6 April 1881 and 8 April 1881; *East Oregonian*, 9 April 1881.

[16]*Oregonian*, 14 April 1881; *Weekly Statesman*, 16 April 1881; *East Oregonian*, 16 April 1881.

[17]*Oregonian*, 17 April 1881.

[18]*Weekly Statesman*, 30 April 1881 and 14 May 1881. Thereafter the trains ran six days a week.

[19]Ibid., 28 May 1881.

[20]Ibid., 25 June 1881.

[21]Ibid., 2 July 1881. Although the palace cars had air brakes the locomotives may not immediately have been equipped to operate them. *Weekly Statesman*, 14 January 1882 reported the arrival of the first train to use such brakes. It was hauled by engine No. 3.

[22]*Weekly Statesman*, 11 June 1881; *East Oregonian*, 11 June 1881. The mixed train made round trips from Walla Walla to South Ainsworth on Mondays, Wednesdays, and Fridays.

[23]*Railroad Gazette*, 20 August 1880, p. 448.

[24]*Times*, 8 April 1880.

[25]Ibid., 21 August, 1880.

[26]*Weekly Statesman*, 9 October 1880.

[27]*Oregonian*, 14 December 1880; *Times*, 6 January 1881.

[28]*Weekly Statesman*, 22 January 1881.

[29]Ibid.

[30]Ibid., 26 February 1881.

[31]Ibid., 2 July 1881.

[32]Ibid., 28 May 1881 and 11 June 1881.

[33]*Oregonian*, 11 May 1881. The rails arrived aboard the *Agnes Oswald* from Cardiff, Wales and the *Merom* from New York. Thielsen fired a gang of men at Walla Walla who demanded overtime pay for unloading rails at night and on Sundays (*Weekly Statesman*, 11 June 1881).

[34]*Weekly Statesman*, 2 July 1881, quotations.

[35]*Times*, 21 July 1881 (quoting correspondence from Dayton, Washington July 15, 1881). The passenger killed instantly was Dr. W. G. Sutherland, who died of a broken neck. Oddly, a loaded pistol, which he was carrying in his pocket, went off when the derailment occurred, simultaneously setting his clothes on fire. The passenger who died the following morning was Ben Hardman. The conductor's name was Howe.

[36]*Weekly Statesman*, 23 July 1881.

[37]Ibid.

[38]*East Oregonian*, 19 August 1881, quotations.

[39]Ibid., 21 July 1882 (from New York "Lumberman"); *Weekly Statesman*, 6 August 1881.

[40]*East Oregonian*, 14 August 1888 reported that the similar Milton flume was finally dismantled.

[41]*Weekly Statesman*, 6 August 1881; *Railroad Gazette*, 26 August 1881, p. 475.

[42]*Weekly Statesman*, 26 February 1881; *Times* 10 March 1881, quotation.

[43]*Oregonian*, 2 April 1881.

[44]*Railroad Gazette*, 11 March 1881, p. 150, quotation.

[45]*Oregonian*, 7 June 1881, quotation.

[46]*Chronicle*, 29 June 1881; *Railroad Gazette*, 1 July 1881, p. 637.

[47]*Weekly Statesman*, 25 June 1881.

[48]*Railroad Gazette*, 12 August 1881, p. 446.

[49]*Times*, 11 October 1881.

[50]*Railroad Gazette*, 12 August 1881, p. 446; *Times*, 16 August 1881 and 4 October 1881; *Weekly Statesman*, 17 September 1881.

[51]*Weekly Statesman*, 15 October 1881. When Villard left Walla Walla he was headed for Dayton. It seems likely that he also went over the Grange City line. His special train consisted of a palace car and a dining car, supervised by steward Fred Ernst, formerly of the steamer *Wide West*.

[52]*Weekly Statesman*, 15 October 1881 and 22 October 1881.

[53]*Times*, 6 December 1881; *Weekly Statesman*, 10 December 1881.

[54]*Weekly Statesman*, 14 January 1882 reported that the Texas Ferry to Colfax line was to be used as a toll road.

[55]*Weekly Statesman*, 6 May 1882 and 12 August 1882. The former reported that OR&N was building a hotel at "South Texas," and the latter intimated that a locomotive fireman named Fitzgerald had fallen off the water tank and been injured at "Riparia." This particular "Texas" was sometimes spelled "Taxsas" (Andrew M. Modelski, *Railroad Maps of North America – The First Hundred Years* (Washington, D.C.: Library of Congress, 1984), p. 110).

CHAPTER 9 THROUGH TO PORTLAND

[1]Gill, *Oregon Historical Quarterly* 25:3 (Sept. 1924): 212-235.

[2]*Oregonian*, 19 January 1881.

[3]Ibid., 14 December 1880.

[4]*Weekly Statesman*, 26 February 1881.

[5]*Oregonian*, 17 April 1881.

[6]Ibid., 31 May 1881.

[7]Ibid., 4 June 1881; *Railroad Gazette*, 28 October 1881, p. 601.

[8]*Weekly Statesman*, 11 June 1881 and 27 August 1881.

[9]Smalley, *History of the Northern Pacific Railroad*, pp. 423-424; *Oregonian*, 4 June 1881; *Weekly Statesman*, 3 March 1882.

[10]*Oregonian*, 4 June 1881; *Chronicle*, 3 August 1881.

[11]*Oregonian*, 4 June 1881.

[12]*Chronicle*, 14 September 1881.

[13]Smalley, *History of the Northern Pacific Railroad*, p. 424; *Railroad Gazette*, 14 April 1882.

[14]*Oregonian*, 2 November 1881.

[15]*Times*, 30 January 1882.

[16]*Oregonian*, 8 March 1882 and 15 March 1882; *Railroad Gazette*, 14 April 1882.

[17]*Oregonian*, 22 May 1882.

[18]Ibid., 18 April 1882; *Weekly Statesman*, 22 April 1882.

[19]*Oregonian*, 26 April 1882.

[20]Ibid., 22 May 1882.

[21]Ibid., 4 June 1881; *Chronicle*, 29 June 1881; *Railroad Gazette*, 1 July 1881, p. 637.

[22]*Oregonian*, 21 May 1881 and 29 September 1881; *Chronicle*, 29 June 1881.

[23]*Oregonian*, 31 January 1881.

[24]Ibid., 8 March 1882 and 7 October 1882.

[25]Ibid., 30 January 1882.

[26]Ibid., 8 March 1882 and 10 March 1882.

[27]Ibid., 19 May 1882.

[28]Ibid., 24 May 1882.

[29] *Weekly Statesman*, 3 March 1882. Between Portland and Sandy River work was supervised by Thielsen's younger son, Julius.

[30] *Oregonian*, 14 February 1882.

[31] Ibid., 11 April 1882.

[32] Ibid., 11 May 1882.

[33] *Railroad Gazette*, 18 August 1882.

[34] *East Oregonian*, 6 October 1882. The location of the last spike was not stated.

[35] *Oregonian*, 4 June 1881, 8 April 1882 and 10 October 1882.

[36] Ibid., 21 November 1882, quotation.

CHAPTER 10   PEND D'OREILLE, CLARK'S FORK AND THE LAST SPIKE

[1] *Weekly Statesman*, 9 April 1881.

[2] Ibid., 21 May 1881.

[3] *Chronicle*, 13 July 1881.

[4] *Times*, 28 July 1881.

[5] Ibid., 9 August 1881.

[6] *Weekly Statesman*, 13 August 1881.

[7] *Times*, 17 August 1881.

[8] *Chronicle*, 7 September 1881. After the Villard takeover miles were given from Wallula instead of Ainsworth and distances were increased by 12 miles. I have used Ainsworth mileages to the Lake Pend d'Oreille crossing at Sand Point, and Wallula mileages beyond that point. For the original alignment in the Athol Granite vicinity refer to NPRR Co. Right-of-Way Plan. Distances on this map are given in miles from Wallula. Note that Rathdrum was at first called Westwood and the Athol area was originally known as Eight Mile Prairie.

[9] *Weekly Statesman*, 10 September 1881.

[10] *Railroad Gazette*, 30 September 1881, p. 545. Before the Villard takeover, Lake Prescott was called Dry Lake. After Villard lost control of Northern Pacific in 1884, it became Granite. Preston includes a map of "Coeur d'Alene Mines and Vicinity," 1884, which shows a settlement called Dry Lake, a body of water called Lake Prescott, and a general area called Granite!

[11] *Weekly Statesman*, 10 December 1881. The end of the track at this point was called Hangtown.

[12] *Railroad Gazette*, 23 December 1881, p. 735.

[13] Smalley, *History of the Northern Pacific Railroad*, p. 414; *Railroad Gazette*, 27 January 1881, p. 63.

[14] *Times*, 2 June 1881; NPRR Co. *Annual Report, 1881*.

[15] *Times*, 12 May 1881; *Oregonian*, 2 November 1881.

[16] *Chronicle*, 24 August 1881.

[17] *Weekly Statesman*, 11 March 1882; Smalley, *History of the Northern Pacific Railroad*, p. 415.

[18] *Times*, 21 July 1881.

[19] *Chronicle*, 17 August 1881.

[20] Smalley, *History of the Northern Pacific Railroad*, p. 415; *Oregonian*, 21 September 1881.

[21] *Oregonian*, 5 November 1881.

[22] *Weekly Statesman*, 10 December 1881.

[23] Ibid., 11 March 1882. Ventnor was on the south shore of the West Arm of Lake Pend d'Oreille, near the bridge.

[24] *Weekly Statesman*, 6 May 1882. An earlier report in *Weekly Statesman*, 22 April 1882, appears to have confused this bridge with the one at Sand Point. This name was later changed to Sandpoint. Also, the Clark Fork River was originally spelled Clark's Fork.

[25] Over the years there have been many line relocations. There were major realignments between Athol and Granite in 1892 and 1965, and at Cocolalla and Algoma in 1910. The Sunnyside headland was bypassed and the original Pack River trestle abandoned at some unknown date; a new line was built along the left bank of the Clark Fork between Trout Creek and Belknap in 1915; the second crossing was relocated to a point between Heron and Noxon and a new line built along the north side of the valley when the Noxon Rapids dam was constructed in 1957.

[26] Smalley, *History of the Northern Pacific Railroad*, p. 416.

[27] *Weekly Statesman*, 5 November 1881.

[28] Ibid., 10 December 1881.

[29] *Sentinel*, 13 April 1882.

[30] *Weekly Statesman*, 22 April 1882; *Oregonian*, 19 April 1882.

[31] Ibid., 6 May 1882.

[32] *Oregonian*, 27 April 1882.

[33] Smalley, *History of the Northern Pacific Railroad*, pp. 416-419; *Oregonian*, 11 July 1882.

[34] *Oregonian*, 11 July 1882; *Chronicle*, 25 July 1882.

[35] *Oregonian*, 1 June 1882.

[36] Ibid., 7 February 1882 re Ellisport; *Oregonian*, 11 May 1882, 1 June 1882 and 1 July 1882, re Cabinet Landing; *Oregonian*, 5 August 1882, re Rock Island City; *Oregonian*, 28 December 1882, re Weeksville; *Oregonian*, 11 May 1883, re Heron. Rock Island City was near the south end of the present Noxon Rapids dam.

[37] *Oregonian*, 7 June 1882, relates that a group of Chinese revolted and refused to complete their journey by train.

[38] *Oregonian*, 9 September 1882.

[39] Ibid., 7 February 1882.

[40] Ibid., 21 November 1883, reported "thirty carloads" of Chinese had arrived at Albina from Missoula.

[41] Ibid., 1 June 1882.

[42] Ibid., 27 April 1882.

[43] Ibid., 14 June 1882, 10 July 1882, 11 July 1882; *Weekly Statesman*, 15 July 1882. The first trains crossed on the falsework; the permanent bridge was not completed until mid-August (*Oregonian*, 12 August 1882). A description of the permanent bridge is given in Smalley, *History of the Northern Pacific Railroad*, p. 417.

[44] *Oregonian*, 1 July 1882 and 6 July 1882.

[45] Smalley, *History of the Northern Pacific Railroad*, p. 417; *Oregonian*, 19 July 1882 and 23 August 1882.

[46] *Oregonian*, 19 July 1882.

[47] Ibid., 7 August 1882.

[48] Ibid., 25 August 1882.

[49] Ibid., 9 September 1882.

[50] *Weekly Statesman*, 14 October 1882 and 4 November 1882.

[51] Ibid., 25 November 1882.

[52] *Oregonian*, 4 December 1882 and 8 December 1882; *Weekly Statesman*, 26 November 1882.

[53] *Oregonian*, 9 November 1882.

[54] Smalley, *History of the Northern Pacific Railroad*, p. 418.

[55] *Oregonian*, 24 January 1883.

[56]*Railroad Gazette,* 2 March 1883 (a premature report); *Oregonian,* 15 March 1883.

[57]*Oregonian,* 8 February 1882 (from Helena *Herald,* 25 January 1882).

[58]Smalley, *History of the Northern Pacific Railroad,* pp. 418-419; Athearn, *Union Pacific Country,* pp. 253 and 262.

[59]*Oregonian,* 12 September 1882, says that the compensation to the Indian band was $16,000. Smalley, *History of the Northern Pacific Railroad,* p. 419 says it was $5000.

[60]*Railroad Gazette,* 2 March 1883, p. 148.

[61]*Oregonian,* 11 May 1883.

[62]*Railroad Gazette,* 1 June 1883, p. 354.

[63]Ibid., 29 June 1883, p. 436.

[64]Ibid., 31 August 1883, p. 584. This article correctly gives the location of the meeting point as 55 miles west of Helena.

[65]Villard, *Memoirs,* pp. 309-310.

[66]*Railroad Gazette,* 14 September 1883, quotation. There is no suggestion here of the ceremonies having been marred by rowdyism as related by Abdill. This article erroneously gives the location of the meeting point as 66 miles west of Helena.

[67]*Oregonian,* 11 September 1883.

[68]Ibid., 14 November 1883. The event was apparently hushed up at the time it happened.

[69]Ibid., 10 September 1883 and 13 September 1883.

[70]Ibid., 12 September 1883.

[71]Ibid., 14 September 1883.

[72]Villard, *Memoirs,* p. 312, quotation.

CHAPTER 11   HENRY VILLARD'S DOWNFALL

[1]Villard, *Memoirs,* pp. 300-301; Daggett, *Railroad Reorganization,* p. 272; Hedges, *Henry Villard,* pp. 108-109.

[2]Daggett, *Railroad Reorganization,* pp. 273-274; Hedges, *Henry Villard,* p. 110.

[3]Villard, *Memoirs,* p. 303; Hedges, *Henry Villard,* pp. 102-103; *Oregonian,* 19 July 1883.

[4]NPRR Co. *Annual Report, 1882*; *Oregonian,* 7 October 1882.

[5]Construction costs of the Northern Pacific's transcontinental line were indeed staggering by the standards of the day, as the following figures indicate:

Construction Costs of Northern Pacific Railroad Divisions as of 30 June 1885.			
Divisions	Miles of Main Track	Total Cost	Average Cost Per Mile
Wisconsin Ashland to NP Junction	37.5	$2,006,099.55	$22,926.85
Missouri Mandan to Glendive	219.3	4,515,242.95	20,589.34
Yellowstone Glendive to Livingston	340.9	10,903,585.77	31,984.70
Rocky Mountain Livingston to Elliston	151.9	4,893,288.75	32,213.88
Missoula Elliston to 3rd crossing	156.7	4,745,245.22	30,282.35
Clark Fork* 3rd crossing to 8 miles east of Sandpoint	120.5	7,425,517.57	61,622.55
Pend d'Oreille Sandpoint to Ainsworth	225.0	5,274,932.09	23,444.14
Cascade (East) Pasco to Yakima	87.5	1,670,869.80	19,095.65
Portland Portland to Hunters	36.3	1,368,407.49	37,697.18
Total	1425.6	$42,803,189.28	$30,024.68

*Includes $237,832.71 cost of the iron bridge at the 2nd crossing of the Clark Fork River near Thompson Falls.

Source: Report of construction for the fiscal year ending June 30, 1885, dated August 10, 1885, Box 10.B.1.6F, Northern Pacific Railroad Company Records, Minnesota Historical Society Archives/Manuscript Division, St. Paul, Minnesota.

[6]Julius Grodinsky, *Transcontinental Railway Strategy, 1869-1893* (Philadelphia: University of Pennsylvania Press, 1962), pp. 204-205.

[7]*Oregonian*, 18 July 1883.

[8]Ibid. This issue reported that O&T then held 162,792 shares of NP common stock, 156,000 shares NP preferred, and 128,000 shares of OR&N. When the O&T holdings were counted on January 1, 1884 there were 147,934 NP common, 153,700 NP preferred, and 152,027 OR&N (*Oregonian*, 2 January 1884). The increase in holdings had thus been largely in OR&N, which was perhaps used as collateral to a greater extent than NP. Refer also to Villard, *Memoirs*, p. 313 and to Grodinsky, *Transcontinental Railway Strategy*, pp. 205-206.

[9]Grodinsky, *Transcontinental Railway Strategy*, p. 206.

[10]Villard, *Memoirs*, p. 308, quotation; *Oregonian*, 2 January 1884.

[11]*Oregonian*, 24 September 1883 (from Philadelphia *Press*, 22 September 1883).

[12]Daggett, *Railroad Reorganization*, p. 274; Hedges, *Henry Villard*, p. 110; *Oregonian*, 22 September 1883.

[13]*Oregonian*, 22 September 1883 (from Philadelphia Press, 21 September 1883).

[14]*Oregonian*, 25 September 1883, editorial.

[15]Daggett, *Railroad Reorganization*, p. 274; Hedges, *Henry Villard*, p. 110.

[16]Daggett, *Railroad Reorganization*, p. 274; Hedges, *Henry Villard*, p. 110; Grodinsky, *Transcontinental Railway Strategy*, p. 206.

[17]*Oregonian*, 13 October 1883 and 1 November 1883; *Chronicle*, 6 December 1883 reported lay-offs at Sprague shops.

[18]*Oregonian*, 3 November 1883.

[19]Villard, *Memoirs*, pp. 313-314; *Oregonian*, 16 October 1883 and 17 October 1883.

[20]Villard, *Memoirs*, p. 314.

[21]*Oregonian*, 22 November 1883.

[22]Ibid., 7 December 1883. The pressure to sell was due to the fact that NP simultaneously made application to list the second mortgage bonds.

[23]*Oregonian*, 17 December 1883.

[24]Villard, *Memoirs*, p. 315, quotation.

[25]*Oregonian*, 18 December 1883.

[26]Ibid., 27 December 1883 (Special to St. Paul *Globe*), and 31 December 1883 (from Philadelphia *Press*, 29 December 1883), quotation.

[27]*Oregonian*, 2 January 1884.

[28]Grodinsky, *Transcontinental Railway Strategy*, p. 207.

[29]*Oregonian*, 15 October 1883 (from Chicago, 13 October 1883).

[30]Ibid., 5 January 1884 (from New York, 4 January 1884).

[31]*Chronicle*, 17 January 1884, quotation.

[32]*Oregonian*, 6 January 1884.

[33]Villard, *Memoirs*, pp. 318-319.

[34]Ibid., p. 315; Grodinsky, *Transcontinental Railway Strategy*, pp. 206-207; *Oregonian*, 10 January 1884 (from New York, 9 January 1884).

[36]Grodinsky, *Transcontinental Railway Strategy*, p. 207; *Oregonian*, 8 February 1884. I have relied upon the latter.

[36]*Oregonian*, 8 January 1884.

[37]Ibid., 18 January 1884 (from New York, 17 January 1884).

CHAPTER 12   THE BRIDGE AT AINSWORTH

[1]*Oregonian*, 17 May 1881.

[2]Wright, *Lewis and Dryden's Marine History*, p. 273; NPRR Co. *Annual Report, 1881*.

[3]*East Oregonian, 1 July 1881; Chronicle*, 6 July 1881.

[4]NPRR Co. *Annual Report, 1881.*

[5]*Oregonian,* 20 May 1882.

[6]*Press,* 9 September 1882.

[7]*Oregonian,* 14 November 1883.

[8]Ibid., 15 November 1881; *Weekly Statesman,* 26 November 1881.

[9]Ibid., 8 March 1882.

[10]For the length of the bridge, NPRR Co. *Annual Report, 1882* gave 1540 ft., Smalley, p. 414 gave 125 ft. ¢ 350 ft. draw ¢ 3(250 ft.) ¢ 2(158 ft.) # 1541 ft. *Oregonian,* 21 April 1884 gave 146 ft. ¢ 346 ft. draw ¢ 4(248 ft.) ¢ 65 ft. # 1549 ft. The latter, as anyone looking at the bridge can see, even today, is the more accurate.

[11]For the drawspan, the *Chronicle,* 29 June 1881 stated that the drawspan purchased for the bridge at Grange City was to be 336 ft. long. There is, therefore, a curious discrepancy of 10 ft. compared with the dimension eventually given in the *Oregonian,* 21 April 1884. I was at first inclined to dismiss this as a newspaper error, but later found a report appearing in the *Oregonian,* 8 January 1886, which stated that the drawspan for the Grange City bridge, found to be too short for use at Ainsworth, would be used instead at the first crossing of the Yakima River, between Yakima and Ellensburg. The engineers appear to have made a 100-ft. mistake in spacing the piers at Ainsworth.

[12]*Weekly Statesman,* 20 March 1882.

[13]*Press,* 9 September 1882.

[14]Smalley, *History of the Northern Pacific Railroad,* p. 414.

[15]*Oregonian,* 21 April 1884 and 15 January 1883.

[16]Ibid., 24 April 1884.

[17]Ibid., 20 September 1883.

[18]Ibid., 14 November 1883.

[19]Ibid., 3 January 1884.

[20]Ibid., 26 January 1884.

[21]Ibid., 21 April 1884. See also note no. 11 above.

[22]Ibid., 14 November 1883 and 3 January 1884.

[23]Ibid., 29 December 1883.

[24]*Chronicle,* 10 January 1884.

[25]*Oregonian,* 26 January 1884 and 11 April 1884.

[26]Ibid., 21 April 1884, quotation.

[27]NPRR Co. *Annual Report, 1884.*

[28]*Railroad Gazette,* 28 September 1883, p. 646.

[29]*Chronicle,* 17 January 1884.

[30]*Railroad Gazette,* 30 May 1884, p. 421.

[31]NPRR Co. *Annual Report, 1884.*

[32]*Oregonian,* 4 June 1883. For a description of the Willamette bridge as first planned see *Oregonian,* 25 September 1883. A railway bridge across the Willamette at Portland was not opened until 1888.

[33]*Oregonian,* 28 June 1884 and 11 December 1884. The *Frederick Billings* remained at Pasco for many years. In 1899 she was purchased by the Central Navigation & Construction Co., which at that time planned to build a railway from Spokane to the Columbia River and run steamers thence to Astoria (*Railroad Gazette,* 15 December 1888). She was at that time reboilered and repainted (*History of the Big Bend Country,* p. 936).

CHAPTER 13   COLUMBIA AND PALOUSE

[1]Hedges, *Henry Villard*, p. 154.
[2]*Times*, 6 December 1881; *Weekly Statesman*, 14 January 1882.
[3]*Weekly Statesman*, 3 March 1882.
[4]Ibid., 27 May 1882.
[5]*Railroad Gazette*, 12 October 1883, p. 682.
[6]*Chronicle*, 20 June 1882.
[7]*Weekly Statesman*, 28 October 1882.
[8]*Oregonian*, 21 November 1882.
[9]*Chronicle*, 25 July 1882 (from Waitsburg *Times*).
[10]*The Channeled Scablands of Eastern Washington* (Washington, D.C.: United States Department of the Interior, Geological Survey, 1972).
[11]*Oregonian*, 3 January 1884.
[12]Information courtesy of Mr. J. Reiser, Division Engineers Office, UPRR Co., Portland, Oregon, March 4, 1983.
[13]*Chronicle*, 20 June 1882.
[14]Ibid., 14 July 1882.
[15]*East Oregonian*, 18 July 1882.
[16]*Railroad Gazette*, 31 March 1882, quotation.
[17]NPRR Co. *Annual Report, 1883*.
[18]*Oregonian*, 11 July 1883.
[19]*Railroad Gazette*, 12 October 1883, p. 682.
[20]*Oregonian*, 21 November 1883.
[21]Ibid., 3 January 1884.
[22]*Railroad Gazette*, 18 January 1884, p. 58.
[23]*Railroad Gazette*, 29 February 1884, p. 176; *East Oregonian*, 4 April 1884.
[24]*Chronicle*, 20 March 1884.
[25]*Oregonian*, 26 May 1884.
[26]*East Oregonian*, 17 June 1884.
[27]*Oregonian*, 30 July 1884.
[28]*History of the Big Bend Country*, pp. 785, 947, and 955.
[29]This train was locally known as "the Sage Hen.'
[30]Personal observation, Sunday, August 10, 1980.

CHAPTER 14   BLUE MOUNTAIN STATION AND CENTERVILLE

[1]*Weekly Statesman*, 15 October 1881.
[2]*Railroad Gazette*, 17 March 1882, p. 174.
[3]*East Oregonian*, 19 June 1882.
[4]*Railroad Gazette*, 26 May 1882, p. 323.
[5]*East Oregonian*, 28 July 1882; *Weekly Statesman*, 29 July 1882.
[6]*Weekly Statesman*, 16 September 1882.
[7]*Railroad Gazette*, 18 August 1882 and 22 December 1882, p. 797. The standard gauge station named Barrett appears to have been the site of the earlier narrow gauge station called Milton.
[8]UPRR Co. Line Data Sheets Nos. 70, 71 & 72, courtesy of Mr. D. L. Monson, Division Engineer, Portland, Oregon, June 9, 1982.
[9]*East Oregonian*, 15 October 1882 and 3 November 1882.
[10]Ibid., 2 December 1882.

[11]Ibid., 4 December 1882, 7 December 1882 and 12 December 1882.

[12]Ibid., 18 January 1883.

[13]Ibid., 22 January 1883.

[14]*Weekly Statesman*, 3 February 1883.

[15]*Oregonian*, 18 April 1883.

[16]Ibid., 17 September 1883.

[17]Ibid., 25 September 1883.

[18]Ibid., 9 November 1883.

[19]Ibid., 29 November 1883.

[20]Ibid., 18 December 1883.

[21]Ibid., 5 January 1884 and 5 February 1884; *Railroad Gazette*, 1 February 1884, p. 100.

[22]*East Oregonian*, 8 February 1884.

[23]Ibid., 12 February 1884.

[24]Centerville was renamed Athena in May 1889. (McArthur, *Oregon Geographical Names*).

CHAPTER 15 OVER THE BLUE MOUNTAINS

[1]Hedges, *Henry Villard*, pp. 59-60; Athearn, *Union Pacific Country*, pp. 311 and 315; *Colorado Rail Annual*, no. 15, p. 51.

[2]Athearn, *Union Pacific Country*, pp. 226-228. At this time the name of the company was changed to Union Pacific Railway. In 1897 it again became Union Pacific Railroad.

[3]Hedges, *Henry Villard*, p. 75.

[4]*Oregonian*, 16 February 1881.

[5]Ibid., 16 November 1882.

[6]UPRR Co. *Brief Historical Sketch of the Origin and Development of the Oregon Short Line Railroad Company*, p. 3. This is a Union Pacific Railroad Co. document, prepared perhaps is a precis of the more formal "Corporate History of Oregon Short Line Railroad Co." submitted realier (possibly in 1916) to the Interstate Commerce Commission. The "Historical Sketch" was issued by UPRR head office at Omaha, Nebraska, date unknown. I received a copy in 1980 through the courtesy of Mr. John Witherbee, Research Specialist, UPRR Co., Omaha, Nebraska.

[7]Athearn, *Union Pacific Country*, p. 315.

[8]*Oregonian*, 26 April 1882.

[9]Hedges, *Henry Villard*, p. 75.

[10]*East Oregonian*, 27 November 1880.

[11]*Oregonian*, 15 December 1880.

[12]Ibid., 14 December 1880.

[13]*East Oregonian*, 1 January 1881 and 10 June 1881.

[14]Ibid., 15 January 1881. The Pendleton depot was eventually built in the Indian Reservation.

[15]*East Oregonian*, 10 June 1881.

[16]Ibid., 1 June 1881.

[17]*Weekly Statesman*, 21 May 1881.

[18]*Oregonian*, 7 June 1881. Homly was the Umatilla chief who fought with the whites against the Paiutes and Bannocks in 1878 (Col. W. Parson and W. S. Shiach, *An Illustrated History of Umatilla County and of Morrow County* (Pendleton, Oregon: W. H. Lever, 1902)). A siding on the main line, established near his grave

in 1928, was named after him (Lewis A. McArthur, *Oregon Geographical Names* (Portland, Oregon: Oregon Historical Society, 1974), p. 365).

[19]*Oregonian*, 29 September 1881 and 12 November 1881.

[20]Foster's. Named for John R. Foster, owner of the 4000-acre Prospect Farm 7 miles northeast of Echo (*Oregonian*, 21 July 1882).

[21]The horseshoe curve can still be seen quite distinctly from the high ground above the present tunnel at Coe. The curve was bypassed by the tunnel, 543 ft. long in 1911, when other changes were also made between Pendleton and Yoakum (*Railway Age Gazette*, 14 January 1910, 26 August 1910 and 3 March 1911. At some time about 1904 *Railroad Gazette* and *Railway Age* merged to publish a new periodical called *Railway Age Gazette*.

[22]*Oregonian*, 2 June 1881; *East Oregonian*, 21 July 1882. The latter states that on the climb from Four Mile House to the first height of land the grade was 53 ft. to the mile (*Railway Age Gazette*, 6 March 1914, reported that the Echo-Coyote (i.e. Munley) cut-off would save 9.4 miles on a journey between Pendleton and Portland (bypassing Umatilla), and save 1560 degrees of curvature and 174 ft. of adverse grade).

[23]Mikecha. The name of this station was a composite of the names of three civil engineers employed on construction of the railway, i.e. *MI*x, *KE*nnedy, and *CHA*lk. (McArthur, *Oregon Geographical Names*, p. 308).

[24]Kamela. An Indian word meaning "pitch pine." (*East Oregonian*, 25 July 1884).

[25]Railroad Canyon is the name now used. It may not have been current in the early days.

[26]The name Pelican Creek was already in use during the railway construction period, as were Stumpton and Black Flat which have fallen into disuse. (*Oregonian*, 28 April 1884).

[27]The line from Umatilla to Baker was located by Engineer Mix. (*Oregonian*, 13 April 1881). The location was filed with the Interior Department about two months later (*Oregonian*, 7 June 1881), and was duly accepted (*Oregonian*, 19 October, 1882). Young Henry (H. B.) Thielsen's claim that *he* chose the Pyle's Canyon route (*Oregonian*, 29 November 1884) was almost certainly an idle boast. H. B. Thielsen did not inherit his father's position as chief engineer of OR&N until April 1884.

[28]Telocaset. An Indian word meaning "the highest ground" (*East Oregonian*, 25 July 1884).

[29]*Oregonian*, 23 October 1882 and 24 December 1883. Antelope Creek tunnel was about 500 ft. in length (*Oregonian*, 28 January 1884). Tunnels Nos. 4 and 5 were both subsequently bypassed by parallel open cuts.

[30]*East Oregonian*, 19 March 1881.

[31]Ibid., 2 April 1881, 16 April 1881 and 19 April 1881.

[32]*Weekly Statesman*, 21 May 1881.

[33]*Oregonian*, 31 May 1881; *East Oregonian*, 29 July 1881; *Weekly Statesman*, 6 August 1881.

[34]*Weekly Statesman*, 25 June 1881; *East Oregonian*, 29 June 1881.

[35]*Oregonian*, 10 February 1881.

[36]Ibid., 29 April 1882.

[37]*Weekly Statesman*, 3 March 1882.

[38]*Railroad Gazette*, 3 March 1882, p. 141.

[39]*Weekly Statesman*, 13 May 1882.

[40]*East Oregonian*, 13 June 1882.

[41]Ibid., 23 June 1882.

[42]*Oregonian*, 10 July 1882 and 19 July 1882.

[43] *East Oregonian*, 28 July 1882.

[44]Ibid., 1 September 1882.

[45]Ibid., 18 August 1882. OR&N was using iron rails at this time because steel rails could not be obtained on less than two years delivery. The rails were probably 56 lbs./yd., 22 ft. long.

[46]*East Oregonian*, 1 September 1882; *Oregonian*, 2 September 1882; *Weekly Statesman*, 9 September 1882.

[47]*East Oregonian*, 12 September 1882; *Weekly Statesman*, 16 September 1882.

[48]*Weekly Statesman*, 22 January 1881.

[49]Ibid., 13 August 1881.

[50]*Oregonian*, 29 September 1881.

[51]Ibid.

[52]Ibid., 29 December 1881.

[53]Ibid., 23 October 1881.

[54]*East Oregonian*, 22 December 1881.

[55]Ibid., 27 June 1882.

[56]Ibid., 18 July 1882.

[57]*Weekly Statesman*, 1 July 1882; *Oregonian*, 19 July 1882.

[58]*Oregonian*, 23 October 1882 and 29 November 1884.

[59]*Weekly Statesman*, 29 January 1882.

[60]UPRR Co., *Brief Historical Sketch of the Origin and Development of the Oregon Short Line Railroad Company*, pp. 2-3; Athearn, *Union Pacific Country*, pp. 237-263. See also Mallory H. Ferrell, "The Utah and Northern," *Colorado Rail Annual* 15 (1981), published by the Colorado Railroad Museum, Golden, Colorado.

[61]Hedges, *Henry Villard*, pp. 103-105.

[62]Athearn, *Union Pacific Country*, pp. 261-262.

[63]*Oregonian*, 8 February 1882 (from Helena *Herald*, 25 January 1882).

[64]Ibid., 6 March 1882.

[65]*East Oregonian*, 12 September 1882.

[66]Ibid., 15 September 1882.

[67]Ibid., 22 September 1882.

[68]Ibid., 26 September 1882.

[69]*Railroad Gazette*, 23 February 1883, p. 132.

[70]*East Oregonian*, 24 November 1882.

[71]*Oregonian*, 12 September 1882.

[72]*East Oregonian*, 29 September 1882.

[73]Ibid., *East Oregonian*, 20 October 1882.

[74]*Oregonian*, 27 December 1882.

[75]*Oregonian*, 16 March 1883. The tunnel was lined with locally felled and sawn timber (*Oregonian*, 20 October 1882).

[76]*Railroad Gazette*, 6 April 1883, p. 224; *Oregonian*, 25 April 1883.

[77]*Railroad Gazette*, 5 October 1883, p. 664; *Oregonian*, 18 October 1883.

[78]*Oregonian*, 27 November 1883 and 6 December 1883.

[79]*Oregonian*, 5 January 1884; *East Oregonian*, 15 January 1884.

[80]*East Oregonian*, 11 January 1884 and 15 January 1884; *Oregonian* 12 January 1884.

[81]*Oregonian*, 5 February 1884.

[82]Athearn, *Union Pacific Country*, p. 324; *Oregonian*, 18 December 1883.

[83]Villard, *Memoirs*, pp. 292 and 302; *Oregonian*, 14 December 1881.

[84]OR&N stock peaked at 180 just after the announcement of the traffic agreement with Northern Pacific in October 1880. As late as April 1883 it was still 144. On the day Villard resigned it was 100.

[85]*Oregonian* 22 January 1884.

[86]*Railroad Gazette*, 29 February 1884, p. 176; *Oregonian*, 24 March 1884.

[87]*Oregonian*, 24 March 1884; *East Oregonian*, 11 April 1884.

[88]*East Oregonian*, 22 February 1884.

[89]Ibid., 19 February 1884.

[90]Ibid., 25 February 1884.

[91]*Oregonian*, 7 April 1884 and 28 April 1884; *East Oregonian*, 11 April 1884.

[92]*East Oregonian*, 13 May 1884.

[93]*Oregonian*, 7 April 1884.

[94]Ibid., 28 June 1884.

[95]*East Oregonian*, 25 July 1884.

[96]*Oregonian*, 8 October 1884.

[97]Ibid., 30 June 1884.

[98]Ibid., 24 December 1883 and 28 January 1884.

[99]Ibid., 30 January 1884, 25 February 1884 and 19 March 1884.

[100]Ibid., 16 June 1884.

[101]Ibid., 7 July 1884.

[102]Ibid., 16 June 1884 and 22 July 1884; *East Oregonian*, 29 August 1884.

[103]*East Oregonian*, 5 September 1884, 11 September 1884.

[104]Encina. This name appears to me to be a corruption of the Spanish "en-cima," meaning "up-there," or simply "summit." I myself doubt the explanation given by McArthur in *Oregon Geographical Names*, p.255.

[105]*Oregonian*, 29 November 1884. The hairpin bend on Pritchard Creek was said to be 8 degrees, laid on a grade of 71 ft. to the mile. Substantially the same alignment is still in use today.

[106]In 1882 it would have been impossible to visualize excavations on the scale later permitting U.S. Interstate Highway 84 to be built through the Burnt River Canyon.

[107]*East Oregonian*, 20 June 1884.

[108]Tunnel No. 6 was abandoned in 1928 when a new concrete lined tunnel was driven just to the west. The north (railway west) end of the tunnel can still be seen from Interstate 84.

[109]Distances per UPRR Co. timetable No. 3, 1980. Elevations courtesy of Mr. D. L. Monson, Division Engineer, UPRR Co., Portland, Oregon, June 9, 1982.

[110]Thomas C. Cochran, *Railroad Leaders, 1845-1890* (Cambridge, Massachusetts: Houghton Mifflin & Company, 1908), p. 117, quotation.

[111]*East Oregonian*, 26 September 1882.

[112]*Oregonian*, 4 December 1882, quotation.

[113]*East Oregonian*, 11 April 1884; *Railroad Gazette*, 2 May 1884, p. 350.

[114]*Oregonian*, 28 June 1884.

[115]*East Oregonian*, 26 August 1884.

[116]*Railroad Gazette*, 14 November 1884, p. 828.

[117]*Oregonian*, 26 November 1884 and 29 November 1884; *Railroad Gazette*, 28 November 1884, p. 860; Athearn, *Union Pacific Country*, p. 318.

[118]*East Oregonian*, 28 November 1884 and 5 December 1884.

CHAPTER 16   "ON THE ROAD – AND OFF"

[1]*Oregonian*, 31 March 1881. These included T. F. Oakes, J. M. Buckley, and J. Muir.

[2]*Weekly Statesman*, 21 May 1881.

[3]*Chronicle*, 14 September 1881.

[4]*Times*, 8 June 1881.

[5]Ibid., 7 July 1881.

[6]*Oregonian*, 27 May 1884.

[7] *Times*, 7 July 1881.

[8] *Chronicle*, 3 January 1883.

[9] *East Oregonian*, 28 November 1882.

[10] OREGONIAN, 16 December 1880, 12 January 1881, and 29 September 1881.

[11] *Weekly Statesman*, 28 January 1882 and 22 April 1882; *Sentinel*, 13 April 1882.

[12] *Weekly Statesman*, 29 April 1882.

[13] *Oregonian*, 25 September 1883 and 6 November 1883.

[14] Ibid., 12 June 1885, 28 September 1886, and 13 October 1886.

[15] Ibid., 16 December 1887, 24 March 1888, 12 November 1888, and 19 October 1889.

[16] Ibid., 11 May 1883.

[17] Ibid., 31 October 1882, 6 January 1883, 13 January 1883.

[18] *East Oregonian*, 4 February 1885 and 12 May 1885.

[19] *Chronicle*, 17 August 1881.

[20] *Weekly Statesman*, 16 September 1882.

[21] *Oregonian*, 2 May 1882.

[22] Ibid., 10 October 1882.

[23] *Chronicle*, 4 January 1883.

[24] Ibid., 15 November 1883.

[25] NPRR Co. Time Schedule No. 8, June 13, 1886.

[26] NPRR Co. *Annual Report, 1883*.

[27] *Weekly Statesman*, 28 January 1882.

[28] *Oregonian*, 1 June 1885.

[29] Ibid., 11 April 1885.

[30] *East Oregonian*, 19 May 1885.

[31] *Oregonian*, 15 March 1885.

[32] Ibid., 25 March 1885.

[33] Ibid., 24 July 1885.

[34] Ibid., 21 August 1885.

[35] *East Oregonian*, 11 March 1884.

[36] Ibid., 29 August 1884.

[37] Ibid., 12 September 1884.

[38] *Union*, 8 August 1885.

[39] *Weekly Statesman*, 14 May 1881.

[40] Ibid., 23 July 1881.

[41] *Oregonian*, 16 May 1885.

[42] Ibid., 13 May 1884.

[43] Ibid., 12 August 1886.

[44] *Weekly Statesman*, 5 March 1881.

[45] *Oregonian*, 7 July 1885.

[46] Ibid., 21 October 1885.

[47] Ibid.

[48] Ibid., 1 October 1883.

[49] Ibid., 6 September 1886.

[50] Ibid., 11 January 1886.

[51] *East Oregonian* 19 June 1885.

[52] *Weekly Statesman*, 28 January 1882.

[53] Ibid., 31 December 1881.

[54] Ibid., 19 August 1882.

[55] *Times*, 25 February 1882.

[56] *Chronicle*, 18 July 1882.

[57] *Oregonian*, 1 November 1886.

[58] Ibid., 29 December 1884.

[59]*Union*, 23 January 1886.

[60]*Oregonian*, 1 December 1885, 20 January 1886, 21 August 1886, and 28 August 1886; *Railroad Gazette*, 1 January 1886.

[61]*Oregonian*, 29 November 1885, 6 December 1885, 8 December 1885, and 10 December 1885.

EPILOGUE

[1]As an example of how railroad connections accelerated the growth of major cities in the Pacific Northwest, see W. Hudson Kensel, "Inland Empire Mining and the Growth of Spokane, 1883-1905," *Pacific Northwest Quarterly* 60 (April 1969): 84-97. See also John Fahey, *Inland Empire—D.C. Corbin and Spokane* (Seattle: University of Washington Press, 1965).

BIBLIOGRAPHY

NEWSPAPERS

Beacon, Kalama, Washington, 1873.
Chronicle, Spokane Falls, Washington, 1881-1884.
East Oregonian, Pendleton, Oregon, 1880-1885.
Oregonian, Portland, Oregon, 1880-1889.
Press, Medical Lake, Washington, 1882.
Railroad Gazette, New York, New York, 1880-1885.
Sentinel, Cheney, Washington, 1882.
Times, Spokane Falls, Washington, 1879-1882.
Union, Walla Walla, Washington, 1880-1887.
Weekly Statesman, Walla Walla, Washington, 1877-1883.

PUBLISHED SOURCES

Abdill, George W. *This Was Railroading*. Seattle, Washington: Superior Books, 1958.

Anonymous. *An Illustrated History of South Eastern Washington*. Spokane, Washington: Western Historical Publishing Co., 1906.

_____. *History of the Big Bend Country*. Spokane, Washington: Western Historical Publishing Co., 1904.

Athearn, Robert G. *Union Pacific Country*. Chicago, Illinois: Rand McNally, 1971.

Baker, W. W. "The Building of the Walla Walla & Columbia River Railroad." *Washington Historical Quarterly* 14 (Jan. 1923): 3-13.

Cochran, Thomas C. *Railroad Leaders, 1845-1890*. Cambridge, Massachusetts: Harvard University Press, 1953.

Daggett, Stuart. *Railroad Reorganization*. Boston: Houghton Mifflin & Co., 1908.

Edwards, Rev. Jonathan. *An Illustrated History of Spokane County*. Spokane, Washington: W. H. Lever, 1900.

Ehrenberger, James L. and Francis G. Gschwind. *Union Pacific Steam-Northwestern District*. Callaway, Nebraska: E. G. Publications, 1968.

Fahey, John. *Inland Empire—D.C. Corbin and Spokane*. Seattle, Washington: University of Washington Press, 1965.

Fuller, George W. *A History of the Pacific Northwest*. New York: Alfred A. Knopf, 1931.

Gill, Frank B. "Oregon's First Railway." *Oregon Historical Quarterly* 25: 3 (Sept. 1924).

Grodinsky, Julius. *Transcontinental Railway Strategy, 1869-1893*. Philadelphia: University of Pennsylvania Press, 1962.

Hedges, James Blaine. *Henry Villard and the Railways of the Northwest*. New Haven, Connecticut: Yale University Press, 1930.

Hofstadter, Richard, William Miller and Daniel Aaron. *The United States: The History of a Republic*. Englewood Cliffs, New Jersey: Prentice Hall Inc., 1957.

Irwin, Leonard B. *Pacific Railways and Nationalism in the Canadian-American Northwest, 1845-1873*. Philadelphia: University of Pennsylvania Press, 1939.

Johansen, Dorothy O. *Empire of the Columbia*. New York: Harper & Row, 1967.

_____. "The Oregon Steam Navigation Company." *Pacific Historical Review* 10 (1942): 179-188.

Kensel, W. Hudson. "Inland Empire Mining and the Growth of Spokane, 1883-1905." *Pacific Northwest Quarterly* 60 (April 1969): 84-97.

Kindleberger, Charles P. *Manias, Panics, and Crashes: A History of Financial Crises.* New York: Basic Books, Inc., 1978.

Larsen, Henrietta M. *Jay Cooke: Private Banker.* Reprint of 1936 edition. New York: Greenwood Press, 1968.

Lewis, Sol H. "A History of Railroads in Washington." *Washington Historical Quarterly* 3 (July 1912): 186-197.

Malone, Michael P. and Richard B. Roeder. *Montana: A History of Two Centuries.* Seattle: University of Washington Press, 1976.

McArthur, Lewis A. *Oregon Geographical Names.* Portland, Oregon: Oregon Historical Society, 1974.

Meinig, Donald W. *The Great Columbia Plain: A Historical Geography, 1805-1910.* Seattle: University of Washington Press, 1968.

Mills, Randall V. *Sternwheelers Up Columbia.* Palo Alto, California: Pacific Books, 1947.

Modelski, Andrew M. *Railroad Maps of North America: The First Hundred Years.* Washington, D.C.: Library of Congress, 1984.

Moore, Miles C. "A Pioneer Railroad Builder." *Oregon Historical Quarterly* 12 (June 1911): 171-189.

Parson, Col. W. and W. S. Shiach. *An Illustrated History of Umatilla County and of Morrow County.* Pendleton, Oregon: W. H. Lever, 1902.

Pelling, Henry. *American Labor.* Chicago: University of Chicago Press, 1960.

Preston, R. N. *Maps of Early Idaho,* n.p., 1972.

Ripley, W. Z. *Railroads: Rates and Regulation.* New York: Longmans, Green & Co., 1912.

_____. *Railroads: Finance and Organization.* New York: Longmans, Green & Co., 1915.

Smalley, Eugene V. *History of the Northern Pacific Railroad.* New York: G. P. Putnam's Sons, 1883.

Smith, C. J. "Early Development of Railroads in the Pacific Northwest." *Washington Historical Quarterly* 13 (October 1922): 243-250.

U.S. Department of the Interior. Geological Survey. *The Channeled Scablands of Eastern Washington.* Washington, D. C., 1972.

Villard, Henry. *Memoirs of Henry Villard: Volume 2.* Boston: Houghton Mifflin & Co., 1904.

Villard, Henry. *The Early History of Transportation in Oregon.* Edited by Oswald Garrison Villard. Eugene, Oregon: University of Oregon, 1944.

Walla Walla City. County Bicentennial Committee. *Dr. Baker's Railroad.* Walla Walla, Washington, 1976.

Washington Water Power Company. *History of the Washington Water Power Company.* Spokane, Washington, n.d.

Wright, E. W., editor. *Lewis and Dryden's Marine History of the Pacific Northwest.* Reprint of 1895 edition. New York: Antiquarian Press, 1961.

RAILROAD COMPANY REPORTS

Northern Pacific Railroad Company. *Annual Reports.* 1872-1886.

_____. Right-of-Way Plan. U.S. National Archives Record Group 49, Tube 38, Map 3.

Union Pacific Railroad Company. *Corporate History of the Oregon Short Line and Utah Northern Railway Company,* n.d.

_____. *Corporate History of the Oregon Short Line Railroad Company,* n.d.

_____. *Brief Historical Sketch of the Origin and Development of the Oregon Short Line Railroad Company*, n.d.

_____. Untitled. An historical outline for the Oregon Short Line Railroad and Oregon, Washington Railroad and Navigation Companies, n.d.

_____. *The Union Pacific Story*. A centennial brochure, 1969.

INDEX